# The Android Game Developer's Handbook

Discover an all in one handbook to developing immersive and cross-platform Android games

Avisekhar Roy

BIRMINGHAM - MUMBAI

# The Android Game Developer's Handbook

Copyright © 2016 Packt Publishing

All rights reserved. No part of this book may be reproduced, stored in a retrieval system, or transmitted in any form or by any means, without the prior written permission of the publisher, except in the case of brief quotations embedded in critical articles or reviews.

Every effort has been made in the preparation of this book to ensure the accuracy of the information presented. However, the information contained in this book is sold without warranty, either express or implied. Neither the author, nor Packt Publishing, and its dealers and distributors will be held liable for any damages caused or alleged to be caused directly or indirectly by this book.

Packt Publishing has endeavored to provide trademark information about all of the companies and products mentioned in this book by the appropriate use of capitals. However, Packt Publishing cannot guarantee the accuracy of this information.

First published: August 2016

Production reference: 1120816

Published by Packt Publishing Ltd.
Livery Place
35 Livery Street
Birmingham B3 2PB, UK.

ISBN 978-1-78588-586-0

www.packtpub.com

# Credits

**Author**
Avisekhar Roy

**Reviewer**
Attilio Carotenuto

**Commissioning Editor**
Edward Gordon

**Acquisition Editor**
Rahul Nair

**Content Development Editor**
Anish Sukumaran

**Technical Editor**
Taabish Khan

**Copy Editors**
Sonia Mathur
Karuna Narayanan

**Project Coordinator**
Izzat Contractor

**Proofreader**
Safis Editing

**Indexer**
Tejal Daruwale Soni

**Graphics**
Disha Haria

**Production Coordinator**
Melwyn Dsa

**Cover Work**
Melwyn Dsa

# About the Author

**Avisekhar Roy** is a B.Tech engineer in computer science. He has had a passion for coding since his school days. However, he had no plans to become a game programmer. His fate landed him in the gaming industry in 2010. Since then, he fell in love with game development.

Avisekhar has worked in many formats of game development environment, ranging from small companies and individual studios to corporate companies and full-scale game development studios. He recently started his own gaming start-up in 2016 and is currently working on games for the mobile platform.

Avisekhar has also worked with some big companies, such as Reliance Games in India, as well as a small-scale studio called Nautilus Mobile. He is now trying to acquire a position in the gaming industry for his own venture, Funboat Games.

> I would like to mention my parents, who have supported me in every step during the journey of my career. I would not be able to write this book without their blessings. I would like to thank Mr. Pritesh Dhawle for his active support in writing the book; he is not just my partner at Funboat Games, but also an intimate friend. I'd also like to express my gratitude to Mr. Kinshuk Sunil, who supported me while writing this book at an early stage. There are many more friends and well-wishers whom I would like thank for their support.
>
> Finally, I would like to express my gratitude toward the people who provided their valuable analysis on specific subjects; their articles and reports have helped me a lot to research more while writing this book.

# About the Reviewer

**Attilio Carotenuto** is a senior game designer and developer with over 7 years of experience in his field. He's the owner and game director at Himeki Games, an indie studio with a focus on hardcore, premium games, currently working on *An Oath to the Stars*, a Japanese-style bullet hell shooter.

Attilio previously worked at companies such as Electronic Arts Playfish, King, and Space Ape Games, creating games that are played by millions of people every day.

He has previously worked with Packt Publishing as a technical reviewer for *Building Levels in Unity*, Volodymyr Gerasimov; *Unity3D UI Essentials*, Simon Jackson; and *Unity 3D Game Development by Example [Video]*, Adam Maxwell.

You can find more about his recent projects, articles, and talks on his personal website at http://www.attiliocarotenuto.com/.

# www.PacktPub.com

## eBooks, discount offers, and more

Did you know that Packt offers eBook versions of every book published, with PDF and ePub files available? You can upgrade to the eBook version at www.PacktPub.com and as a print book customer, you are entitled to a discount on the eBook copy. Get in touch with us at customercare@packtpub.com for more details.

At www.PacktPub.com, you can also read a collection of free technical articles, sign up for a range of free newsletters and receive exclusive discounts and offers on Packt books and eBooks.

https://www2.packtpub.com/books/subscription/packtlib

Do you need instant solutions to your IT questions? PacktLib is Packt's online digital book library. Here, you can search, access, and read Packt's entire library of books.

## Why subscribe?

- Fully searchable across every book published by Packt
- Copy and paste, print, and bookmark content
- On demand and accessible via a web browser

# Table of Contents

| | |
|---|---|
| **Preface** | **xvii** |
| **Chapter 1: Android Game Development** | **1** |
| **Android game development** | **1** |
| Features and support | 3 |
| Challenges | 4 |
| User experience | 4 |
| Design constraints | 5 |
| **A game is not just an application** | **5** |
| Games versus applications | 5 |
| Life cycle of Android application and games | 6 |
| Performance of games and applications | 7 |
| Memory management of games and applications | 7 |
| **Choosing the target device configuration** | **8** |
| Game scale | 8 |
| Target audience | 9 |
| Feature requirement | 9 |
| Scope for portability | 10 |
| **Best practices for making an Android game** | **10** |
| Maintaining game quality | 11 |
| Minimalistic user interface | 11 |
| Supporting maximum resolutions | 12 |
| Supporting maximum devices | 12 |
| Background behavior | 13 |
| Interruption handling | 13 |
| Maintaining battery usage | 14 |
| Extended support for multiple visual quality | 15 |
| Introducing social networking and multiplayer | 15 |
| **Summary** | **16** |

## Chapter 2: Introduction to Different Android Platforms — 17
- Exploring Android mobiles — 18
- Exploring Android tablets — 22
- Exploring Android televisions and STBs — 24
- Exploring Android consoles — 28
- Exploring Android watches — 33
- Development insights on Android mobiles — 35
- Development insights on Android tablets — 38
- Development insights on Android TV and STBs — 39
  - UI and game design — 41
  - Overscan — 41
- Development insights on Android consoles — 42
- Development insights on Android watches — 42
  - Creating and setting up a wearable application — 43
  - Including the correct libraries in the project — 44
  - Hardware compatibility issues with Android versions — 44
- Platform-specific specialties — 44
  - Android mobiles — 45
  - Android tablets — 45
  - Android televisions and STBs — 45
  - Android consoles — 46
  - Android watches — 46
- Summary — 46

## Chapter 3: Different Android Development Tools — 49
- Android SDK — 50
- Android Development Tool — 50
- Android Virtual Device — 51
  - Configuring AVD — 51
- Android Debug Bridge — 53
  - Using adb on an Android device — 54
- Dalvik Debug Monitor Server — 55
- Other tools — 56
  - Eclipse — 56
  - Hierarchy Viewer — 57
  - Draw 9-Patch — 58
  - ProGuard — 59
  - Asset optimization tools — 60
    - Full asset optimization — 60
    - Creating sprites — 61

| | |
|---|---|
| **Tools for testing** | **61** |
| Creating a test case | 61 |
| Setting up your test fixture | 61 |
| Adding test preconditions | 63 |
| Adding test methods to verify an activity | 63 |
| **Performance profiling tools** | **64** |
| **Android Studio** | **65** |
| Android project view | 65 |
| Memory and CPU monitor | 66 |
| **Cross-platform tools** | **67** |
| Cocos2d-x | 68 |
| Unity3D | 69 |
| Unreal Engine | 70 |
| PhoneGap | 71 |
| Corona | 72 |
| Titanium | 73 |
| **Summary** | **74** |
| **Chapter 4: Android Development Style and Standards in the Industry** | **75** |
| **The Android programming structure** | **76** |
| Class formation | 76 |
| Call hierarchy | 77 |
| **Game programming specifications** | **78** |
| Gameplay programming | 78 |
| Graphics programming | 79 |
| Technical programming | 79 |
| Sound programming | 80 |
| Network programming | 80 |
| Game tool programming | 80 |
| Research and development programming | 81 |
| **Technical design standards** | **81** |
| Game analysis | 82 |
| Design pattern and flow diagram | 82 |
| Technical specification | 82 |
| Tools and other requirements | 83 |
| Resource analysis | 83 |
| Testing requirements | 83 |
| Scope analysis | 84 |
| Risk analysis | 84 |
| Change log | 84 |

| | |
|---|---|
| **Game design standards** | **85** |
| Game overview | 85 |
| Gameplay details | 85 |
| Game progression | 86 |
| Storyboard and game elements | 86 |
| Level design | 86 |
| Artificial intelligence | 86 |
| Art style | 86 |
| Technical reference | 87 |
| Change log | 87 |
| **Other styles and standards** | **87** |
| **Different styles for different development engines** | **88** |
| Different programming languages | 88 |
| Different work principles | 88 |
| Different target platforms | 89 |
| **Industry best practices** | **89** |
| Design standards | 89 |
| Programming standards | 90 |
| Testing standards | 91 |
| **Summary** | **91** |
| **Chapter 5: Understanding the Game Loop and Frame Rate** | **93** |
| **Introduction to the game loop** | **94** |
| User input | 94 |
| Game update | 95 |
| State update | 96 |
| Rendering frames | 96 |
| **Creating a sample game loop using the Android SDK** | **97** |
| **Game life cycle** | **101** |
| **Game update and user interface** | **102** |
| **Interrupt handling** | **106** |
| **General idea of a game state machine** | **107** |
| **The FPS system** | **110** |
| **Hardware dependency** | **112** |
| Display or rendering | 113 |
| Memory load/unload operations | 113 |
| Heap memory | 113 |
| Stack memory | 114 |
| Register memory | 114 |
| ROM | 114 |
| Logical operations | 114 |

| | |
|---|---|
| Balance between performance and memory | 115 |
| Controlling FPS | 116 |
| Summary | 117 |
| **Chapter 6: Improving Performance of 2D/3D Games** | **119** |
| 2D game development constraints | 119 |
|   2D art assets | 120 |
|     Sets of 2D art assets | 120 |
|     Same asset set for multiple resolutions | 120 |
|     Number of assets drawn on screen | 120 |
|     Use of font files | 121 |
|   2D rendering system | 122 |
|   2D mapping | 123 |
|   2D physics | 125 |
|     Box2D | 125 |
|     LiquidFun | 126 |
|     Performance impact on games | 126 |
|   2D collision detection | 126 |
|     Rectangle collision | 127 |
|     Rectangle and circle collision | 129 |
|     Circle and circle collision | 131 |
|     Performance comparison | 132 |
| 3D game development constraints | 133 |
|   Vertices and triangles | 133 |
|   3D transformation matrix | 133 |
|   3D object and polygon count | 134 |
|   3D rendering system | 135 |
|   3D mesh | 135 |
|   Materials, shaders, and textures | 136 |
|     Textures | 136 |
|     Shaders | 137 |
|     Materials | 137 |
|   Collision detection | 137 |
|     Primitive colliders | 137 |
|     Mesh colliders | 137 |
|   Ray casting | 138 |
|   Concept of "world" | 139 |
|     Elements of the game world | 139 |
|     Light sources in the game world | 139 |
|     Cameras in the game world | 143 |
| The rendering pipeline in Android | 145 |
|   The 2D rendering pipeline | 145 |
|   The 3D rendering pipeline | 146 |

## Optimizing 2D assets — 147
- Size optimization — 147
- Data optimization — 147
- Process optimization — 148

## Optimizing 3D assets — 148
- Limiting the polygon count — 148
- Model optimization — 148

## Common game development mistakes — 149
- Use of non-optimized images — 149
- Use of full utility third-party libraries — 149
- Use of unmanaged networking connections — 149
- Using substandard programming — 150
- Taking a shortcut — 150

## 2D/3D performance comparison — 151
- Different look and feel — 151
- 3D processing is way heavier than 2D processing — 151
- Device configuration — 152
  - Processor — 152
  - RAM — 152
  - GPU — 153
  - Display quality — 153
  - Battery capacity — 153

## Summary — 154

# Chapter 7: Working with Shaders — 155

## Introduction to shaders — 156
- What is a shader? — 156
- Necessity of shaders — 156
- Scope of shaders — 158

## How shaders work — 158

## Types of shaders — 159
- Pixel shaders — 159
- Vertex shaders — 159
- Geometry shaders — 159
- Tessellation shaders — 159

## Android library shaders — 160
## Writing custom shaders — 161
## Shaders through OpenGL — 163
## Use of shaders in games — 169
- Shaders in a 2D game space — 169
- Shaders in a 3D game space — 170

## Summary — 173

# Chapter 8: Performance and Memory Optimization — 175

## Fields of optimization in Android games — 176
### Resource optimization — 176
- Art optimization — 176
- Sound optimization — 177
- Data file optimization — 177

### Design optimization — 177
- Game design optimization — 177
- Technical design optimization — 178

### Memory optimization — 178
- Don't create unnecessary objects during runtime — 179
- Use primitive data types as far as possible — 180
- Don't use unmanaged static objects — 180
- Don't create unnecessary classes or interfaces — 180
- Use the minimum possible abstraction — 181
- Keep a check on services — 181
- Optimize bitmaps — 181
- Release unnecessary memory blocks — 182
- Use external tools such as zipalign and ProGuard — 182

### Performance optimization — 183
- Using minimum objects possible per task — 183
- Using minimum floating points — 184
- Using fewer abstraction layers — 185
- Using enhanced loops wherever possible — 185
- Avoid getter/setters of variables for internal use — 185
- Use static final for constants — 185
- Using minimum possible inner classes — 186

## Relationship between performance and memory management — 186
## Memory management in Android — 186
### Shared application memory — 187
### Memory allocation and deallocation — 187
### Application memory distribution — 188

## Processing segments in Android — 188
### Application priority — 188
- Active process — 189
- Visible process — 190
- Active services — 190
- Background process — 190
- Void process — 190

### Application services — 191
- Service life cycle — 191

### Resource processing — 191
- Drawable resources — 192
- Layout resources — 192
- Color resources — 192
- Menu resources — 192

| | |
|---|---|
| Tween animation resources | 192 |
| Other resources | 192 |
| **Different memory segments** | **193** |
| Stack memory | 193 |
| Heap memory | 194 |
| Register memory | 195 |
| **Importance of memory optimization** | **195** |
| **Optimizing overall performance** | **196** |
| Choosing the base resolution | 196 |
| Defining the portability range | 197 |
| Program structure | 197 |
| Managing the database | 197 |
| Managing the network connection | 198 |
| **Increasing the frame rate** | **198** |
| **Importance of performance optimization** | **198** |
| **Common optimization mistakes** | **199** |
| Programming mistakes | 199 |
| Design mistakes | 200 |
| Wrong game data structure | 200 |
| Using game services incorrectly | 200 |
| **Best optimization practices** | **201** |
| Design constraints | 201 |
| Development optimization | 201 |
| Data structure model | 202 |
| Asset-using techniques | 202 |
| Art assets | 203 |
| Audio assets | 203 |
| Other assets | 204 |
| Handling cache data | 204 |
| **Summary** | **205** |
| **Chapter 9: Testing Code and Debugging** | **207** |
| **Android AVDs** | **207** |
| Name of the AVD | 209 |
| AVD resolution | 209 |
| AVD display size | 210 |
| Android version API level | 210 |
| Android target version | 210 |
| CPU architecture | 210 |
| RAM amount | 210 |
| Hardware input options | 211 |

| | |
|---|---:|
| Other options | 211 |
| Extended AVD settings | 211 |
| **Android DDMS** | **211** |
| Connecting an Android device filesystem | 212 |
| Profiling methods | 213 |
| Thread information monitoring | 213 |
| Heap information monitoring | 213 |
| Tracking memory allocation | 213 |
| Monitoring and managing network traffic | 214 |
| Tracking log information using Logcat | 214 |
| Emulating device operations | 214 |
| **Android device testing and debugging** | **215** |
| Device testing | 215 |
|     Prototype testing | 216 |
|     Full or complete testing | 216 |
|     Regression testing | 216 |
|     Release testing or run testing | 216 |
| Device debugging | 217 |
|     Use of breakpoints | 217 |
| **Monitoring the memory footprint** | **217** |
| Checking log messages | 218 |
|     Dalvik message log | 218 |
|     ART message log | 218 |
| Checking heap updates | 219 |
| Tracking memory allocation | 220 |
| Checking overall memory usage | 221 |
|     Private RAM | 221 |
|     Proportional set size (PSS) | 221 |
| Tracking memory leaks | 222 |
| **Strategic placement of different debug statements** | **222** |
| Memory allocation | 222 |
| Tracking the object state at runtime | 223 |
| Checking the program flow | 223 |
| Tracking object values | 223 |
| **Exception handling in Android games** | **224** |
| Syntax | 224 |
| Scope | 226 |
|     Null pointer exceptions | 226 |
|     Index out of bound exceptions | 227 |
|     Arithmetic exceptions | 228 |
|     Input/output exceptions | 228 |
|     Network exceptions | 229 |
|     Custom exceptions | 229 |

| | |
|---|---|
| Debugging for Android while working with cross-platform engines | **230** |
| **Best testing practices** | **230** |
| Tools and APIs | 230 |
| Testing techniques | 231 |
|     Local test | 231 |
|     Instrumented test | 232 |
| **Summary** | **232** |
| **Chapter 10: Scope for Android in VR Games** | **233** |
| **Understanding VR** | **234** |
| Evolution of VR | 234 |
| Modern VR systems | 235 |
| Use of VR | 235 |
|     Video games | 235 |
|     Education and learning | 236 |
|     Architectural design | 236 |
|     Fine arts | 236 |
|     Urban design | 236 |
|     Motion pictures | 236 |
|     Medical therapy | 237 |
| **VR in Android games** | **237** |
| History of Android VR games | 237 |
| Technical specifications | 237 |
| Current Android VR game industry | 238 |
| **Future of Android in VR** | **238** |
| Google Daydream | 238 |
| **Game development for VR devices** | **239** |
| VR game design | 239 |
| VR target audience | 239 |
| VR game development constraints | 240 |
| **Introduction to the Cardboard SDK** | **240** |
| Cardboard headset components | 241 |
| Cardboard application working principle | 241 |
| Upgrades and variations | 241 |
| **Basic guide to develop games with the Cardboard SDK** | **242** |
| Launching and exiting the VR game | 242 |
|     Hitting the Back button | 242 |
|     Hitting the Home button | 243 |
| VR device adaptation | 243 |
| Display properties | 243 |
| In-game components | 243 |
| Game controls | 244 |
|     Control concepts | 244 |

## VR game development through Google VR — 246
### Google VR using the Android SDK — 246
### Google VR using Android NDK — 248
## Android VR development best practices — 248
### Draw call limitations — 248
### Triangle count limitations — 249
### Keeping a steady FPS — 249
### Overcoming overheating problems — 249
### Better audio experience — 250
### Setting up proper project settings — 250
### Using a proper test environment — 250
## Challenges with the Android VR game market — 250
### Low target audience — 251
### Limited game genres — 251
### Long game sessions — 251
### Limited device support — 251
### Real-time constraints — 252
## Expanded VR gaming concepts and development — 252
## Summary — 253

# Chapter 11: Android Game Development Using C++ and OpenGL — 255
## Introduction to the Android NDK — 256
### How the NDK works — 256
#### Native shared library — 256
#### Native static library — 257
### Build dependency — 257
#### Android SDK — 257
#### C++ compiler — 257
#### Python — 258
#### Gradle — 258
#### Cygwin — 258
#### Java — 258
### Native project build configuration — 258
#### Android.mk configuration — 258
#### Application.mk configuration — 260
## C++ for games – pros and cons — 261
### Advantages of using C++ — 261
#### Universal game programming language — 261
#### Cross-platform portability — 261
#### Faster execution — 262
#### CPU architecture support — 262
### Disadvantages of using C++ — 262
#### High program complexity — 262

| | |
|---|---|
| Platform-dependent compiler | 263 |
| Manual memory management | 263 |
| Conclusion | 263 |
| **Native code performance** | **264** |
| **Rendering using OpenGL** | **265** |
| OpenGL versions | 265 |
| OpenGL 1.x | 265 |
| OpenGL 2.0 | 265 |
| OpenGL 3.0 | 266 |
| OpenGL 3.1 | 266 |
| Detecting and setting the OpenGL version | 266 |
| Texture compression and OpenGL | 267 |
| ATC | 267 |
| PVRTC | 267 |
| DXTC | 267 |
| OpenGL manifest configuration | 268 |
| Choosing the target OpenGL ES version | 269 |
| Performance | 269 |
| Texture support | 269 |
| Device support | 269 |
| Rendering feature | 270 |
| Programming comfort | 270 |
| **Different CPU architecture support** | **270** |
| Available CPU architectures | 270 |
| ARM | 270 |
| x86 | 271 |
| Neon | 271 |
| MIPS | 271 |
| Advantages and disadvantages of integrating multiple architecture support | 271 |
| **Summary** | **272** |
| **Chapter 12: Polishing Android Games** | **273** |
| **Requirements for polishing** | **274** |
| Development polishing | 274 |
| Memory optimization | 274 |
| Performance optimization | 274 |
| Portability | 275 |
| Art polishing | 275 |
| UI polishing | 275 |
| Animation polishing | 275 |
| Marketing graphics | 275 |
| Design polishing | 276 |
| Designing UX | 276 |
| Polishing the game flow | 276 |
| Polishing the metagame | 276 |

*Table of Contents*

| | |
|---|---|
| Game economy balance | 276 |
| Game difficulty balance | 277 |
| **Play testing** | **277** |
| User gameplay difficulty levels | 277 |
| User actions during gameplay | 278 |
| User actions while browsing the game | 278 |
| Whether the user is paying or not | 278 |
| Whether the game is running smoothly | 279 |
| Whether the user can adopt the gameplay | 279 |
| User retention | 280 |
| **Taking care of the UX** | **280** |
| Visual effects | 280 |
| Sound effects | 281 |
| Theme music | 281 |
| SFXs | 281 |
| Transaction effects | 281 |
| Action feedback | 281 |
| **Android-specific polishing** | **282** |
| Optimum use of hardware buttons | 282 |
| Sticking to basic Android features and functionalities | 282 |
| Longer background running | 283 |
| Following Google guidelines for Play Store efficiency | 283 |
| **Game portability** | **283** |
| Support for various screen sizes | 283 |
| Support for multiple resolutions | 284 |
| Support for multiple hardware configurations | 284 |
| **Summary** | **285** |
| **Chapter 13: Third-Party Integration, Monetization, and Services** | **287** |
| **Google Play Services** | **288** |
| Google Analytics | 288 |
| Significance | 288 |
| Integration tips | 289 |
| Best utilization | 289 |
| Google IAB | 289 |
| The Google IAB model | 289 |
| Integrating Google IAB | 290 |
| Advantages and disadvantages of Google IAB | 290 |
| Google Leaderboard | 291 |
| Significance | 291 |
| Integrating Google Leaderboard | 291 |
| Variety of leaderboards | 292 |
| Options for storing and displaying leaderboards | 292 |

| | |
|---|---:|
| Push notifications | 293 |
| Database | 293 |
| Server | 293 |
| Target device | 293 |
| GCM service | 294 |
| Integrating push notifications | 295 |
| Significance of push notifications | 298 |
| **Multiplayer implementation** | **299** |
| Real-time multiplayer | 299 |
| Turn-based multiplayer | 300 |
| Single-screen real-time multiplayer | 301 |
| Pass and play turn-based multiplayer | 301 |
| Local network multiplayer | 302 |
| **Analytic tools** | **302** |
| Requirement of analytics tools | 302 |
| User behavior | 303 |
| Game crash reports | 303 |
| Game event triggers | 303 |
| Gameplay session timing | 303 |
| Gameplay frequency | 303 |
| Game balancing | 303 |
| User retention | 304 |
| Piracy prevention | 304 |
| Monetization aspects of analytic tools | 304 |
| Identify popular regions of the game | 304 |
| Identify a user's likes and dislikes | 305 |
| Validate and improve the metagame | 305 |
| Track paying users | 305 |
| Track and count advertisement display | 305 |
| Some useful analytic tools | 305 |
| Flurry | 306 |
| GameAnalytics | 306 |
| Crashlytics | 306 |
| AppsFlyer | 306 |
| Apsalar | 306 |
| Mixpanel | 306 |
| Localytics | 307 |
| Appcelerator | 307 |
| **Android in-app purchase integration** | **307** |
| What are in-app purchases? | 307 |
| In-app purchase options | 308 |
| Store billing services | 308 |
| Career billing services | 309 |
| Types of in-app purchases | 310 |
| Consumable items | 310 |
| Non-consumable items | 310 |
| Subscriptions | 310 |

## Android in-game advertisements — 311
- Requirement for advertisements — 311
- Terminologies in advertisement monetization — 312
  - eCPM — 312
  - CPC/CPA — 312
  - CPI — 312
  - RPM — 312
  - Fillrate — 313
- Types of advertisements — 313
  - Banner advertisements — 313
  - Interstitial advertisements — 314
  - Video advertisements — 315
  - In-game dynamic advertisements — 315

## Monetization techniques — 315
- Premium model — 316
- Free model — 316
- Freemium model — 316
- Try-and-buy model — 316

## Planning game revenue — 316
- Revenue versus profit — 317
- Revenue sources — 317
  - Advertisement revenue — 317
  - In-app purchase revenue — 317
  - Other revenue sources — 318
- Regional variations of revenue plan — 318
  - User base variations — 319
  - User behavior variations — 319

## User acquisition techniques — 319
- Game promotion channels — 320
  - YouTube channels — 320
  - Android forums — 320
  - Sports forums — 320
  - Facebook promotion — 321
  - Twitter and other social platforms — 321
- Game blogs and forum discussions — 321
- Paid user acquisition — 321
- Other techniques — 322

## User retention techniques — 322
- Daily bonus — 323
- Leaderboards and achievements — 323
- Offerwall Integration — 323
- Push notifications — 323
- Frequent updates — 324

| | |
|---|---|
| **Featuring Android games** | **324** |
| Creativity and uniqueness | 324 |
| User reviews and ratings | 324 |
| Download count | 325 |
| Revenue amount | 325 |
| **Publishing Android games** | **325** |
| Self publishing | 325 |
| Publishing through publishers | 326 |
| **Summary** | **326** |
| **Index** | **327** |

# Preface

Fun is the keyword that creates the necessity for entertainment in life. There are many platforms made for entertainment, and games are one of those platforms. There are many types of games available around the world. There were times when gaming was limited to sports, board games, card games, and the like. Then, games entered the digital domain with specific gaming devices. Gradually, they have come to the mobile platform now. Android is one of the most promising platforms. The Android market is growing each day and Android gaming is growing with it.

This book is mainly aimed at game programmers. Many people consider game programming the same as any other programming job. However, my personal opinion differs—game programming is not about sitting with an open code editor and typing in a computer language, it's about creating a medium of spreading entertainment.

This book is focused on the technical part of developing a game, especially for Android. It will help a developer create games in a better way. Game programming is far more logical than technical. I have tried to clear that logic in this book with my experiences throughout my career so far.

## What this book covers

*Chapter 1*, *Android Game Development*, will introduce you to the guidelines and rules of game development on the Android platform.

*Chapter 2*, *Introduction to Different Android Platforms*, will disclose the current variants of Android devices, such as smartphones, TVs, tablets, and smartwatches. It will elaborate all the possible difficulties while creating a game on these platforms and the possible solutions.

*Chapter 3, Different Android Development Tools,* will expose the different tools available to develop an Android application and how to choose suitable tools for specific purposes.

*Chapter 4, Android Development Style and Standards in the Industry,* will cover the current development style and standards in the game development domain. This will mainly talk about Java game coding standards and styles on the Android SDK.

*Chapter 5, Understanding the Game Loop and Frame Rate,* will demonstrate the creation and maintenance of game loop using the Android SDK (Java). This chapter will also cover the effects of game loop on the frame rate.

*Chapter 6, Improving Performance of 2D/3D Games,* will explain all the constraints of 2D and 3D game development on Android, along with the common mistakes and ways to avoid them in order to improve performance.

*Chapter 7, Working with Shaders,* will describe the use of shaders on the Android platform. It exposes the use of shaders through OpenGL and its scope in game development.

*Chapter 8, Performance and Memory Optimization,* will provide in-depth knowledge of optimizing any Android game.

*Chapter 9, Testing Code and Debugging,* will teach you the different ways to debug an Android game.

*Chapter 10, Scope for Android in VR Games,* will introduce you to virtual reality for game development on Android. This chapter describes various scopes of VR and its future in game development.

*Chapter 11, Android Game Development Using C++ and OpenGL,* will briefly explain game development using C++ and OpenGL.

*Chapter 12, Polishing Android Games,* will focus on the completion of an Android game and make it ready for release.

*Chapter 13, Third-Party Integration, Monetization, and Services,* will elaborate the possible integration of any third-party tools or SDKs in order to monetize the game.

# What you need for this book

It is assumed that the reader is already a game developer who has worked on the Android platform. You need to have a clear idea about Android programming using Java and C++.

The reader needs to work on various Android development platforms; most of the code works with the Android SDK. You also need to know the concept of several third-party SDKs regarding advertisements, analytics, in-app purchases, and more.

# Who this book is for

This book is ideal for any game developer with prior knowledge of developing games for Android. A good understanding of game development and basic knowledge of the Android platform application development and Java/C++ will be appreciated.

# Conventions

In this book, you will find a number of text styles that distinguish between different kinds of information. Here are some examples of these styles and an explanation of their meaning.

Code words in text, database table names, folder names, filenames, file extensions, pathnames, dummy URLs, user input, and Twitter handles are shown as follows: "We can include other contexts through the use of the include directive."

A block of code is set as follows:

```
<application
<!-- other declarations and tags -->
android:isGame="true"
<!-- other declarations and tags -->
>
```

Any command-line input or output is written as follows:

```
cd platform-tools
```

**New terms** and **important words** are shown in bold. Words that you see on the screen, for example, in menus or dialog boxes, appear in the text like this: "In the **Configure Project** window, enter a name for the application."

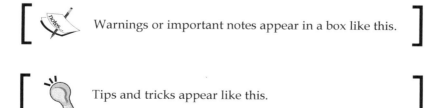

## Reader feedback

Feedback from our readers is always welcome. Let us know what you think about this book—what you liked or disliked. Reader feedback is important for us as it helps us develop titles that you will really get the most out of.

To send us general feedback, simply e-mail feedback@packtpub.com, and mention the book's title in the subject of your message.

If there is a topic that you have expertise in and you are interested in either writing or contributing to a book, see our author guide at www.packtpub.com/authors.

## Customer support

Now that you are the proud owner of a Packt book, we have a number of things to help you to get the most from your purchase.

## Errata

Although we have taken every care to ensure the accuracy of our content, mistakes do happen. If you find a mistake in one of our books—maybe a mistake in the text or the code—we would be grateful if you could report this to us. By doing so, you can save other readers from frustration and help us improve subsequent versions of this book. If you find any errata, please report them by visiting http://www.packtpub.com/submit-errata, selecting your book, clicking on the **Errata Submission Form** link, and entering the details of your errata. Once your errata are verified, your submission will be accepted and the errata will be uploaded to our website or added to any list of existing errata under the Errata section of that title.

To view the previously submitted errata, go to https://www.packtpub.com/books/content/support and enter the name of the book in the search field. The required information will appear under the **Errata** section.

## Piracy

Piracy of copyrighted material on the Internet is an ongoing problem across all media. At Packt, we take the protection of our copyright and licenses very seriously. If you come across any illegal copies of our works in any form on the Internet, please provide us with the location address or website name immediately so that we can pursue a remedy.

Please contact us at copyright@packtpub.com with a link to the suspected pirated material.

We appreciate your help in protecting our authors and our ability to bring you valuable content.

## Questions

If you have a problem with any aspect of this book, you can contact us at questions@packtpub.com, and we will do our best to address the problem.

# Android Game Development

Developing games has become a very popular profession through the last decade. Previously, it was limited to PCs, consoles, and a few embedded gaming devices. Today's world is fully equipped with modern gadgets with better technology, better portability, better flexibility, and better quality. This has opened up the doors for developers to create games with better quality and fewer limitations.

Android is a modern age operating system, and is being used widely for many hardware platforms. Hence, the world of Android has become a target for game developers. The most efficient and useful targets are Android smartphones and tablets. According to surveys of the global market share for mobile OS, Android tops it with a 78-80% share in 2015. Android is now not only a mobile OS, it is being used in TVs and smart watches also. Hence, the popularity of Android is touching the sky among game developers.

This book will be helpful for those who already have a background in Android game development. Let's start with the following topics:

- Android game development
- A game is not just an application
- Choosing target device configuration for your game
- Best practices while making a game on Android

## Android game development

Let us now focus on the main topic of this book. Although game development covers many platforms and technologies, we will only focus on Android in this book.

Android is a mobile operating system based on the Linux kernel. Currently, it is being developed by Google. The OS has released many versions since 2008 to date. But after the release of Android 2.2 (Froyo) and Android 2.3 (Gingerbread), this OS caught the attention of many game developers. Android uses what is called the **Dalvik Virtual Machine (DVM)**, which is an open source implementation of a **Java Virtual Machine** (JVM). There are several differences between Dalvik and a standard JVM, some subtle, some not so subtle. The DVM is also not aligned to either Java SE or Java ME, but to an Apache implementation called Apache Harmony Java. All of this makes for a slight learning curve if you happen to be transitioning from Java ME. Google introduced an alternative to DVM called **Android RunTime (ART)** from Android 4.4 (KitKat), and ART replaced DVM from Android 5.0 (Lollipop). ART mainly features **Ahead-of-time (AOT)** compilation, and an improved garbage collection process, and it provides a smaller memory footprint in order to optimize memory operations. However, most game developers use DVM to support older versions of Android devices.

Android game development started extensively when this OS was adapted by many hardware platforms. Android is mostly being used on the mobile and tablet platforms. When the mobile game industry started migrating from Symbian or Java to Android or other smart mobile OSes, Android game development started to boom.

There are a few reasons for the success of Android games:

- Smooth user interface
- Better interactivity
- Touch interface
- Better look and feel
- Better hardware platform
- More design flexibility

It is always easier to use a common operating system than an embedded **real-time operating system (RTOS)**. The user need not spend time on different hardware to learn its usability. Android is one such easy-to-use operating system.

The visual user interface is very attractive in Android, as it always runs on better hardware configuration than Symbian, Java, or an embedded OS. It enhances user experience, which is one of the reasons why it got adapted by so many organizations. As the user base of Android increased, many more game developers started targeting this platform.

From the perspective of game design, the enhanced Android features list gave flexibility to explore more in mobile games. Thus, the game design style was enhanced.

The current world has various types of hardware that run on Android. Apart from mobile phones, Android is being used on tablets, televisions, wristwatches, consoles, digital cameras, PCs, and other devices. Nowadays, game developers are targeting almost every Android platform.

## Features and support

**Direct manipulation interface** is the top feature of Android. It interacts with the user through a continuous representation of objects of interest, dynamic real-time action, and dynamic feedback. Android mainly uses a touch interface with real-time action such as swiping, dragging, tapping, and multi-touch, which are widely used in game development for Android.

Android application development is mainly based on Java (SDK) and C++ (NDK), which are the most common programming languages in the world. Hence, developing a game has become much easier.

**Excellent support for multimedia** took Android a step further in gaining popularity. Game developers can now use multimedia objects freely inside the game in order to increase the game quality.

Since version 2.2 (Froyo), Google has developed an integrated service called Google Play Services. It is a closed system-level API service provider, which has proved to be very useful in game development.

A large number of third-party tools available for Android development have also eased the job of game developers. Some of the tools we can mention are Android Studio, App Inventor, Corona, Delphi, Testdroid, Sample Directmedia Layer, Visual Studio, Eclipse IDE, and RubyMotions.

**Android device hardware** configuration has to follow a minimum configuration list, so it becomes very easy for the developers to identify the configuration. Moreover, it has to maintain a minimum standard to run applications easily.

There are plenty of sensors associated with Android devices (mostly on mobiles or tablets), which are a very good option for designing the controls of a game.

Android supports awesome connectivity through Bluetooth, Wi-Fi, GSM/CDMA/EDGE, LTE, NFC, IDEN, and the like. These help game developers to create multiplayer games easily.

**Virtual reality** is another field where Android is being used through Cardboard SDK. We will discuss this topic more later on.

These are the features that a game developer should keep in mind. The rest of the features are less important for game development. However, there is always a chance to explore more, and create a few specific-feature oriented games.

## Challenges

The main challenge in developing a game on an Android platform is to make the most use of the features in an efficient way.

The range of Android device configurations is wide. So, designing a game targeting most of them is a big challenge.

Many of the Android game developers design and build games for specific hardware configurations, like Tegra, or Snapdragon, or a particular device like Xperia Play. Nvidia's Tegra is the most commonly used chip in these situations; the *THD* branding often indicates that a game was built for Tegra only. Nvidia has a lot of experience working with developers on the desktop side, and has brought that expertise to mobiles. Android game developers are encouraged to make use of Tegra-specific APIs to build their games. The problem with this scenario is that most users don't have Tegra in their phones. In fact, many LTE handsets that might have otherwise had that gaming-friendly chip are being moved over to Snapdragon S4. Now, for a developer, it is very difficult to maintain performance across different graphic processors.

## User experience

Android games can provide awesome user experience through their features.

Game controls can use the accelerometer or gravity sensor for a physics-based mechanism (if supported by the hardware), which is always an added advantage for real-time interactivity.

On-touch screen devices, and dynamic controls like swiping, dragging, pinching, and multi-touch, can be experienced through Android.

Android supports OpenGL for better graphic rendering, which enhances the visual quality of the game.

Miracast in Android is another feature which enables games to use multiple displays and screen sharing for a better experience.

## Design constraints

Development of any game requires a design Android is not an exception. The design of Android games requires a lot of knowledge about the target hardware. There are thousands of varieties available for Android. Designers have to choose their target very carefully, and then design the game scope.

As previously stated, it is a challenge not only for the programmers but for the designers as well. Different Android devices have different configurations, but it is very important for a designer that the common features should be targeted.

## A game is not just an application

It is a very common practice for an application developer to switch to game development and vice versa. Many do not change their style, and approach game development accordingly. Every developer of games should keep in mind that *a game is not just an application*.

## Games versus applications

A game can be termed an interactive entertainment system, in brief. The main objective of games is to provide fun, be it a software or physical exercise. On the other hand, the main objective of an application is to make life easier with a mechanical job. So the development approaches for these two are completely different. However, this still remains a point of discussion, as every game is an application. Any application can adapt the features of games in order to provide a better user experience.

It is difficult to differentiate between the complexities of development of a game versus an application. However, game development has an edge. Most of the application developers do not have to focus much on speed performance, whereas all game developers have to focus on speed and the frame rate of the game.

Every game is an application for sure, but every application is not a game. This statement itself conveys the message that on a single reference scale, game development has more parameters than applications, yet it has to have all the features of an application.

Application development is technology-oriented, whereas game development is fun-oriented. This increases the difficulties in game development. Fun is an emotion, there is no parameter to calculate that. So, while making games, a developer can never know what exactly the game is going to achieve in terms of fun. On the other hand, an application developer is very much certain that the application target can be achieved if all the specifications meet the requirement.

Game development very rigorously needs mathematics to work on the physics or graphics side; even AI needs a lot of mathematics for the low-level stuff. Applications are more technology driven, with limited use of graphics.

Any application that qualifies as a game must fulfill the following criteria:

- It must entertain a set of users in terms of fun
- There must be a set of milestones to achieve for the users of the application
- It should reward the users for achieving a milestone
- It should have a more dynamic user interface
- There must be better visual impact
- It should be performance driven rather than feature driven

# Life cycle of Android application and games

The application life cycle applies to any game made on the same platform. But a game has more to the cycle, as you can see in the following diagram:

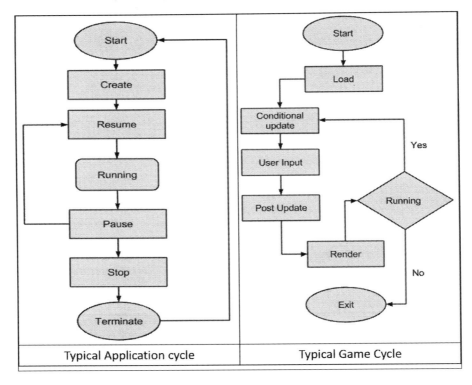

The application life cycle is simpler a game life cycle. The game cycle runs within the running phase of the application life cycle. This is typically termed the **game loop**. This will be discussed later in detail.

This game loop runs on game states. The application may have only one running state, but there are multiple game update states. In a typical system of game development, there are a minimum of two update states. One depends on the game loop execution, and the other depends on the time interval. The second one actually controls the **frame rate**.

## Performance of games and applications

There are noticeable differences between the performance management systems for games and applications. Performance is one of the biggest requirements in game development, whereas it is only a recommended feature for an application, as the frame rate does not affect the quality.

It is an accepted truth that games are heavier than applications on the same scale. A game runs on repetitive frames—one set of tasks runs on one frame. This increases the instruction traffic for the processor. In an application, there are generally no loops; the state of the application depends on user action. In this case, the processor gets plenty of time to execute the instruction as no instructions are being sent repetitively.

## Memory management of games and applications

Applications which are not games have different memory management than games. In case of games, multimedia assets are the main objects, which occupy a larger portion of the heap than class objects. But in the case of applications, it is just the opposite. Applications need to load only the object they require for the state, that is, class objects.

For any game developer, memory optimization is a must. Because of the extensive use of memory, a developer cannot afford to have unused objects loaded in memory, or any memory leakage caused by mishandled memory pointers. This has a direct effect on running games. For an application, memory optimization is obviously a good practice, but most of the time it has no direct or indirect effect on running the application. However, a good programmer should always have knowledge about memory optimization.

# Choosing the target device configuration

As mentioned earlier, Android has a variety of device configurations. So, it is very important for an Android game developer to choose the target very carefully. The general approach should have these parameters:

- Game scale
- Target audience
- Feature requirement
- Scope for portability

## Game scale

This is basically the scale on which the game is being made. The larger the scale, the better the configuration that it'll need. This includes mainly the game size, which means the amount of memory it will consume on a device. Many Android devices are configured with very low RAM and internal memory storage. If the targeted device does not have the required configuration, the game will not run. Even if the game is fully optimized, it can fail depending on the hardware platform it is running on.

Every game requires a set of processes to be executed recursively, which requires processor speed. If a game is process-heavy, and the targeted device has a slow processor, the game will experience some horrible frame rate issue, or crash.

Every Android game developer must be aware of the requirements of memory, processor, and other constraints when choosing the target device.

Let's take the example of an Android game which requires at least 120 MB of disk space to install, 512 MB of RAM to run, and a 1.2 GHz processor speed to achieve a decent frame rate. Now consider a mobile device which matches these specifications exactly, but being a developer, one must not assume that the device will not have any other application installed or running in parallel. So, in this case, there is a fair assumption that the game will not have the required support even if the device meets its requirement. Hence, for this example game, the target device must have a higher configuration than the minimum requirement.

Now, let's take a look at the opposite scenario. Assuming the same game requirements, consider a device having 8 GB of available storage, 2 GB of RAM, and a 2 GHz multicore processor. There is no doubt that the game will run on that device with maximum performance, but the device could have supported a larger-scale game. So the resource utilization is not efficient in this scenario. This is where porting comes in. A game developer should upscale the game quality, and create a different build for those high-end configuration devices.

It is a very common practice in the industry to exclude a few devices from the targeted device list to make the game run properly. In a few cases, the game developer creates separate game builds to support most of the devices and maintain the game quality.

## Target audience

The target audience is the particular group for which the game is made. It is assumed that a particular set of people will have most fun from the game, or that they will play the game more than other people.

Every game design has its target audience. The set of target devices are the direct consequence of the set of target audience. For example, if the target audience is working professionals between the ages of 25 to 40, it makes no sense to create the game for an Android TV no matter what the game scale is. This is because this specific audience will mostly use mobile devices, as they have less time to sit in front of a television set. So, the list of target devices should contain mobile devices for this target audience.

We can see a lot of difference between devices in the same category. For now, let's take the example of Android mobile phones, as this is the most-used Android category. We can see a range of Android devices available in the market. Most of the Android phones are comparatively cheaper, and have fewer features. A major section of the target audience that uses such phones belongs in particular to Asia or the third world countries. So while making a game for this target audience, the developer should consider the minimum configuration target.

## Feature requirement

Feature requirement depends completely on the game design. When we talk about games on Android, the major focus is on mobile and tablet platforms. Mostly, Android games are made for these devices.

If we consider other platforms like watches, TVs, or consoles, the feature set varies. Televisions provide a bigger display with less user control, watches have limited display area and minimum configuration, consoles have better graphic quality with dedicated controls, and so on. It is very important to identify the feature list which is required to recognize the hardware devices.

There might be a scenario where an accelerometer, Bluetooth, Wi-Fi, or some other special feature is being used in a game, so the selected hardware platform must have those features. However, common mobile and tablet devices have almost the same set of features that a game developer might generally use. This feature dependency becomes very specific when Android games are made for some particular hardware platform like consoles or VR devices.

## Scope for portability

While choosing the target hardware device, every game developer must consider the scope for portability of games. The more portable a game becomes, lesser the effort required to select or choose the target hardware.

The portability of games always depends on the vision of the game developer. Porting can take two different approaches: platform porting and hardware porting. We will only focus on hardware porting here, as we have already fixed the platform to be Android.

A game developer should focus on the following points to increase the portability of a game:

- Creating different sets of assets
- Designing different sets of controls
- Finding and listing alternatives for a feature
- Controlling memory usage
- Controlling the frame rate

A good portable game is a balanced combination of all of these preceding points. Most of the time, the target hardware is chosen first depending on the other parameters, and only then does the developer work on the portability of the game.

## Best practices for making an Android game

Making an Android game is not a big deal. But making the game in the right way through which the game looks great, and performs well across as many devices as possible, is very important. The best practices should focus on the following points:

- Maintaining game quality
- Minimalistic user interface
- Supporting maximum resolutions
- Supporting maximum devices
- Background behavior
- Interruption handling
- Maintaining battery usage
- Extended support for multiple visual qualities
- Introducing social networking and multiplayer

Let's discuss these in brief here. We will elaborate on this in detail later as the book progresses.

## Maintaining game quality

There are millions of games available in the market, and thousands being introduced every week. So, just making a good game is not enough nowadays. Every developer should maintain their game periodically to cope with the quality of other improved games.

The developer should keep a constant eye on the reviews and complaints from the users. The game quality can be improved a lot based on this feedback. No one can predict the exact user reaction to the game before it is out in the market. So, in most cases, it is noticed that the game goes through a drastic change in design, or other means, to keep the consumer happy.

There are a few other ways to track the behavior of consumers/players. There are several tools available to do this job efficiently, such as Google Analytics, Game Analytics, Flurry, and so on. Besides these internal integrations, user comments on stores or blogs are helpful to maintain the quality of a game.

Fixing bugs in a game is another major factor in increasing the quality of the game. It is not possible to get rid of all the bugs inside the game during development. The App Store bug report tool is useful for tracking major crashes and ANRs when the game is out in the market. Besides this, the developer can use Android error reporting to track errors and bugs from real users. Android provides this feature in Android versions 2.2 and later.

Two more parameters that improve the quality of the game are stable gameplay, and consistent frame rate.

## Minimalistic user interface

This is a typical design practice for Android games. A common mistake that many developers make is that they design a long and hectic user interface to take the user to the gameplay. This section should be as short as possible. The player should experience the game with minimum effort the very first time. Most users leave games because of the heavy UI interface.

Technically, a developer should take care of the device UI options like Menu, Back, and Home. These are the most common options for the Android mobile and tablet platforms. The behavior of all these options should be controlled within the game, as the user might press/touch them accidentally while playing the game. Also, there should be a quick interface to quit the game.

Basically, having a minimum user interface and fewer screen transactions saves a lot of time, which has a direct impact on gameplay sessions.

## Supporting maximum resolutions

This is a very obvious point for creating a good Android game. A game must support as many resolutions as possible. Android, in particular has many different screen sizes available in the market.

Android has a series of different resolution sets:

- LDPI (approximately 120 dpi)
- MDPI (approximately 160 dpi)
- HDPI (approximately 240 dpi)
- XHDPI (approximately 320 dpi)
- XXHDI (approximately 480 dpi)
- XXXHDPI (approximately 640 dpi)

If they do not follow multiple resolution specifications, the developer can also opt for the screen compatibility option available as a last resort. However, it is recommended not to use this feature of Android, because it can reduce the visual quality significantly. This option is, by default, disabled from Android API version 11.

## Supporting maximum devices

Other than the different screen sizes, Android has a variety of device configurations. Most developers filter the device list only by screen resolution, which is a bad practice. An Android game developer should always consider the target device configuration along with the resolution.

When building their applications, developers should remember not to make assumptions about specific keyboard layouts, the touch interface, or other interactive systems unless, of course, the game is restricted so that it can only be used on those devices.

Optimizing the application in terms of memory and performance is also helpful in supporting more devices. The developer should not restrict them to only a few sets of devices. Optimal use of disk space and the processor opens up the opportunity to increase the support range.

A single game application build can support more devices with some simple tricks. On Android activity launch, the developer should detect hardware information, and use that to create some sort of rules by which the entire game quality and processing speed can be controlled.

## Background behavior

A few tasks in a game may run in the background while the main thread is running. These are called asynchronous tasks, mostly used for loading a large file or fetching something from the Internet.

Another type of background task is called services, which works even when the main application thread is not running. This is a very useful feature for communicating with the device on which the game is installed.

It is a good practice for any game developer to use these features in the game properly. A large chunk of data usually takes longer time, but it should not pause the game loop. In another scenario, asynchronous tasks are used when the game communicates with the Internet or other connectivity. This feature helps to keep the main thread running, and provides dynamic feedback.

Background services are useful for increasing the communication between the developer and user. They can provide user activity information to improve the game as well as notifying users about the latest update or information.

## Interruption handling

Interruption handling is one of the trickiest parts of game development. As we discussed earlier about the game loop, the loop pauses or, sometimes, terminates on any external interruption. In an ongoing game cycle, the interruption should not harm the gaming experience. It is a very common problem for developers that the game restarts after being interrupted. Android is most likely to kill the game activity if it remains in an idle state for a long time, or if some other activity needs provision to run. In these cases, most of the time, the player loses his/her progress.

It is good practice to save the user progress periodically to avoid any loss of data or progression. But saving data may cause lags in the game loop, and can drop the frame rate significantly. The game developer should identify the states where the data can be saved without affecting the gaming experience.

The way to handle this issue in a multi-activity application is to detect and pause/resume all the running threads. Many times, the game developer keeps running the thread, as the primary objective is just to pause/resume the game loop properly on interruption. In most cases, all of the background processes do not pause, causing unusual behavior by the game.

## Maintaining battery usage

One of the reasons for the success of an Android game is power efficiency. Most likely, the Android hardware platform will be a mobile device, which has a limited source of power. So power-saving applications are always preferred.

A major chunk of the battery is consumed by rendering and network connectivity. From the gaming perspective, rendering and connectivity are both necessary. So, there is a fair chance that the game uses up a lot of power.

Most game developers focus a lot on visual appearance. It increases the graphic quality as well as battery consumption. So it is a very good practice for the developer to always focus more on the technical quality of the graphical assets. Assets should not boost up processing or rendering, as, developers often use non-optimized assets.

Another process which consumes a lot of battery is background services. These are used widely for better connectivity with consumers or for some web-based services. Technically this process pings frequently to stay connected with the desired network. Developers can control this frequency. Another way to avoid this is by killing a service which is not connected for a long time or was disconnected from the network, with the help of Android **PackageManager**.

In many cases, it is seen that a game becomes popular, or has a better user count than another, better-quality game, just because of lower battery consumption.

If the developers can determine that connectivity is lost, then all of the receivers except the connectivity-change receiver can be disabled using native APIs. Conversely, once the developers are connected, then they can stop listening for connectivity changes, and simply check to see if the application is online immediately before performing an update; they can then reschedule a recurring update alarm.

Developers can use the same technique to delay a download that requires higher bandwidth to complete simply by enabling a broadcast receiver, which will listen for connectivity changes, and initiate the download only after the application is connected to Wi-Fi. This significantly reduces battery use.

# Extended support for multiple visual quality

This section actually starts with supporting multiple resolutions. We have already discussed multiple-size screens with different dpi. The following list is another standard that Android devices follow:

- QVGA (low PPI)
- WQVGA (medium-low PPI)
- HVGA (medium-high PPI)
- WVGA (medium-high PPI)
- SVGA (high PPI)
- VGA (very high PPI)

Creating graphics using this standard is always beneficial in order to achieve the best possible visual quality across devices. This notation mainly depends on the screen size, irrespective of the resolution. It is very common for Android devices to have the same resolution running on different screen sizes. Creating assets specially optimized for targeted devices will always help to increase the visual quality.

# Introducing social networking and multiplayer

The gaming industry's style and standards are changing rapidly. Now gaming is being used for social connectivity, which is, connecting more than one real user on a single platform. Very careful use of this social element can increase the user base and retention rate significantly.

In many games, there is the possibility of more than one user being able to experience the same game state together, and to improve the game play by real-time interaction. A few board games such as Chess, Ludo, and Snakes and Ladders, are examples of such a possibility. Beside those, some real-time online multiplayer games are also at their peak.

Google has its own multiplayer features through Google Play Services. Besides popular turn-based and real-time multiplayer support, Google has also introduced a feature to connect players in close proximity on a single platform through Wi-Fi, called **Google Nearby**. There are many other third-party platforms that support multiplayer.

# Summary

Making an Android game is not difficult, making a successful game is. From a technical point of view, a successful game must provide smooth gameplay to provide users with an excellent, swift gaming experience. Great visual quality with better graphics always attracts users and other potential players nearby, while fewer bugs removes the irritation of users during gameplay, and the game can perform according to plan. A wide range of device support can increase the number of users and gameplay sessions, optimal use of resources ensures the minimum possible application package size, and finally, a good relationship between the developer and users, through excellent communication skills, can eliminate the few doubts and confusions of the users.

We have covered all of these points in brief to give you an idea about how to make a successful Android game. Making an Android game is no different to making any software. However, a game must follow some practices in order to achieve its fun element. You will learn in detail about making an efficient Android game later in this book. You will also eventually learn about several aspects of game development for the Android platform. You will recognize and realize the current state of available Android devices made by various manufacturers. There are many types of devices, which we will have a look into.

We will try to explore a better and efficient approach for Android game development ,with many development procedures, styles, and standards for different hardware platforms. We will further dig deep, with game-specific development standards for 2D, 3D, and virtual reality games. We will further discuss native development, with shaders and various optimization techniques.

Then, finally, we will explore various ways to make a successful game, which is good enough from the monetization point of view. Since developers must know about each and every user behavior to make the game better, you can realize the power of data collected from users through this book.

# Introduction to Different Android Platforms

The first commercially released Android device was the **HTC Dream**. In 2008, this mobile phone introduced a new Linux-based operating system, Android. Since then, thousands of manufacturers have been using Android for their devices. At first, Android became popular among mobile operating systems such as Symbian, Java ME, Blackberry, and iOS. New generation technology had a demand for a new, lightweight, user-friendly, and affordable operating system. Android fulfilled these requirements, and gained its momentum faster than Blackberry and other competing operating systems.

According to the latest market study, in the first quarter of 2016, Android holds 76% of the market share, which itself explains its success. With the passage of time, Android has expanded its territory from mobile to other useful hardware platforms like tablets, televisions, watches, consoles, and so on.

In this chapter, we will explore these platforms from the perspective of game development. Let's have a quick look at the topics we are going to cover:

- Exploring Android mobiles
- Exploring Android tablets
- Exploring Android televisions
- Exploring Android consoles
- Exploring Android watches
- Development insight on Android mobiles
- Development insight on Android tablets
- Development insight on Android television and STB

- Development insight on Android consoles
- Development insight on Android watches
- Each platform has its own specialty
- Going cross-platform for the same game
- Required limitation measurement before design

We will try to understand all platforms and their details in order to develop games. The modern world has witnessed that games are now not just limited to PCs or consoles. They have become a part of almost everything. So, it is very important for Android game developers to have a decent knowledge of all possible hardware that might be useful for gaming, and which opens up opportunities for few more.

## Exploring Android mobiles

Android mobile devices are the most important devices for game developers. Mobile technology has undergone a huge revolution during the last decade, from the black and white pixel phone to modern age smartphones. Currently, Android mobile devices are leading the market by a huge margin compared to its nearest competitor, the iPhone.

Initial Android gaming got its momentum after the release of Android version 1.6, followed by Android 2.3. Even today, there are many devices running on Android 2.3. That is why many of the popular cross-platform gaming engines support Android 2.3.

There was a time when Android used to run with a minimum requirement of 32 MB of RAM, 32 MB of disk space, and a 200 MHz processor as well. If we take a look at current device specifications, a drastic change can be noticed. Nowadays, Android mobile devices have 1 GB RAM, 1 GHz processor, and 4 GB disk space on an average. Most of the devices have multicore processing units. However, this rise did not simplify the life of the game developer; on the contrary, it increased the complexity even more.

Let's have a look at the specifications of a low-budget Android device with a comparatively low configuration. The following example table shows the configuration of a Micromax Bolt A24:

| Processor | Cortex A5 |
|---|---|
| **Speed** | 1 GHz |
| **RAM** | 256 MB |
| **Flash memory** | 512 MB |

| Screen mode | NA |
|---|---|
| Screen resolution | 480x640 |
| Screen size | 2.8 inch |
| Android version | 2.3 (Gingerbread) |

Here is what it looks like (image source: `http://www.androided.in/wp-content/uploads/2014/02/Micromax-BoltA24.jpg`):

Now take a look at a very high-budget Android device with a very high configuration. The following table shows the configuration of a Samsung Galaxy S6:

| Processor | Cortex A57 |
|---|---|
| Speed | 2.1 GHz quadcore |
| RAM | 3 GB |
| Flash memory | 128 GB |
| Screen mode | NA |
| Screen resolution | 1440x2560 |
| Screen size | 5.1 inches |
| Android version | 5.0.2 (Lollipop) |

Here is what it looks like (image source: `http://talishop.ru/data/big/eew.jpg`):

Every Android game developer should be well aware of the fact that a single game build cannot achieve best performance across all configurations. It is pretty obvious that if the game runs well on a Micromax Bolt A24 device, then it will surely underperform on the Samsung Galaxy S6. By the word "underperform", we mean the quality of the game on Samsung Galaxy S6 would be far below expectations. So it is a very good line of thinking to have some idea on game portability. We will discuss this in detail later on.

The following chart shows the market shares of mobile phones since 2012:

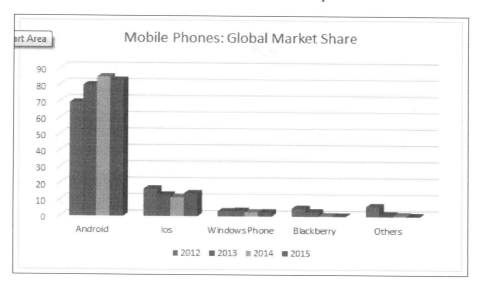

As you can see, the majority of the market is captured by Android, and iOS trails behind with a huge gap in between.

The rest of the mobile operating systems such as Windows Phone, BlackBerry, Java, Symbian, Bada, QT, and others are nowhere near them. So, it can be predicted that the future mobile phone market will be dominated by Android and iOS.

The Android mobile market is getting bigger day by day. Both design and development is getting tougher, trickier, and more market-intense. Every day, around tens of thousands of new games are being launched for Android mobiles on stores like Google Play Store, Amazon App Store, a few career-specific stores, and many more individual online sites.

We have discussed earlier about the target audience of the game. While exploring Android mobile devices, we need to understand the user group. In most cases, the user category is recognized by the device configuration or the price group.

# Exploring Android tablets

Android tablets are very similar to Android mobile phones. The main specification difference between an Android phone and an Android tablet is the physical size and screen resolution. Generally, Android tablets work on lower PPI than a mobile. However, there is no hard-and-fast rule or any specific system to measure that.

The minimum requirement to run Android was a 200 MHz processor, 32 MB RAM, and 32 MB disk space. Android requires an ARMv5 or higher processor, although Android 4 requires ARMv7. Previously, starting age tablets had almost the minimum hardware system.

Tablets evolved from the concept of a tablet computer; they consist of a touchscreen display, camera, microphone, speaker, and a few physical buttons. Tablets are typically larger than phones or PDAs.

One of the minimum configured Android tablet is Coby Kyros MID7047, which is shown here (image source: `http://www.evisionstore.com/catalogo/coby_mid7012-4g.jpg`):

The following table shows its specifications:

| Processor | Cortex A5 |
|---|---|
| Speed | 1 GHz |
| RAM | 512 MB |
| Flash memory | 4 GB |
| Screen mode | WVGA |
| Screen resolution | 800x480 |
| Screen size | 7.00 inch |
| Android version | 4.0 (ICS) |

In the year 2013, Android tablet sales were about 62% with a volume of more than 121 million devices. To add more to the number, the Amazon Kindle Fire sold about 7 million devices.

As the volume of Android tablets has increased, the configuration is getting better. Let's have a look at a tablet configuration released in June 2015 by Sony. The model is called the Sony Xperia Z4 (image source: `https://tecneticoc1.wpengine.com/wp-content/uploads/2015/03/z4tab.png`):

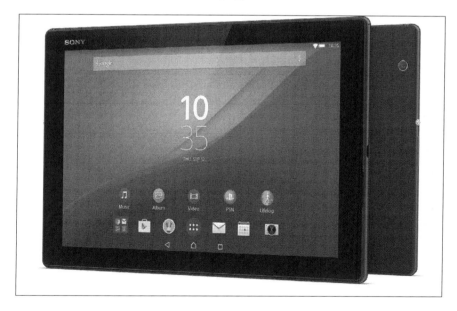

The following table shows its specifications:

| Processor | Snapdragon 810 |
|---|---|
| Speed | 2 GHz octacore |
| RAM | 3 GB |
| Flash memory | 32 GB |
| Screen resolution | 2560x1600 |
| Screen size | 10.1 inch |
| Android version | Android 5.0 (Lollipop) |

We can clearly observe the huge configuration difference between the two tablets. The funny fact is that both the configurations coexist in the market even today, and people are buying them.

Android tablets are generally bigger and heavier than smartphones. They also have better battery capacity. So games for tablets should be energy efficient. However, modern age tablets do not differ much from smartphones. The size of the smartphone is getting bigger, and smartphone features are being added to tablets. Now, one can even use a tablet as a phone.

# Exploring Android televisions and STBs

After the success of Android mobiles and tablets, Android started expanding its territory towards other hardware platforms. Television became the next target, as the concept of smart TV was already in the market. Thus, a television set became interactive through Android. Google has released a few additional accessories for Android televisions to increase the user experience.

The first Android television device launched for consumers was the Nexus Player on November 3, 2014. The specification of this is as follows:

- Intel Atom Z3560 1.8 GHz quadcore processor
- 1 GB RAM
- 8 GB Flash storage
- Android 5.1.1 Lollipop

Here's what it looks like (image source: `http://1.bp.blogspot.com/-H1rp1fboU6g/VX2Huu6ClyI/AAAAAAAA3hA/5te4NZ65Tgg/s1600/nexus_player.jpg`):

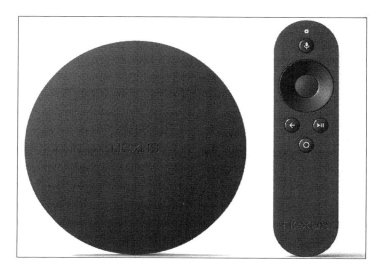

This was the first kind of Android television device, very similar to Google TV and comparable with Apple TV also.

Apart from Nexus Player, there are a few more Android-enabled STB devices:

- **Freebox Mini 4K**: This is a 4K capable TV STB, originally offered by a French ISP with fiber modem.
- **Forge TV**: This is a television/microconsole with high hardware specs, which was announced by Razer on January 6, 2015. It features a Qualcomm Snapdragon 805 processor, 2 GB RAM and 16 GB of Flash storage.
- **Shield Android TV**: This device was announced by NVIDIA on March 3, 2015. This claims to give tough competition to the eighth-generation consoles. This hardware set comes with an NVIDIA-branded game controller.
- **OgleBox Android TV**: This device mainly provides region-based content in Australia. It was announced in March 2015.
- **LG UPlus Android TV**: The Korean telecoms company LG UPlus introduced an Android TV on U+ tvG 4K UHD and U+ tvG Woofer IPTV STBs.
- **Arcadyan BouygtelTV**: In June 2015, a French telecom company, Bouygues Telecom, announced an integrated STB codenamed "Miami" based on Android TV.

*Introduction to Different Android Platforms*

Besides these STB/console-based Android devices, many television manufacturers are targeting the launch of Android television sets. Sony, Sharp, Philips, LG, Samsung, and other companies are migrating to Android. Philips has announced that 80% of their upcoming television models will be running on Android (image source: `http://www.techdigest.tv/wp-content/uploads/2014/07/kogan-smart-tv-may-2013.jpg`):

Let's take a look at the specifications of an example smart TV:

- **Model**: VU 32K160M LED TV
- **Operating system**: Android v4.4 KitKat
- **Processor**: 2.0 GHz octacore GPU with Amlogic quadcore S802 ARM Cortex processor CPU
- **Display**: 32" LED screen (1366x768 px) with achromatic technology and full color optimizer, which provides a world class viewing experience for images, videos, games, and so on
- **Design**: The model is covered in A+ grade pure prism panel which makes pictures more sharp and detailed. And it is surprisingly thinner than the common smart TV models. Its dimensions are 29 inch x 19 inch x 7 inch, and it weighs 7.3 kg.
- **RAM and storage**: The Vu 32K160M TV has 2 GB DDR3 RAM and 8 GB NAND Flash storage.

- **Video**: It plays 1080p videos @60fps, and supports various file formats.
- **Connectivity**: Vu TV supports Bluetooth v4.0, Wi-Fi, and Ethernet. It lets the user browse their favorite sites and check mails from the TV screen. It has three USB ports and two HDMI ports.

This specification is good enough to attract a game developer to get active with his/her next game.

Google has also released an Android TV development kit called ADT-1. This hardware development kit was given to application developers during Google I/O (image source: `http://chezasite.com/media/2014-post-icon/adt-1-android-tv-reference-design-1920x1080.jpg`):

One of the things that early Google TV devices were criticized for was underperforming specs. Thankfully, Google has tried to remedy that, as they came out the gate strong with some pretty impressive specs:

- Tegra 4 chipset
- 2 GB RAM
- 16 GB of internal storage
- 2×2 MIMO dual-channel Wi-Fi
- Bluetooth 4.0
- Ethernet port
- HDMI port
- Android L developer Preview

Android TV is fully unlocked out of the box, so Google is inviting developers to come up with anything they can to help this platform. It's far too early to tell what will be the result of such openness, but it should not take long for developers to explore and develop for this device.

## Exploring Android consoles

A small piece of adapter connected to a television and a controller device to control the adapter, together are called a console set. Android is a cheap, low-budget operating system, which can be used on any mobile hardware platform with ease.

One of the first Android-based consoles is OUYA (image source: `http://cdn2.pu.nl/media/misc/ouya_wall_ins.jpg`):

These consoles are called microconsoles. A few years ago, the specification of such consoles was the following:

- **Model**: OUYA
- **Processor**: ARM Cortex A9
- **Speed**: 1.7 GHz quadcore
- **System chip**: NVIDIA Tegra 3
- **Flash memory**: 8 GB
- **RAM**: 1 GB DDR3
- **Display**: HD (720p) or Full HD (1080p)
- **Graphics processor**: NVIDIA GeForce ULP GPU
- **Android version**: Android 4.1 Jelly Bean
- **Connectivity**: Wi-Fi, Bluetooth and LAN

Now let's have a look at the modern age Android console specification:

- **Model**: NVIDIA Shield
- **Processor**: ARM Cortex A57 + A53 (64 bit)
- **Speed**: 1.9 GHz quadcore + 1000 MHz quadcore
- **System chip**: NVIDIA Tegra X1
- **Flash memory**: 500 GB HDD
- **RAM**: 3 GB
- **Connectivity**: Wi-Fi, Bluetooth, LAN, USB, and HDMI
- **Display**: 4K resolution support

Here is the NVIDIA Shield Android console (`https://cdn0.vox-cdn.com/thumbor/72vPz7fqWT7ButeiG17cW_jjP2Y=/0x0:1920x1080/1600x900/cdn0.vox-cdn.com/uploads/chorus_image/image/45812214/shield-hero-image.0.0.jpg`)

*Introduction to Different Android Platforms*

Let's now take a look at another modern age Android gaming console called Razor Forge TV (image source: `http://android.hu/img/2015/04/gallery-04.jpg`):

Its specifications are as follows:

- **Model**: Razor Forge TV
- **Processor**: Qualcomm Snapdragon 805
- **Speed**: 2.5 GHz quadcore
- **GPU**: Adreno 420
- **Flash memory**: 16 GB
- **RAM**: 2 GB
- **Connectivity**: Wi-Fi, Bluetooth, LAN, USB, and HDMI
- **Android version**: 5.0 Lollipop

A console is a specific device for gaming. However, nowadays, consoles can be used for various purposes, but the main objective remains the same.

From the previous example specifications, we can have an idea of how Android console gaming is improving. Developers work on a specific target device for consoles. Even if the game is portable, console quality has to be maintained.

In a recent market study, it was said that PlayStation 4, Xbox One, and the Nintendo Wii U will be the dominant platforms for hardcore console gamers. However, Android console offerings from Amazon, Google, and others are projected to grow at a much faster rate, and offer the casual to mid-core gamer an affordable way to play from the couch. It is pretty much clear that over time, the broader base of console gamers will likely consider Android.

This opens up a new era of Android game development. Console games are different to typical mobile games, which maximum Android game developers are into. However, with the growing number of Android consoles since 2014, more and more developers are taking interest in this.

Apart from the consoles discussed earlier, there are few more, such as the following:

- **Game Stick**: This is a small dongle-sized console powered by Android Jelly Bean, having 1 GB DDR3 RAM and 8 GB Flash memory. However, this specification is being boosted (image source: http://cdn2.knowyourmobile.com/sites/knowyourmobilecom/files/styles/gallery_wide/public/5/05/gamestick-4.jpg?itok=kYGDnKgr):

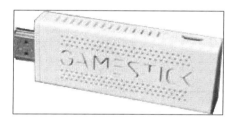

*Introduction to Different Android Platforms*

- **Mad Catz MOJO**: This is a normal microconsole having 2 GB RAM, 16 GB Flash memory, and a Tegra 4 processor. This device runs on Android 4.2.2 (image source: http://cc.cnetcontent.com/inlinecontent/mediaserver/3m/8f8/607/8f8607ed9d2b4cee981f651125046895/original.jpg):

- **GamePop**: BlueStacks has manufactured this next generation Android gaming console with a target to set a subscription model like other top consoles. Most of the Android gaming consoles use store-based content. This is certainly a new venture with great expectations.

  A new feature introduced in this console is that this device is capable of running iOS games with the help of a visualization tool called Looking Glass. It would be wise to wait until the unit is in the wild before getting too excited about how this all works. But if it does, then the results could be astounding.

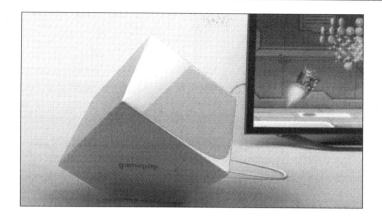

The evolution of consoles running Android may be the future of gaming; however, it is established that the existence of other top consoles will not become extinct. The user base is increasing day by day, and so is the number of games on those platforms.

Being an Android game developer, one must not stick to the conventional gaming platforms such as smartphones and tablets. The era is changing rapidly. Developers should keep themselves up to date.

# Exploring Android watches

In the smart era of technology, it was expected that every possible gadget would work smarter. Wristwatches were no exception. The type of watches changed from analog to digital, and now to purely computerized smartwatches. Being a very flexible open source operating system, Android is one of the most favorite option for smartwatches (image source: `http://photos.appleinsidercdn.com/bigger-wimm-130830.jpg`):

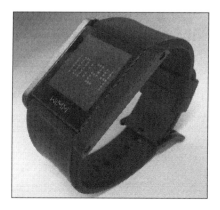

From the very early versions, Android watches were well capable of playing games, thus entering the game development domain. Advanced devices are as good as small computers. They consist of the Internet, sensors, cameras, Bluetooth, Wi-Fi, speakers, card slots, and have many more features.

Like other computers, a smartwatch may collect information from internal or external sensors. It may control, or retrieve data from, other instruments or computers. It may support wireless technologies like Bluetooth, Wi-Fi, and GPS. However, it is possible that a "wristwatch computer" may just serve as a frontend for a remote system, as in the case of watches utilizing cellular technology or Wi-Fi.

Android Wear was first announced on March 18, 2014 by Google. At the same time, many manufacturers of electronic gadgets were announced as partners of Android Wear. These companies include Samsung, Motorola, LG, HTC, ASUS, and others.

In December 2014, the operating system was upgraded to Android 5.0 (Lollipop). We can see a series of Android Watch releases around this period of time. LG started shipping LG G Watch, Motorola announced Moto 360, and ASUS released ZenWatch.

The latest advanced watches offer a set of attractive features. Users can find directions by voice from the phone, choose a transport mode, including a bike, and start a journey. While travelling, the watch shows directions, and will actually use tactile interaction to indicate turns by feel, helping the wearer travel without looking at a phone, or even the watch screen. Users can use their Android Wear watch to control their phone. Music can be requested (for instance, "OK Google, play the Rolling Stones"). The screen then shows a card for play-control, volume, skip, and media images, and music can be controlled from the wrist with the user free to move around.

Let's look at a few specifications of Android wearable devices. First, the LG G Watch:

| Processor | Qualcomm Snapdragon 400 |
| --- | --- |
| Flash memory | 4 GB |
| RAM | 512 MB |
| Battery | 400 mAh |
| Connectivity | Bluetooth 4.0 |
| Sensors | Gyro, accelerometer, compass |
| Android version | 4.3 |
| Display | 1.6 inch |
| Resolution | 280x280 |

This configuration does not exist anymore in the market, but users do. So while making a game for an Android wearable, the developer should take into account these configurations as well.

Android wearable manufacturers are also upgrading their devices with massive hardware changes. Now let's have look at the evolution of devices by comparing two releases:

|  | Sony Smartwatch 2 | Sony Smartwatch 3 |
| --- | --- | --- |
| Processor | ARM Cortex M4 | ARM A7 quadcore |
| Speed | 180 MHz | 1.2 GHz |
| Flash memory | 256 MB | 4 GB |
| RAM | 64 MB | 512 MB |
| Battery | 225 mAh | 420 mAh |
| Connectivity | Bluetooth 3.0 | Bluetooth 4.0 and Wi-Fi ready |
| Sensors | Gyro, accelerometer, compass, proximity, ambient light, and IP57 dust and water resistant | Gyro, accelerometer, compass, proximity, ambient light, and IP68 dust and water resistant |
| Android version | 4.0 | 4.3+ |
| Display | 1.6 inch | 1.6 inch |
| Resolution | 220x176 | 320x320 |

We can observe a huge boost in terms of technical and hardware upgradation here. This is how the market is growing, and the applications as well.

# Development insights on Android mobiles

As we discussed earlier, the main development target for any game developer on the Android platform are Android mobiles. We have also noticed the various technical specifications for Android mobiles. When a game developer targets this platform at its maximum possible scope, they must take a note of the device category.

Mostly, all Android devices support a common touch interface, a physical Home button, a physical Lock button, a Back button, and volume Up-Down keys for user interaction. Besides these, an accelerometer can be also a good medium for the user interface.

Gaming is mostly visual, so game developers should always look for the graphic performance of the device. There is a separate graphics processor in the latest Android mobiles, but the quality varies.

Visual excellence does not depend on GPU only—the display screen quality also matters a lot. Low PPI screens cannot deliver a high quality display. The first-generation Android G1 mobile had a screen resolution of 240x320, falling in the LDPI resolution category. Hence, the visual quality of the game could not be excellent, no matter how hard the developer tried. Fortunately, with time, device manufacturers put in a lot of effort in to improving the visual quality along with performance. But this feature came with a price of battery life. The more quality it gained, the more battery it consumed.

Previously, few Android phones (for example, Android HTC Dream G1) had a physical QWERTY keypad. This made it much easier to port the game control system from Symbian or BlackBerry to Android (image source: `http://s.androidinsider.ru/2015/02/htc-dream.@750.jpg`):

Nowadays, the control system for Android games has changed completely to cope with the control style of other smartphone games in the market.

In the current scenario, the average capacity of a mobile battery is around 2750 mAh. A few manufacturers provide higher battery capacity by reducing the display quality. It is not possible to increase battery capacity beyond a certain limit due to the physical size and weight constraints for a mobile device.

Targeting the maximum devices is always a good idea as long as the balance between performance and gaming experience is maintained.

The device market is open for various devices. Although old configurations are not being manufactured further, those devices are not yet obsolete. This is why developers have a minimum requirement for their games.

Smartphones are the major target for any game development organization. The increasing user base and upgrading of Android helps this platform grow faster. There was a time when BlackBerry was considered to be the only smartphone. But the current market says that times have changed, and so have the developers.

For Android mobile game development, a developer should keep in mind the following constraints and features:

- Small display area
- Wide range of resolution and pixel density
- Full-screen multitouch interface
- Sensor support for gyro, accelerometer, compass, ambient light, and so on
- Wide range of RAM
- A variety of processors and performance
- Battery life
- More chances of interruption

Android mobiles are one of the more profitable platforms now. When it comes to market share, there is no other mobile OS that can compete with Android. So, developers always jump into Android. Few economical reasons for the success of this platform are as follows:

- Availability of a massive user base, which attracts advertisers as an advertising platform
- Easy monetary transactions through well-established stores
- Ease of cross promotion of games and apps

# Development insights on Android tablets

Android game development was mainly limited to smartphones before Android tablets came into the picture. It was much more fun to play a game on a tablet. Tablet gaming became popular over a short period of time because of the following reasons:

- **Bigger screen**: Although a bigger screen with the same resolution compromises the visual quality, it provides bigger visibility. Bigger visibility enhances the art asset to reveal its details, which is not always possible for a small screen smartphone.
- **Bigger physical size**: Bigger physical size forces the player to play with both hands, which results in better grip on the device and better controls.
- **Bigger space/playable area**: Bigger playable area can provide more control space. That means that the player need not to be accurate while using the touch control system, so he/she can concentrate more on the game alone. Thus, it enhances the gaming experience.
- **Less constraints**: Continuous playing of games causes a serious amount of battery drainage. In case of phones, the primary objective is to stay connected with a network. So, keeping the device alive is very necessary. But a tablet does not have a particular goal. It is a multipurpose utility device. One of the purposes can be playing games. Therefore, there is no hardcore necessity to save power for jobs other than gaming.
- **Less interruption**: We all know how any interruption can be irritating during an ongoing job. The same goes for the gaming experience as well. Any interruption causes a major pause in gaming, and most of the time, players quit at that point in time. On a tablet, there are fewer chances of automated interruption than manual or physical interruption; this means less irritation while playing on a tablet.

For Android tablet game development, a developer should keep the following constraints and features in mind:

- Big display area
- Wide range of resolution, and comparatively low pixel density
- Full-screen multitouch interface
- Sensor support for gyro, accelerometer, compass, ambient light, and so on
- Wide range of RAM
- A wide range of processors and performance
- Fewer chances of interruption

Tablets evolved from the idea of a small portable computing device, which could be the bridge between smartphones and PCs/laptops.

A bigger screen always helps the user to interact with the game more easily. Game designers have more space to utilize. However, this slightly increases the headache for developers, as the visual quality has to be maintained within the same hardware limitation.

Previously, most tablets used mobile processors, but tablet manufacturers are using laptop processors for tablets now. Intel Atom is an example of this. The more capable the processor used in a device, the better the quality it can deliver.

There was a time when Android games were targeted for mobiles first, and then those were ported for tablets. But the table has turned now. Now there is a very thin line between the development of smartphone games and games for tablets. Most of the time, the same APK can support both phones and tablets with almost the same quality and performance. There is no more exclusive porting for tablets.

# Development insights on Android TV and STBs

Firstly, Android TV game development requires a focus on two specific things:

- Large shared display
- Landscape resolution with lower dpi

A large display is always a plus from a player's perspective, but that increases the overhead for graphic designers to optimize the assets accordingly. At the same time, the display can be shared with multiple users, so the developer has to make sure that all the user actions can always be synced with the display.

TVs are big in comparison to any other Android devices. The stretch from a 5" to 50" to a 150" screen can expose poor graphical quality. So, the following points need to be considered while developing games for Android TVs:

- Check the textures of the game—low resolution textures often look poor when stretched on Android TV
- 3D models might have jagged curves on TV because there are too few polygons
- Particle effects may need reworking for the TV's big screen if there are too few emitters, patterns, or colors
- Anti-aliasing is often not required on Android devices with small screens that have a high pixel density, but it effects a considerable visual difference for a TV.

Now the next challenge is the input control system. There can be multiple controllers for the game. The TV can be directly controlled by some other Android device, or by a remote control.

However, any Android console or STBs can be used as well. In this case, a game controller or a D-pad control is much more useful for games.

To use a controller or a D-pad, a game developer should be very specific about using the proper control button for each functionality. When multiple players are playing a game, each with their own controller, it is important to map each player-controller pair.

It is an optional advantage to specify the game inside the `AndroidManifest.xml` file under the `application` tag, as follows:

```
<application
<!-- other declarations and tags -->
android:isGame="true"
<!-- other declarations and tags -->
>
```

This will help separate the game from other regular applications, and will show it under the games category on the Android TV home page.

There are a few other declarations that can be made according to the requirements.

To declare support for game controllers, use the following code:

```
< uses-feature android:name="android.hardware.gamepad"
  android:required="true"/>
```

The developer must include the "touchscreen required false" declaration in the `AndroidManifest.xml` file, as it is used by Play Store for filtering. If it is missing, Play Store does not show the app to Android TV users in the search results:

```
< uses-feature android:name="android.hardware.touchscreen"
  android:required="false"/>
```

It is very good practice for all Android TV game developers to specify the non-required features of Android to get rid of the extra library hassle. For example, a TV does not have an accelerometer or gravity sensor, so marking them as non-required is a good development practice. This can be done as follows:

```
<manifest ...>
  <application ...>
  ...
    <!-- Requiring the camera removes this listing from Android TV
      search results -->
```

```xml
    <uses-feature android:name="android.hardware.camera"
      android:required="true" />

    <!-- Making accelerometer optional has no impact on Android TV
      filtering -->
    <uses-feature android:name=
      "android.hardware.sensor.accelerometer"
        android:required="false" />
  </application>
</manifest>
```

## UI and game design

Each game UI has to follow the design that will support the control scheme, that is, the UI should completely support the input controller and elements, and the screen has to be designed accordingly. This is a major difference between mobile/tablet game development and Android TV game development.

As we are discussing the development on Android TV, a developer must consider how it would feel to play a game on Android TV from a distance of 4-10 feet while sitting on a couch or on a bean bag. Here is the check list that a developer should look for:

- All text should be clearly readable
- UI buttons and other elements should match the overall layout without harming the readability and visibility of the whole screen
- A controller must control all the possible tasks while playing the game, as nobody would like to get up frequently to control the TV

## Overscan

Unlike phone and tablet screens, TVs can lose some space at the edges of the screen to **overscan**. Although many TVs now use fixed-pixel technologies like LCD, many brands still lose edge detail. Be sure to leave a region around the outside of the TV screen free from important UI and gameplay elements. A good rule-of-thumb is to have a 5-10% margin of totally free space, and a 10-20% margin before drawing important elements.

If developers are using standard Android components for their UI, then they can use the built-in overscan support that was made available in Android Jelly Bean. If the UI is custom OpenGL or OpenGL ES code, or is using a game engine's UI system, the developer will have to cater for overscan in the Android TV interface design.

# Development insights on Android consoles

Today's modern mobile devices are well capable of running a moderate quality game with limited processing power, comparable with PC and consoles. It is being anticipated that the revenue for mobile games will surpass that of consoles and PC by the year 2015-2016. Now the question arises, "Will the console game market survive?" The answer is *Yes*.

Consoles are specially designed and configured to provide the best gaming experience, where smartphones are designed for better communication and networking with limited computing power. Android, as an operating system for consoles, has proved to be a success.

There is not much difference between the configurations of an Android mobile and an Android console. Processor, memory capacity, and another few changes can be seen, but the major and the most important difference is the input system. Mobiles, tablets, wearables, all have a touch interface, whereas consoles use the typical gaming controller.

Android gaming consoles are placed between mobiles and PCs from a development perspective. So, apart from the design, the engineering or programming section of console game development depends on mainly two parameters: controls and the use of hardware.

We have already discussed the various types of consoles available in the market. As a development platform, it does not have much uniqueness.

# Development insights on Android watches

Wearable games run directly on the wearable device, giving the developer access to low-level hardware such as sensors, activities, services, and more, right on the wearable. A companion handheld game that contains the wearable app is also required when the developer wants to publish to the Google Play Store. Wearables don't support the Google Play Store, so users download the companion handheld game, which automatically pushes the wearable game to the wearable. The handheld game is also useful for doing heavy processing, network actions, or other work and sending the results to the wearable.

To develop games on Android wearables, there are some technical steps to be followed. This is not general Android game development:

- The Android SDK tool has to be updated to version 23.0 or higher
- The Android platform support within the SDK has to be updated with Android 4.4.2 (API 20) or higher
- An Android wearable device or emulator is required for development

## Creating and setting up a wearable application

This can be done as follows:

Select **New Project** in Android Studio. In the **Configure Project** window, enter a name for the application and a package name. In the **Form Factors** window, perform the following steps:

1. Select **Phone and Tablet** and select **API 9: Android 2.3 (Gingerbread)** under **Minimum SDK**.
2. Select **Wear**, and select **API 20: Android 4.4 (KitKat Wear)** under **Minimum SDK**.
3. In the first **Add an Activity** window, add a blank activity for `mobile`.
4. In the second **Add an Activity** window, add a blank activity for `wear`.

When the wizard completes, Android Studio creates a new project with two modules, `mobile` and `wear`. Developers now have a project for both their handheld and wearable apps for which they can create activities, services, and custom layouts. The handheld app does most of the heavy lifting, such as network communications, intensive processing, or tasks that require long amounts of user interaction. When the app completes these operations, the application should notify the wearable of the results through notifications or by syncing and sending data to the wearable.

> The `wear` module also contains a `Hello World` activity that uses a `WatchViewStub`. This class inflates a layout based on whether the device's screen is round or square. The `WatchViewStub` class is one of the UI widgets that the wearable support library provides.

## Including the correct libraries in the project

There is a lot of library support for Android apps/games. Every developer needs to identify their correct requirements to include the correct libraries.

The following is a list of a few useful libraries for game development on wearable devices:

- **Notifications**: The Android v4 support library (or v13, which includes v4) contains the APIs to extend the existing notifications on handhelds to support wearables. For notifications that appear only on the wearable (meaning, they are issued by an app that runs on the wearable), the developer can just use the standard framework APIs (API level 20) on the wearable, and remove the support library dependency in the `mobile` module of the game or application.
- **Wearable Data Layer**: To sync and send data between wearables and handhelds with the Wearable Data Layer APIs, developers need the latest version of Google Play services. If developers are not using these APIs, remove the dependency from both modules.
- **Wearable UI support library**: This is an unofficial library that includes UI widgets designed for wearables. The Android platform encourages developers to use them in applications, because they exemplify best practices, and yet they can change at any time. However, if the libraries are updated, the applications won't break, since they are compiled into the project. To get new features from an updated library, developers just need to statically link the new version, and update the application accordingly. This library is only applicable if a developer creates wearable apps.

## Hardware compatibility issues with Android versions

Now let's have another look at the absolute minimum hardware requirements, as we already know that Android is not compatible with ARM v4 processors, and Android 4.0+ requires ARM v7 or higher. Android wearables run on Android 4.4 or higher. So the developer must support ARM v7 onwards.

## Platform-specific specialties

We have already discussed about all the Android hardware platforms till now. Each platform has its own specialties in terms of configuration, size, shape, utilities, and features.

Let's summarize the platform-specific points that should be taken into consideration while developing a game for the same.

## Android mobiles

This type of Android hardware platform is the most famous and widely used device across the world. Typical Android mobile-specific features are:

- Small screen
- High dpi display
- Wide range of hardware configurations
- Full touchscreen
- Maximum sensor support
- Multipurpose use
- Maximum user base

## Android tablets

This type of Android hardware platform is the second most famous and widely used devices across the world, with slightly different utilities. Typical Android tablet-specific features are:

- Comparatively bigger screen
- Low dpi display
- Full touchscreen
- Specific use device

## Android televisions and STBs

This type of Android hardware platform is spreading rapidly as smart TVs with more features and abilities than a simple television gain popularity. Typical Android television- and STB-specific features are:

- Biggest display unit
- No touch interface
- D-pad or controller-based input system
- Fixed landscape orientation
- Limited hardware support
- Suitable for multiplayer games

## Android consoles

Beside famous gaming consoles such as the PS3, PS4, and Xbox, Android gaming consoles are also gaining popularity nowadays. Typical Android console-specific features are:

- Dedicated hardware system for gaming
- Full controller-based input system
- Multiresolution large display support
- Hardware-specific development
- Best Android platform for multiplayer gaming experience

## Android watches

This is the most used wearable platform on Android. The main feature of this device is to provide health information. However, gaming is also spreading on this device. Typical Android watch-specific features are:

- Very small display
- Limited hardware support
- Less memory and processing power
- Touchscreen interface
- Very portable
- Separate wearable development environment needed

## Summary

Before starting development, a developer must have clear knowledge about hardware and software specifications. In this chapter, you have learned about the possible different hardware platforms running on Android. Through this knowledge, you, as a developer, can easily identify your target audience. It is much easier to choose a specific set of hardware platforms to target.

In the near future, Android will be stepping into the world of virtual reality with different technologies. We will discuss these later in this book. Till now, you have come to know that mobiles, tablets, televisions, STBs, consoles, and watches are the various hardware platforms. All of them are capable of running Android games. However, Android consoles are the only dedicated hardware platform for games.

Though consoles are a dedicated gaming platform, Android mobiles and Android tablets are the most targeted platforms for developers. These provide all the necessary support and facilities to run almost every kind of game. These platforms have the added advantage of the number of users. Most developers target these platforms to acquire as many users as possible.

# 3
# Different Android Development Tools

We have already discussed the different Android target devices for game development. In this chapter, we will take a look at the different ways and tools to develop games for Android. Other than development skill and knowledge, it is very important to know about the helpful software that can make the development process easier and effective.

Android game development is supported or backed by many powerful tools and libraries. Let's have a look at the list of mandatory tools for the development process:

- Android SDK
- Android Development Tool
- Android Virtual Device
- Android Debug Bridge
- Dalvik Debug Monitor Server

These are the must-have tools that should be installed in an Android game developer's system. Without these, it is impossible to develop anything for the Android platform. Although ADB and AVD are not mandatory for development, they are required to test and deploy the game on physical as well as virtual devices in order to debug the game.

# Android SDK

Android SDK is the main development kit required to build any application for Android. Without going into details, it can be said that the SDK is the skeleton for any Android development. This SDK itself comes with dozens of support tools. It contains platform details, APIs, and libraries along with ADT and AVD. So having Android SDK integrated in the system provides the developer with all the necessary tools. It is a very good practice to always update the SDK with the latest platforms and other tools.

Upgrading can be done through the Android SDK manager. However, platform selection is manual, and it is recommended to have only the necessary platforms as per requirements. Another best practice is to have the latest released platform along with the minimum targeted version of Android (image source: `http://photos4.meetupstatic.com/photos/event/1/1/0/f/highres_441724367.jpeg`):

# Android Development Tool

**Android Development Tool (ADT)** is a plugin for the Eclipse IDE that is designed to give a powerful, integrated environment in which to build Android applications.

ADT extends the capabilities of Eclipse to let the developer quickly set up new Android projects, create an application UI, add packages based on the Android framework API, debug the applications using the Android SDK tools, and even export signed (or unsigned) `.apk` files in order to distribute the application.

Developing in Eclipse with ADT is highly recommended, and is the fastest way to get started. With the guided project setup it provides, as well as tools integration, custom XML editors, and the debug output pane, ADT gives an incredible boost to developing Android applications.

However, ADT support for Eclipse is being pulled by Google, so developers are recommended to switch to Android Studio.

## Android Virtual Device

An **Android Virtual Device (AVD)** is a software-produced model of a real device, which can be configured with custom hardware specifications. It can be a virtual copy of the real device as well. This is one of the most important tools for any Android developer. This lets the developer test the application in a typical Android environment without using an actual hardware device, to cut short the development time (image source: http://www.geeknaut.com/images/2014/08/top-android-emulators-for-windows3.png):

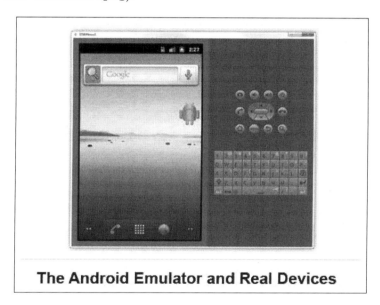

The Android Emulator and Real Devices

## Configuring AVD

An AVD consists of the following:

- **Hardware profile**: This profile describes the hardware features of the virtual device. This can be configured with hardware options like a QWERTY keypad, camera, integrated memory, and so on.
- **System image mapping**: The running Android platform version can be configured depending on the installed set of Android platforms. Android platforms can be installed by the Android SDK manager.

- **Dedicated disk space**: Dedicated storage area on your development machine can be set with this feature, which saves the emulator's user data and the virtual SD card.
- **Other features**: The developer can even specify the look and feel of the virtual device such as device skin, screen dimension, and appearance.

The following is the brief procedure to create an AVD through AVD manager, which is located in the `<SDK Path>/tools` directory:

1. On the main screen, click on **Create Virtual Device**.
2. In the **Select Hardware** window, select a device configuration such as **Nexus 5**, then click on **Next**, then click on **Finish**.
3. To begin customizing the device by using an existing device profile as a template, select a device profile and then click on **Clone Device**. Or, to create a complete custom emulator, click on **New Hardware Profile**.
4. Set the following to create a new custom emulator:
    - Device name
    - Screen size
    - Screen resolution
    - RAM
    - Input options
    - Supported states
    - Camera options
    - Sensor options
5. After setting every property, click on **Finish**.

The developer can also create a new custom emulator using the command line, as follows:

```
android create avd -n <name> -t <targetID> [-<option> <value>] ...
```

Here, the following options can be set:

- `name`: This will be the custom AVD name
- `targetID`: This will be the custom ID
- `option`: This can include options such as device screen density, resolution, camera, and so on.

The developer can execute this command to use a previously defined AVD:

`android list targets`

Then, the developer can run the following command:

`emulator -avd <avd_name> [options]`

## Android Debug Bridge

**Android Debug Bridge** (**adb**) is a tool used to establish communication between the development environment and a virtual device or the connected Android device. It is a client-server command-line program, which works on three elements:

- **Client on the development machine**: Works as the client, which can be invoked by adb commands. Other Android tools such as the ADT plugin and DDMS also create adb clients.
- **Daemon**: A background process that runs in the background on each emulator or device instance.
- **Server on the development machine**: This is a background process that runs on the development machine and manages the communication between the client and server.

On starting adb, the client first checks whether there is an adb server process already running. If there isn't, it starts the server process. When the server starts, it binds to the local TCP port `5037` and listens for commands sent from adb clients—all adb clients use port `5037` to communicate with the adb server.

The server then sets up connections to all running emulator/device instances. It locates emulator/device instances by scanning odd-numbered ports in the range `5555` to `5585`, the range used by emulators/devices. Where the server finds an adb daemon, it sets up a connection to that port. Note that each emulator/device instance acquires a pair of sequential ports—an even-numbered port for console connections and an odd-numbered port for adb connections.

Once the server has set up connections to all emulator instances, the developer can use adb commands to access those instances. Because the server manages connections to emulator/device instances, and handles commands from multiple adb clients, the developer can control any emulator/device instance from any client (or from a script).

*Different Android Development Tools*

# Using adb on an Android device

One of the first things to remember is to put the development device in the USB debugging mode. This can be done by navigating to Settings, tapping on **Developer options**, and checking the box named **USB debugging** for Android 5.0 and above (for other Android versions, refer to `https://www.recovery-android.com/enable-usb-debugging-on-android.html`). Without doing this, the development PC won't recognize the device.

The most important thing to know is simply how to get to the adb folder via the command line. This is done with the `cd` (change directory) command. So, if (on Windows) the SDK folder is called `android-SDK`, and it's in the root (`c:`) directory, you can enter the following command:

```
cd c:/android-SDK
```

Then, to get into the adb folder, use this:

```
cd platform-tools
```

At this point, the prompt will say this:

```
C:\android-SDK\platform-tools>
```

Now the developer can connect the device, and test the adb connection, after locating and installing the drivers for a particular device:

```
adb devices
```

If everything is set up properly, there should be a list of devices attached. The phone or tablet will have a number assigned to it, so don't be surprised if it doesn't say "Droid Razr" or "Galaxy Nexus".

For average users, adb is more of a tool for basic hacking tasks than it is a task in itself. Unless the developers know what they are doing, they probably shouldn't go poking around too much without clear instructions. When rooting the device, knowing these basics can help save some time and let the developer be prepared in advance.

Beside the specific instructions to root a particular device, the next thing the developer needs will be the drivers for the phone or tablet.

The easiest way to do this is usually to simply Google search for the *specific device plus drivers*. So if the developer has a Droid Razr, he/she should search for `Droid Razr Windows Drivers`. This will almost always direct the developer to the best link.

Another option, which will only work for stock Android devices, is to download the USB drivers from the SDK. To do this, launch the SDK manager again. Go to the **Available packages** tab on the left, expand the **Third party add-ons** entry, and then expand the **Google Inc. add-ons** entry. Finally, check the entry for the **Google USB Driver** package.

Note that the USB driver package isn't compatible with OS X.

## Dalvik Debug Monitor Server

The **Dalvik Debug Monitor Server (DDMS)**, whether it's accessed through the standalone application or the Eclipse perspective with the same name, provides handy features for inspecting, debugging, and interacting with emulator and device instances. You can use DDMS to inspect running processes and threads, explore the filesystem, gather heap and other memory information, attach debuggers, and even take screenshots. For emulators, you can also simulate mock location data, send SMS messages, and initiate incoming phone calls:

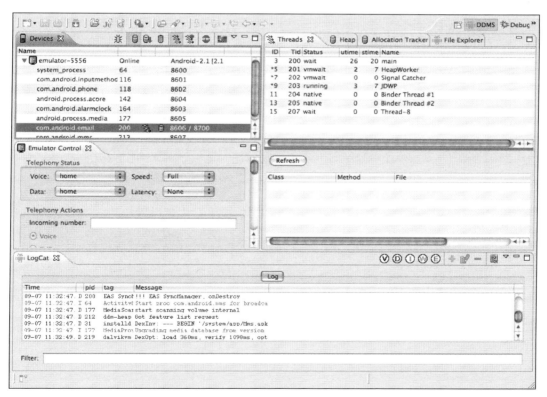

As the preceding screenshot shows, DDMS can primarily track, update, and display the following information:

- All running processes
- All running threads per process
- Consumed heap per process
- All log messages

On Android, every application runs in its own process, each of which runs in its own virtual machine. The debugger can be attached to the exposed port of VM. DDMS connects to adb on start. On successful connection, a VM monitoring service is created between adb and DDMS, which informs DDMS upon starting and ending a VM on the device. DDMS retrieves the VM's process ID via adb, and opens a connection to the VM's debugger when there is an active VM running through the adb daemon on the device. DDMS can now communicate to the VM using a custom wire protocol.

DDMS also listens on the default debugging port, called **base port**. The base port is a port forwarder, which can accept VM traffic from any debugging port and forward it to the debugger. The traffic that is forwarded is determined by the currently selected process in the DDMS **Devices** view.

# Other tools

The elements mentioned in the previous sections are the minimum requirement for Android development, with which a full application can be created. However, the development process can become much easier with the support of a few other tools. Let's have a look at a few of such tools. These tools are not mandatory for Android development, but they are recommended to be used for a better development process.

# Eclipse

Although Eclipse is not the only Java development environment that can be used to develop Android applications, it is by far the most popular. This is partially due to its cost (free!), but mostly due to the strong integration of Android tools with Eclipse. This integration is achieved with the ADT plugin for Eclipse, which can be downloaded from the Android website.

Use of Eclipse for Android development is a well-known practice for many developers. Some of the reasons for this are as follows:

- Free Eclipse IDE
- Direct Android plugin support
- Direct DDMS support
- Simple interface
- Android NDK support

The launch of Android Studio reduced the popularity of Eclipse among Android developers, because Android Studio has everything inbuilt to support any Android development. Moreover, it is a much simplified tool to use in design view. Google itself is promoting the new tool massively.

There are a few drawbacks in Eclipse Android development, because it uses Android SDK as a third-party tool. The significant drawbacks are as follows:

- Debugging through Eclipse is sometimes difficult
- ADB configuration is tricky
- Android manifest has to be managed manually
- The design view is very complex through Eclipse IDE

Eclipse is an excellent standalone IDE, but when it comes to Android development, Android Studio wins the race.

## Hierarchy Viewer

Hierarchy Viewer, whether it's accessed through the standalone application or the relatively new Eclipse perspective, is used to see how your layouts and screens resolve at runtime.

It provides a graphical representation of the layout and view hierarchy of your application, and can be used to diagnose layout problems (image source: `https://media-mediatemple.netdna-ssl.com/wp-content/uploads/2012/03/da_hierarchy_viewer.png`):

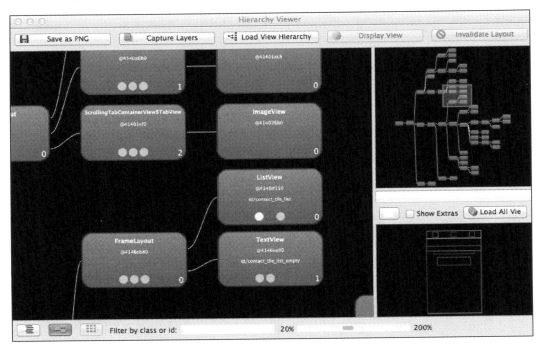

# Draw 9-Patch

When it comes to graphics design, the Draw 9-patch tool comes in handy. This tool allows you to convert traditional PNG graphic files into stretchable graphics that are more flexible and efficient for mobile development use. The tool simplifies the creation of NinePatch files in an environment that instantly displays the results:

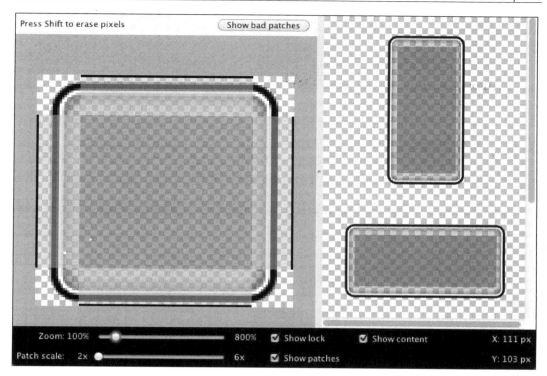

## ProGuard

ProGuard is not directly associated with Android development, but it helps in protecting the intellectual property of the developer. It is a very common practice for Android game developers to use ProGuard.

ProGuard basically wraps the members and methods to a non-readable code structure. This tool can be configured to obfuscate the resulting binary. ProGuard also helps in optimizing the binary, so that the overall package size is reduced.

ProGuard can be difficult to use when developers try to integrate pre-compiled JARs into the Android project. Sometimes conflicts are created in class structures if the JAR is already optimized through ProGuard. In those situations, ProGuard must be configured to exclude the precompiled JARs in order to achieve a successful build.

It is always recommended to use ProGuard to protect the game classes from reverse engineering or decompilation.

## Asset optimization tools

We all know the vast range of Android hardware configurations. It is always necessary to optimize the assets to reduce runtime memory usage and unnecessary data processing. In games, graphical assets take most of the storage and memory.

## Full asset optimization

An unoptimized asset may hold some unnecessary data, like transparency information in an opaque asset, EXIF data, unused color information, extra bit depth, and so on.

Asset optimizer tools help to get rid of this burden. However, it is tricky to use such tools as the asset quality may be lost. A developer should be very cautious while using these tools.

For example, if an asset is supposed to be at 24 bit, but was optimized with an 8 bit optimizer tool, it will surely lose its visual quality. So, over-optimization is never recommended for any games, and it is the developer's responsibility to use proper optimization techniques to maintain the game quality.

The following are a few such asset optimizer tools:

- PNGOUT
- TinyPNG
- RIOT
- JPEGmini
- PNGGauntlet

With the help of such tools, art assets can be optimized up to 80-90% of their size. But many developers don't prefer to use them on a regular basis because of the following reasons:

- The developers do not optimize each asset separately, which results in quality loss for a few assets.
- It is really difficult to choose the right tools for optimization. Sometimes, multiple tools are required for the same job, which slows down the overall development process.

## Creating sprites

In many cases, it is noticed that a large number of small art assets are being used in games individually. This may cause critical performance lag for the game. It is recommended to use a sprite building tool to merge those assets into one to save space and time. SpriteBuilder and TexturePacker are two good examples of such tools.

# Tools for testing

For any development process, testing is of major importance. For Android game development too, there are a few tools and processes to make testing easier.

## Creating a test case

Activity tests are written in a structured way. Make sure to put your tests in a separate package, distinct from the code under test. By convention, your test package name should follow the same name as the application package, suffixed with `.tests`. In the test package you created, add the Java class for your test case. By convention, your test case name should also follow the same name as the Java or Android class that you want to test, but suffixed with `Test`.

To create a new test case in Eclipse, perform the following steps:

1. In Package Explorer, right-click on the `/src` directory for your test project, and select **New** | **Package**.
2. Set the **Name** field to `<package_name>.tests` (for example, `com.example.android.testingfun.tests`), and click on **Finish**.
3. Right-click on the test package you created, and select **New** | **Class**.
4. Set the **Name** field to `<activity_name>Test` (for example, `MyFirstTestActivityTest`), and click on **Finish**.

## Setting up your test fixture

A test fixture consists of objects that must be initialized for running one or more tests. To set up the test fixture, you can override the `setUp()` and `tearDown()` methods in your test. The test runner automatically runs `setUp()` before running any other test methods, and `tearDown()` at the end of each test method execution. You can use these methods to keep the code for test initialization and clean up separate from the tests methods.

To set up a test fixture in Eclipse, follow the steps listed next:

1. In Package Explorer, double-click on the test case that you created earlier to bring up the Eclipse Java editor, then modify your test case class to extend one of the subclasses of `ActivityTestCase`. For example:

   ```
   public class MyFirstTestActivityTest extends ActivityInstrumentati
   onTestCase2<MyFirstTestActivity> {
   ```

2. Next, add the constructor and `setUp()` methods to your test case, and add variable declarations for the activity that you want to test. For example:

   ```
   public class MyFirstTestActivityTest
           extends ActivityInstrumentationTestCase2<MyFirstTestActivi
   ty> {

       private MyFirstTestActivity mFirstTestActivity;
       private TextView mFirstTestText;

       public MyFirstTestActivityTest() {
           super(MyFirstTestActivity.class);
       }

       @Override
       protected void setUp() throws Exception {
           super.setUp();
           mFirstTestActivity = getActivity();
           mFirstTestText =
                   (TextView) mFirstTestActivity
                       .findViewById(R.id.my_first_test_text_view);
       }
   }
   ```

The constructor is invoked by the test runner to instantiate the test class, while the `setUp()` method is invoked by the test runner before it runs any tests in the test class.

Typically, in the `setUp()` method, you should invoke the superclass constructor for `setUp()`, which is required by JUnit

You can initialize your test fixture state by:

1. Defining the instance variables that store the state of the fixture.
2. Creating and storing a reference to an instance of the activity under test.
3. Obtaining a reference to any UI components in the activity that you want to test.

Developers can use the `getActivity()` method to get a reference to the activity under test.

## Adding test preconditions

As a sanity check, it is good practice to verify that the test fixture has been set up correctly, and the objects that you want to test have been correctly instantiated or initialized. That way, you won't have to see tests failing because something was wrong with the setup of your test fixture. By convention, the method for verifying your test fixture is called `testPreconditions()`.

For example, you might want to add a `testPreconditions()` method like this to your test case:

```
public void testPreconditions() {
    assertNotNull("mFirstTestActivity is null",
      mFirstTestActivity);
    assertNotNull("mFirstTestText is null", mFirstTestText);
}
```

The assertion methods are from the Junit `Assert` class. Generally, you can use assertions to verify if a specific condition that you want to test is true.

If the condition is false, the assertion method throws an `AssertionFailedError` exception, which is then typically reported by the test runner. You can provide a string in the first argument of your assertion method to give some contextual details if the assertion fails.

If the condition is true, the test passes. In both cases, the test runner proceeds to run the other test methods in the test case.

## Adding test methods to verify an activity

Next, add one or more test methods to verify the layout and functional behavior of your activity.

For example, if your activity includes a TextView, you can add a test method like this to check that it has the correct label text:

```
public void testMyFirstTestTextView_labelText() {
    final String expected =
            mFirstTestActivity.getString(R.string.my_first_test);
    final String actual = mFirstTestText.getText().toString();
    assertEquals(expected, actual);
}
```

The `testMyFirstTestTextView_labelText()` method simply checks that the default text of the TextView, which is set by the layout, is the same as the expected text defined in the `strings.xml` resource.

When naming test methods, you can use an underscore to separate what is being tested from the specific case being tested. This style makes it easier to see exactly what cases are being tested.

When doing this type of string value comparison, it's a good practice to read the expected string from your resources instead of hardcoding the string in your comparison code. This prevents your test from easily breaking whenever the string definitions are modified in the resource file.

To perform the comparison, pass both the expected and actual strings as arguments to the `assertEquals()` method. If the values are not the same, the assertion will throw an `AssertionFailedError` exception.

If you added a `testPreconditions()` method, put your test methods after the `testPreconditions()` definition in your Java class.

You can build and run your test easily from the Package Explorer in Eclipse. To build and run your test, follow these steps:

1. Connect an Android device to your machine. On the device or emulator, open the **Settings** menu, select **Developer options**, and make sure that **USB debugging** is enabled.
2. In the Project Explorer, right-click on the test class that you created earlier, and select **Run As | Android JUnit Test**.
3. In the **Android Device Chooser** dialog, select the device that you just connected, then click on **OK**.
4. In the JUnit view, verify that the test passes with no errors or failures.

# Performance profiling tools

Putting pixels on the screen involves four primary pieces of hardware: the CPU computes display lists, the GPU renders images to the display, the memory stores images and data, and the battery provides electrical power. Each of these pieces of hardware has constraints; pushing or exceeding those constraints causes your app to be slow, worsens the display performance, or exhausts the battery.

To discover what causes your specific performance problems, you need to take a look under the hood, use tools to collect data about your app's execution behavior, surface that data as lists and graphics, understand and analyze what you see, and improve your code.

Android Studio and your device provide profiling tools to record and visualize the rendering, computing, memory, and battery performance of your app.

# Android Studio

Android Studio is the official IDE for Android application development, based on IntelliJ IDEA. On top of the capabilities you expect from IntelliJ, Android Studio offers the following among many others:

- Flexible Gradle-based build system
- Build variants and multiple .apk file generation
- Code templates to help you build common app features
- Rich layout editor with support for drag and drop theme editing
- lint tools to catch performance, usability, version compatibility, and other problems
- ProGuard and app-signing capabilities
- Built-in support for the Google Cloud platform, making it easy to integrate Google Cloud messaging and App Engine

If you're new to Android Studio or the IntelliJ IDEA interface, this section provides an introduction to some key Android Studio features.

## Android project view

By default, Android Studio displays your project files in the Android project view. This view shows a flattened version of your project's structure, which provides quick access to the key source files of Android projects, and helps you work with the Gradle-based build system. The Android project view:

- Shows the most important source directories at the top level of the module hierarchy
- Groups the build files for all modules in a common folder

- Groups all the manifest files for each module in a common folder
- Shows resource files from all Gradle source sets
- Groups resource files for different locales, orientations, and screen types in a single group per resource type

The Android project view shows all the build files at the top level of the project hierarchy under `Gradle Scripts`. Each project module appears as a folder at the top level of the project hierarchy, and contains these four elements at the top level:

- `java/`: Source files for the module
- `manifests/`: Manifest files for the module
- `res/`: Resource files for the module
- `Gradle Scripts/`: Gradle build and property files

> For example, the Android project view groups all the instances of the `ic_launcher.png` resource for different screen densities under the same element.
>
> The project structure on disk differs from this flattened representation. To switch back to the segregated project view, select your project from the **Project** drop-down menu.

## Memory and CPU monitor

Android Studio provides a memory and CPU monitor view so that you can easily monitor your app's performance and memory usage to track CPU usage, find deallocated objects, locate memory leaks, and track the amount of memory the connected device is using. With your app running on a device or emulator, click on the **Android** tab in the lower-left corner of the runtime window to launch the **Android runtime** window. Click on the **Memory | CPU** tab.

When you're monitoring memory usage in Android Studio, you can initiate garbage collection, and dump the Java heap to a heap snapshot in an Android-specific HPROF binary format file at the same time. The HPROF viewer displays classes, instances of each class, and a reference tree to help you track memory usage and find memory leaks.

Android Studio allows you to track memory allocation as it monitors memory use. Tracking memory allocation allows you to monitor where objects are being allocated when you perform certain actions. Knowing these allocations enables you to adjust the method calls related to those actions to optimize your app's performance and memory use.

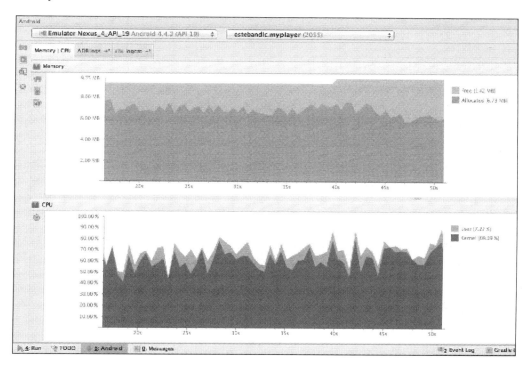

# Cross-platform tools

Although we are only talking about Android game development, game development cannot be efficient without cross-platform support. We have already discussed game design flexibility. From a typical technical perspective, it should be possible to deploy the game for various platforms such as iOS, Windows, consoles, and the like.

Always keep in mind that cross-platform mobile development isn't quite as simple as writing the code once, putting it through a tool for translation, and publishing both an iOS and Android app to the respective app stores.

Using a cross-platform mobile development tool can reduce the time and cost associated with developing apps on both platforms, but the UI needs to be updated to match each system. For example, adjustments are needed between the two so that the menu and control commands match the UX of how Android devices and iOS devices inherently operate in different ways.

There are plenty of tools that support cross-platform development. Let's take a look at a few of them:

## Cocos2d-x

Cocos2d is primarily used in two-dimensional game development. It gives developers the option of five different forks or platforms to develop on, based on their preferred programming languages, such as C++, JavaScript, Objective C, Python, and C# (image source: http://www.cocos2d-x.org/attachments/802/cocos2dx_landscape.png):

Primarily, this tool is efficient for Android, iOS, and Windows Phone. The development platform is mainly 2D; however, from Cocos2d-x 3.x it is possible to develop games in 3D also.

Cocos2d-x works with native Android, and can support different processor architectures separately. This tool works in a Unix-based environment.

There is a huge developer community that develops games on Cocos2d-x. Here are the pros and cons of this cross-platform development engine from the Android game development perspective:

The pros are as follows:

- Supports the most common programming languages such as C++
- Works in the native environment
- Lightweight and optimized library
- Common OpenGL rendering system
- All smartphone features supported for 2D development
- Completely free open source Engine

The cons are as follows:

- Majorly supports 2D development
- Cross-platform deployment is tricky and complicated
- Performance and memory optimization is weak
- No visual programming support
- No debugging tool is provided within the engine
- Mostly works on mobile phone platforms

## Unity3D

Unity3D is the most popular cross-platform engine among Android and iOS game developers. Although it is mainly optimized for mobile platforms, it is powerful enough to deploy games for other major gaming platforms as well, for example, PC, Mac, consoles, web, Linux, Xbox, PlayStation, and so on. Currently, it supports 17 different platforms for game development (image source: http://img.danawa.com/images/descFiles/3/545/2544550_1_1390443907.png):

Once you've got your game on all your chosen platforms, Unity3D will even help you distribute it to the appropriate stores, get social shares, and track user analytics.

Unity3D has the largest game developer community, with huge support on almost every aspect of game development. It has its separate store where you can find an effective prebuilt custom library, prebuilt plugins, and so on, which helps a developer in terms of reducing development time significantly. Here are the main pros and cons of Unity3D.

The pros are as follows:

- Supports 17 different platforms for gaming
- Very simple deployment procedure
- Visual editor to support visual programming
- Inbuilt powerful debug tool
- Huge library support
- Hassle-free development
- Inbuilt powerful memory and performance optimizer

The cons are as follows:

- Comparatively bigger library size
- Slightly performance heavy (however, it is improving day by day)
- Supports only scripting languages (C#, JavaScript, and Boo)
- Not completely free for commercial purposes
- Mainly works well with 3D

## Unreal Engine

The recently released Unreal Engine 4 is a very powerful cross-platform game engine. Previously, this engine focused on the console and PC platforms only, but it has extended its support to mobile gaming platforms such as Android and iOS (image source: http://up.11t.ir/view/691714/1425334231-unreal-engine-logo.png):

There have been a lot of debates about whether Unreal Engine 4 is better than Unity3D. They both have their own pros and cons. Let's have a look at the pros and cons of Unreal Engine 4:

The pros are as follows:

- The Blueprint feature allows flexible visual programming
- Generic C++ language is more developer friendly
- Graphic processing is excellent
- Inbuilt dynamic shadow system
- Simple to understand and start making games
- Vast support in terms of device scalability
- In-editor material designing

The cons are as follows:

- Mobile optimization is still not up to the mark
- Lack of 2D development tools
- Lack of availability of third-party plugins
- Working with sprites is a pain for mobile development
- Still focused on high configuration hardware platforms

# PhoneGap

Owned by Adobe, PhoneGap is a free resource that first-time app developers can use to translate code from HTML5, CSS, and JavaScript.

They maintain SDKs at their end for each of the platforms you can develop an app for, so it's one less thing you have to worry about. And once your app is completed, you can share it with your team members for review to see if you need to make any improvements.

Beyond iOS and Android, PhoneGap also creates apps for BlackBerry and Windows. So it is truly a cross-platform mobile development tool (image source: http://blogs.perceptionsystem.com/wp-content/uploads/2016/03/phonegap.png):

PhoneGap features the following pros:

- Supports almost all mobile platforms
- Lightweight application build
- Supports HTML, CSS, and JavaScript
- Cordova apps install just like a native application
- PhoneGap is open source and free

It has the following cons:

- Lack of platform support
- Lack of third-party plugins
- Native UI is still difficult to use

## Corona

Corona's SDK comes with the promise that you can start coding your new app in as little as five minutes after the download. It's another cross-platform mobile development tool that's optimized for 2D gaming graphics, and helps you make games 10 times faster than it would take to code everything from scratch (image source: https://qph.ec.quoracdn.net/main-qimg-fad64a16e531773325448e6ca699d117):

Corona's programming language is Lua, which is written in C, making it a cross-platform language. Corona chose Lua because they found it to be really robust, with a small footprint for mobile apps.

Corona has the following pros:

- Good application performance in terms of FPS
- Good inbuilt emulator
- Light application build

It has the following cons:

- Uses the less popular scripting language Lua
- Not free
- Less plugin support
- No on-device debugging support

# Titanium

Using JavaScript, Titanium's SDK creates native iOS and Android apps while reusing anywhere from 60% to 90% of the same code for all the apps you make, thereby saving you a significant amount of time (image source: http://mobile.e20lab.info/wp-content/uploads/sites/2/2014/04/titanium.png):

Because Titanium is an open-source tool, hundreds of thousands of your fellow developers are constantly contributing to it to make it better, and give it more functionality. And if you happen to find a bug in its system, you can do so too.

The pros are as follows:

- Quick-start flexibility for the initial phase
- Lightweight application build
- Common JavaScript language
- Web and mobile support on Android and iOS
- Open source

The cons are as follows:

- Lack of plugin support
- Lack of platform support range
- Script-based development increases complexity and effort
- Performance varies with different platforms
- Poor optimization compared to other tools

# Summary

Development tools are essential for any game development; however, they have always been low priority in game design and the pre-development analysis stage. The necessity for these tools is realized when they are required.

We have discussed all the mandatory tools for Android development only. But modern age game development demands flexibility across hardware platforms as well as operating systems. This is where cross-platform development engines come into the picture. These tools help the development process to become faster and more efficient; however, this comes at the cost of a little drop in performance and a larger build size. In most cases, developers have limited control over the cross-platform engine, but full control can be gained if the game is developed on native SDKs.

Development tools are not just useful for development and debugging—they are very efficient in optimizing the game along with data protection, which might not have a direct impact on games. A good developer must use optimization tools to deliver a better performing game.

# 4
# Android Development Style and Standards in the Industry

There is no written rule or direction to write code in Android, other than the syntactical grammar. However, most developers across the globe follow a few fundamental styles and standards for writing Android code. Android is based on Java, so most of the stylization follows Java standards.

When it comes to Android game development, there are a few design styles that should be followed. They do not cover game design, rather more technical design. These kinds of styles and standards indicate a proper project structure, class structure, and folder/file management.

Typical game design also involves following some rules while working on the Android platform. A few styles are being followed in the industry in terms of game design.

In this chapter, we will have a look at these styles and standards through the following topics:

- The Android programming structure
- Game programming specifications
- Technical design standards
- Game design standards
- Other style and standards
- Different styles for different development engines
- Industry best practices

# The Android programming structure

Android style or recommendation is not a definite programming rule. However, a good programming practice always includes a set of rules. To code in Android, the code structure follows the Android base structure and hierarchy.

Android typically follows the standards and style of Java. So, the Android programming structure is basically Java structure, which follows the OOP style.

## Class formation

Java class formats should be consistent and follow the Javadoc rule; a standard structure should follow this sequence:

1. Copyright information
2. License information
3. Package declaration
4. Library imports
5. Class description and purpose
6. Class definition
7. Global variables
8. Constructor
9. Methods

This is the copyright and license information format:

```
/*
 * Copyright (C) <year> authority
 *
 * <License information and other details>
 */
```

This is the class and method description format:

```
/*
 * <Description>
 * <Purpose>
 */
```

# Call hierarchy

Like the coding style, there is no defined call hierarchy. However, in Android gaming, most developers follow a basic approach. In this approach, there are mainly three kinds of classes in the project structure:

- Managers and controllers
- Associates
- Utility classes

A game requires the managers and controllers to implicate game rules and regulations. It is also used to control the behavior of game elements and states. Most games consist of multiple sections or screens, for example, menu, level selection, game play, and so on.

These sections can be termed as states, and the elements used inside these are called associates. Associates may be separate classes by themselves. Utility classes basically support development by providing predefined functionality, such as in-game sound implementation, record store management, common utilities, network connectivity, and so on:

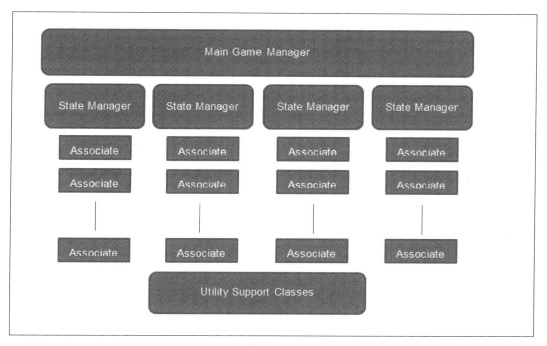

Call hierarchy

Inside the game loop, the main Android game thread loops hand over control to the main game manager. The main game manager is responsible for passing on the thread and rendering control to the required state manager. The main game manager is also responsible for the initialization and destruction of state managers, depending on the current thread. Moreover, the main game manager is active throughout the game cycle and manages the main game activity as well.

State managers are responsible for managing a state (main menu, level selection, in-gameplay, and so on) and all the required associate classes. State managers pass the call to the respective associates to carry out a specific task.

Utility classes are accessible from any layer in the hierarchy, depending on the requirements.

This is a generic architecture that is not mandatory. Many developers design the call hierarchy differently. Everything is good, and the game flow is also running properly without sacrificing the class/data security.

# Game programming specifications

Game programmers are not very different from any other software programmer. However, game programming requires stronger logical skill than software programming. The sense of game design is also different.

A game is an interactive entertainment system. A software or an application is meant to reduce a human calculative real-time task. So, it is clear that a game serves a very different purpose than a software or an application.

This is why game programming has to follow a few specifications and protocols.

Game programming can be divided into these following categories:

- Gameplay programming
- Graphics programming
- Technical programming

# Gameplay programming

This is the most relevant programming for the gaming division. Gameplay programming requires a strong logical, mathematical, and analytical skill. A sense of game design is also required. Gameplay programming includes AI, user control, physics, display control, and so on.

Gameplay programmers are the ones who deal with the most responsible designers for prototyping the game.

## Graphics programming

All the visual effects and impacts are made by graphic programmers. They are responsible for the visual quality of the game. There is a vast scope to manipulate graphic assets while the game is running.

Graphics programming is all about getting the maximum from the GPU. Nowadays, most games are graphics heavy. The latest devices have separate, powerful GPUs to support heavy graphics.

Modern-age games represent an excellent quality of graphical display. All new 3D real-time lighting, particle system effect, visual motion effect, and so on entirely depend on the graphical programmer. The challenge is to increase the visual quality without affecting the game performance.

Most of the time, game performance drops significantly due to heavy art asset processing, which is never a desired situation. Shaders or graphics programmers have to balance quality and performance.

This is mostly effective when games are ported across different platforms. As we have discussed earlier, a range of hardware platforms with a wide range of hardware specifications run on Android. Separate shaders and assets are required for this kind of porting. A shader program instructs the graphic processor to render each pixel in a particular way.

## Technical programming

This part of programming has not much to do with games; however, it ensures the game performance. Besides the performance, network management, plugin development, optimization, and so on are also part of technical programming. Here is a list of the possible areas for technical programming:

- Sound programming
- Network programming
- Game tool programming
- Research and development programming

## Sound programming

Nowadays, sound is a mandatory part of games. Some games are even made around music. Sound programming has therefore become a part of game programming. A sound programmer mainly has knowledge of digital signal processing. Sound programmers have to work with sound designers.

Modern-age games use 3D sound systems. Sound programming plays a critical role in delivering quality sound without affecting the performance.

## Network programming

Old-age games were mostly made to run on a single instance. Most of the time, the game did not communicate with other instances, so there was not much need for network programming at that point in time. The modern age is the age of networking; just one instance is not enough. Multiplayer games are very common today; even standalone games communicate with other game instances just for socialization and monetization.

Network programming takes care of network latency, packet optimization, connection handling, and maintaining communication. The network programmer is also responsible for managing client-server communication and creating the architecture.

Some games run on the server. The client acts as a display device for the game instance running on the server. The transaction follows real-time syncing. Few games even follow asynchronous communication. Network programming assures the smooth and proper transition in this architecture.

## Game tool programming

Game development cannot be completed without the support of certain tools. Tool programmers can make other developers' lives a living hell or heaven. Proper game tool programming can ease the development process a lot. A lot of time and effort can be saved with the help of development tools.

We have already discussed a few development tools. However, it is not necessary for all of the tools to be game independent. There may be few tools that can be game specific. For example, a tool can be made to generate a required database to be used in a game.

# Research and development programming

This kind of programming is not primarily for making a game. Instead, this programming helps make gaming better and finds new techniques to be used for upcoming games.

This type of programming requires strong skills in technical understanding, hardware platforms, and native development. Programmers should have knowledge of native language and assembly or hardware-level language as well.

In the case of Android game development, research programmers are assigned to explore new Android devices along with a new feature and specification. These programmers then try to discover how to use the feature in the best possible way in games.

This programming is solely responsible for games having features like the use of various sensors such as gravity, light, accelerometer, and so on. The recent development of virtual reality with Android devices is a practical example of such experiments.

# Technical design standards

Mostly, game development revolves around game design; however, the development process is controlled by technical design. Technical design considers each and every possible aspect of the real-time feasibility of the actual game design and requirements.

A technical design contains the following sections:

- Game analysis
- Design pattern and flow diagram
- Technical specification
- Tools and other requirements
- Resource analysis
- Testing requirements
- Scope analysis
- Risk analysis
- Change log

## Game analysis

This section of technical design analyzes the game design thoroughly and figures out the sections where technology plays a major role. Game play logic development is not a part of this section. However, when game logic requires hardware dependency, then this section is also considered in technical design.

Many developers and organizations have a habit of making a technical design document after creating the game design and before starting the actual development process. This helps define the timeline and predict upcoming challenges, with possible solutions.

## Design pattern and flow diagram

This section designs the class diagram and hierarchy for the game. The game flowchart and server-client architecture (if required) are also defined here.

This section of game technical design gives a clear picture of upcoming development for a developer. Each and every part of game modules, program structure, call hierarchy, third-party tool integration, database connectivity, and server-call management should be clearly declared in this part of the technical design document.

The visual display of such a diagram, showing the flowcharts, is always a headstart for any development process.

## Technical specification

The technical specification specifies the development platform, target device set, and target operating system. It may also mention what hardware system and software is required to develop the project.

This identification is essential before starting the actual development. For any software to run, it requires a hardware platform that is well capable of supporting the software. Developers must know the target devices and must be provided with these devices to carry out unit testing. Any additional requirement is also identified in this section of technical design.

So, basically, there are two different sections in this specification. First is to specify the target system on which the game is designated to run. Second is to identify the system required to create the game according to the design.

# Tools and other requirements

This section in technical design refers to the additional tools and system requirements. In many cases, this section is included in the technical specification. However, this part serves a different purpose.

This may create the requirement to develop a new tool for the actual game development. Therefore, tool programmers are referred to this section. Android game development is not out of scope for this section. Although most of the tools are readily available for Android development, a few scenarios may demand a game-specific tool as well. In this case, the tool design and separate technical design, and the use of the tool is mentioned in this section.

# Resource analysis

Resource analysis is a report on staff dependency, staff skill level, technical dependency, and other resource dependencies. This helps estimate project cost and decide the development timeline.

# Testing requirements

This is another important part of technical design. Testing is an integral part of a game development process. Technical design should define the testing procedure along with the defined test cases.

The development head of the game identifies the stages of testing and its requirements. Testing tools may be declared in this section. We have already mentioned testing tools in the previous chapter. In some cases, a customized tool may be required.

Testing requirements have four main sections:

- Testing resource requirements
- Testing tool requirements
- Test cases
- Testing timeline

## Scope analysis

Every game has a predefined limited scope. Especially in Android devices, where the variety is maximum, a scope definition is required. Running a game with the same design on all Android platforms is next to impossible.

This section of technical design indicates the probable scope of the game. This may identify the minimum required configuration, recommended configuration, and target configuration to run the game at its maximum performance.

The game scope defines the minimum and maximum range of the hardware platform. Most developers like to minimize the game design scope to target maximum hardware devices. A technical design document is a good reference for developers to get an idea of the performance of the game within the scope.

## Risk analysis

A technical design document is made before the production is started, so there are many fields that have to be assumed beforehand. This obviously increases the risk of the project. However, having a clear idea of the risk always helps developers get the solution when the actual problem occurs.

This is the reason risk analysis is mandatory for any technical design standard. The risk may be analyzed in different fields.

While developing a game, the technical requirements or game design may change. So, risk should be calculated to accommodate these changes without affecting the main project pipeline.

Technology is evolving quickly. So, in the risk analysis section, change of technology should also be addressed. In a common scenario in game development, technology may change during development to increase the game quality.

## Change log

A change log is the list containing all the changes in technical document from the first draft and according to the date and version number. This helps in keeping track of the evolution of the game.

# Game design standards

Game design is documented in almost every organization in the gaming industry. This is one of the standards used most often by almost all developers. Technical design is sometimes skipped to save some time, and some designers include the most required segments from a technical document in game design. However, this approach is not recommended.

A basic approach to maintain a standard game design contains the following sections:

- Game overview
- Gameplay details
- Game progression
- Storyboard and game elements
- Level design
- Artificial intelligence
- Art style
- Technical reference
- Change log

## Game overview

This section defines the nature of the game along with its target audience. This section contains a brief about the game concept, gameplay, and the look and feel. The working title is mentioned beforehand.

Game overview is basically the brief on almost all aspects of the game to be made. This section may project a market study to support the game concept and genre chosen for the game.

## Gameplay details

Gameplay controls and the preferred user interface to control the gameplay is defined in this section. This is one of the most important parts of the game. Gameplay should be optimized for each hardware platform it is targeting. The game might be deployed for a mobile, tablet, and a console as well. So, different control schemes are defined for obvious reasons.

## Game progression

Game progression defines the game life cycle and its evolution through time. A game is a dynamic entertainment system. So, users cannot be bored at any point in time, and this section is responsible for user retention.

## Storyboard and game elements

This part of game design defines the background of the game concept. This does not mean having an actual story-based game background. However, every game must have some elements or objects around which the gameplay works.

For example, a side scrolling runner game will have a character, a few obstacles, environmental objects, and so on. They are termed as game elements. The reason for running is the background story.

In another example, let's assume a game of Tic-Tac-Toe. A background story is not necessary; however, crosses, circles, and the grid are the elements of the game, which need to be designed and stylized.

## Level design

Levels are the consequence of game progression. Each level has a synopsis, introduction, materials or elements, and an objective. More information can be given depending on the game.

## Artificial intelligence

Artificial intelligence helps the gameplay to be experienced in a real-time scenario. It may be the opponent, enemy, obstacle, friendly support, situation detection, collision detection, pathfinding, or anything that determines a state of the game automatically.

Artificial intelligence is mandatory for each and every game. It should imply a mathematical or physical algorithm to carry out a certain task within a domain.

## Art style

A game design document also includes the style and direction of the look and feel. The designer may include few references as well. This gives the artist a headstart in thinking about the art direction. Art is the most powerful part of the game to attract users initially.

This section does not include the technical specification for the art. Developers may include a few technical directions here to optimize the asset to be used inside the game.

## Technical reference

In this section of a design document, all the technical references are included. For Android game development, this section may include a range of devices with minimum specification, targeting platforms, base graphics engine, development engine, and so on. This is a miniature version of the actual technical design document. When a developer or an organization chooses not to make any separate technical document, they mention all the tech specs in this scope.

## Change log

The change log holds a history of changes in the document with versions and dates. This serves the same purpose as any change log documentation.

## Other styles and standards

The standard mentioned in the previous sections defines the general process of making a game. We will discuss a few of these processes that are used widely in the game development industry.

Most large-scale organizations follow a certain project management and tracking system. This may make the development process slower, but effective enough to minimize risk and improve game quality. A few small organizations or individual developers do not follow such processes in order to finalize the product as early as possible.

These styles are opposite to each other, and have different consequences. However, it is recommended that you follow a procedure that helps in the long run. A quick fix cannot be a permanent solution.

One more commonly used practice is patching code to resolve bugs. This is also extremely vulnerable to threats such as project crash, deadline failure, and creation of a major bug. In game development, the most common problem is a device crashing, which is least expected on any hardware platform. In most of the cases, it happens because of handling exceptions badly.

It is very necessary to play and understand games to make games. Most game development organizations encourage developers to play and study games. For Android developers also, it is very good practice to play a lot of games from different platforms. It is already established that Android is the best mobile or small-scale hardware operating system. It has its foot in large-scale platforms as well. Being an Android developer, it is always a good practice to keep an eye on other platforms' features and development and try to implement them in Android. It is the job of the Android game research and development team.

# Different styles for different development engines

We have already discussed a few development tools and engines. The current gaming industry does not encourage the development of a game only for a specific hardware or operating platform. We can find a lot of games that are platform exclusive, but this implies a business decision.

It is quite obvious that the same development is not applicable on every development engine. For example, the development style in native Android will differ from the development style in the Unity3D game engine. The basic reasons are:

- Different programming languages
- Different work principles
- Different target platforms

## Different programming languages

Each and every programming language has its own style and structure of programming. Developing games with Android NDK through C++ is not the same as making games in Android SDK using Java. Developing games using third-party cross-platform engines is also different.

We are not talking about the syntactical difference here. It is about the coding style. Using C++ for Android NDK is different from using C++ for Unreal Engine 4 or Cocos2d-x. Although the C++ core library remains the same, each tool guides the developer to a different direction of styles to get the best result.

Not only C++ and Java, but also C#, Python, JavaScript, Lua, Boo, and so on are being used in the gaming industry. Many of the engines support multiple programming languages to attract maximum developers.

## Different work principles

Different game engines or game making tools follow different working principles. A developer should be flexible enough to become accustomed to these different systems. There are always different code structures, folder structures, and program hierarchies for different engines.

For native development, it is the developer who sets the standard. Engines come with an integral set of standards, and it is expected that all the developers working on that particular engine will follow the same principle.

For example, the work principle of Unity3D is far different to Unreal Engine or Cocos2d-x. Cocos2d-x does not support visual programming, whereas Unreal Engine Blueprint has full visual programming support. So, the development approach must be different despite having the same deployment target.

## Different target platforms

Modern age cross-platform game development tools have already minimized the difference in style and standard. However, for a very few tools, the style and standard is still different.

Now, if we talk only about Android here, then consider the different hardware platforms on it. Development style does not always mean programming. It is about maintaining the complete project, starting from design to deployment. Android console development is different from Android mobiles.

From the gameplay point of view, the general style of design varies with play session time, control, and look. An average session on a console may last up to 2 hours, whereas mobile session length is almost 5 percent of that. A touch interface is far different from a key interface, which also differs from a game controller interface. So, even if the developer plans to deploy the same game made with the same engine, the style of designing the interface changes for very obvious reasons.

## Industry best practices

Although there are plenty of styles and standards out there, most developers like to maintain some common standards to create stability in the game development procedure. Let's discuss some of these area of standards commonly practiced by the industry:

- Design standards
- Programming standards
- Testing standards

## Design standards

Design and concepts vary for every game. The best design standard practice is to make it properly documented along with scope for improvement. The document must be clear enough for the users to understand. No matter what the concept is, developers cannot implement it without a proper understanding of the standard.

The design scope must not be so widely open that it can change the entire game; this causes serious delay in production time. However, it should always have a limited scope to improve the production time over time with ideas.

Design must specify the target genre and audience along with a valid reason. This should also include probable target hardware platforms.

For Android development, mobile gaming is the largest industry in the present day. So, most Android developers mainly have their focus on mobile games. However, designers should always leave scope for the game to be deployed on other platforms, such as wearables, consoles, and so on.

## Programming standards

Programming is the execution of the design. It is the most significant part of the production of any game. A standard piece of code should be readable, modular, and properly documented. Previously, there were two programming approaches: procedural and object-oriented. In the case of the modern day gaming industry, developers follow an object-oriented approach. For this reason, programming standards have changed a lot. Previously, it was common practice to use `m_` and `l_` as prefixes to variables to indicate their status in the object-oriented structure. There were a few other notations such as `i`, `f`, and `b` and so on to indicate variable types.

Modern day standards follow mainly the Camel and Pascal casing system for their naming convention. Common practice is to use Pascal casing for all classes, interfaces, enums, events, structures, namespaces, and method names, and other elements should use the Camel casing system.

Camel casing in programming language means that the first letter of a name should be in lowercase, which is specifically **Lower CamelCase**. The Pascal casing system states that the first letter should be capitalized, which is termed **Upper CamelCase**.

There is no limitation technically to the number of arguments in a method or the number of words per line while programming in any language. However, common industry practice says that the number of arguments should be within eight, and the number of letters per line of coding should not exceed 20.

The reason for this manual limitation is to have less complexity and better readability of the code. For the same reason, a method body should be limited to 200 lines, and a split class structure is always preferred.

## Testing standards

Testing is the validation process for the implementation of the design. Testing also checks the development standard, and it also ensures the quality of the game.

In most cases, there are mainly two parts of testing procedure involved, automated testing and manual testing. The programmer must write the automated testing code for checking the core development. This part is called the test code, which must not be included in the main development project. It requires dedicated testers to carry out manual testing. Their job is to ensure the quality of the game from the user point of view.

Most game development companies follow a checklist for the testing procedure. This checklist often contains defined test cases. Test cases are mainly defined by the developer and designer, and testers need to execute these cases. We will discuss testing in detail in a later chapter.

## Summary

Any software development must follow a certain protocol and standard. Game development is not an exception. Following a standard helps the product sustain for a longer period of time. The modern age Android game life cycle includes many updates after launch, and in many cases the game sustains for years. For an organization, the same developer might not be working on the same game for a long period time, which is a very common scenario in the game industry.

The development project must be readable enough to be adopted by new developers and be flexible enough to accommodate new changes for updates to the game.

Finally, let's summarize the mandatory tasks, which are common in the Android game development industry. Game developers should follow the game development principles. First, they must create a proper game design document to make it easy for programmers and artists to understand clearly. Then, they should create a proper technical design document to supply all the possible technical information to programmers and game engineers. A specific development process in an organization defines and maintains development standards. Programmers must write code in modules to avoid future changes and to increase the reusability of codes. A proper naming convention always helps in understanding the code better, and prepares it for easy editing and reuse.

Another practice that a game developer should follow to make games is to play and enjoy a lot of games.

# 5
# Understanding the Game Loop and Frame Rate

The game loop is the operational body of a game, and the frame rate is the consequence. A game cannot be made without a defined game loop, and the performance cannot be judged without measuring the frame rate.

These two aspects of game development are common throughout any game development project. However, the scalability and nature of the game loop vary across different devices, and there might be different scales to measure frame rates across different platforms.

For native development, the game loop is created and maintained by developers only. However, in most game engines, the loop is already defined with all the necessary controls and scope.

We will have a detailed look at these two most important parts of game development through the following topics:

- Introduction to the game loop
- Creating a sample game loop using the Android SDK
- Game life cycle
- Game update and user interface
- Interrupt handling
- General idea of a game state machine
- The FPS system
- Hardware dependency
- Balance between performance and memory
- Controlling FPS

# Introduction to the game loop

The game loop is the core cycle in which user input, game update, and rendering are executed sequentially. This loop ideally runs once per frame. So, the game loop is the most important part of running a game with frame rate control.

A typical game loop has three steps:

1. User input
2. Game update
3. Rendering

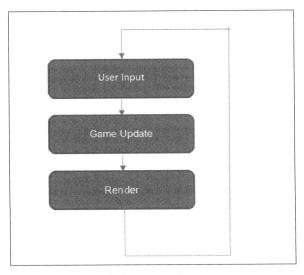

A simple game loop

# User input

This section checks the UI system of the game for any external input that has been given to the game. It sets the required changes to be made in the game for the next update. On a different hardware platform, this portion of the game loop varies the most. It is always a best practice to create common functionality for different input types to make a standard.

The input system is not considered as part of the game loop; however, user-given input detection is part of the game loop. This system continuously monitors the input system, whether an event has occurred or not.

A user can trigger any event at any point of time during gameplay when an active game loop is running. Normally, there are queues maintained by the input system. Each queue represents different types of possible input events, such as touch, key press, sensor reading, and so on.

The user input monitor checks those queues at a particular interval following the loop sequence. If it finds any event in the queue, it makes the required changes that will have an impact on the next update call in the game loop:

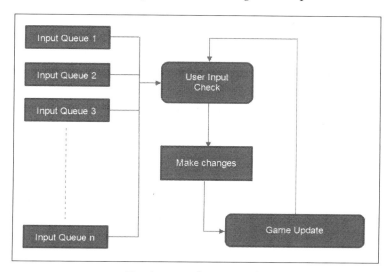

User input working principle

## Game update

The complete game state is managed and maintained by the game update section of the game loop. This section is also responsible for running the game logic, changes in game states, loading/unloading assets, and setting the rendering pipeline.

The game control is usually managed by the game update section. Usually, the main game manager works at the top level of this game update section. We discussed game program structure in the previous section.

Any game runs a particular state at a time. The state can be updated by either user input or any automated AI algorithm. All AI algorithms work on the game update cycle frame by frame.

## State update

As stated earlier, the state can be updated from game update. The state is also initiated and destroyed by the game update. Initialization and destruction happens once per state, and state update can be called once per game cycle.

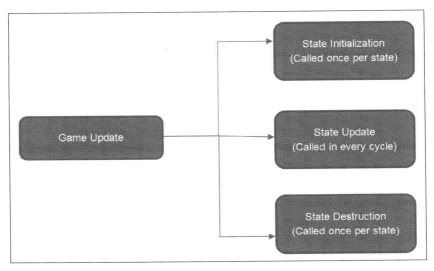

State update call flow

## Rendering frames

The rendering section inside a game loop is responsible for setting the rendering pipeline. No update or AI algorithm runs on this section of the game loop.

There was time when a developer had full control over the rendering pipeline. The developer could manipulate and set each and every vertex. The modern age game development system has not much to do with this rendering system. The graphics library takes care of all the control of the rendering system. However, at a very high level, a developer can only set the order and quantity of rendering vertices.

Rendering is one of the most important roles when it comes to frame rate control, keeping other continuous processes constant. Display and memory operations take the most time to execute from the processing point of view.

Typical Android graphics rendering follows the OpenGL pipeline:

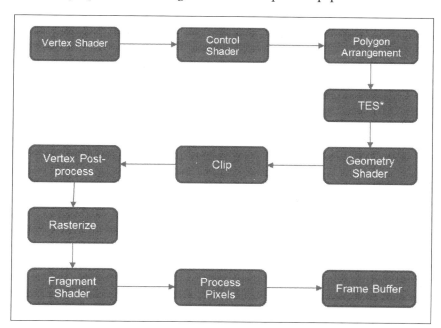

# Creating a sample game loop using the Android SDK

Android SDK development starts with an activity, and the game runs on single or multiple views. Most of the time, it is considered to have a single view to run gameplay.

Unfortunately, the Android SDK does not provide a predefined game loop. However, the loop can be created in many ways, but the basic mechanism remains the same.

In the Android SDK library, the View class contains an abstract method OnDraw() in which every possible rendering call is queued. This method is called upon any change in the drawing, which invalidates the previous rendering pipeline.

## Understanding the Game Loop and Frame Rate

The logic is as follows:

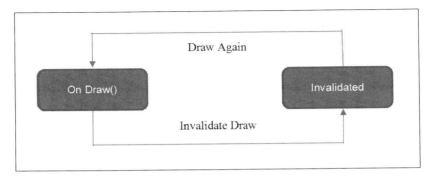

Let's have a look at a basic game loop created with Android View. Here, a custom view is extended from the Android View:

```
/*Sample Loop created within OnDraw()on Canvas
 * This loop works with 2D android game development
 */
@Override
public void onDraw(Canvas canvas)
{
  //If the game loop is active then only update and render
  if(gameRunning)
  {
    //update game state
    MainGameUpdate();

    //set rendering pipeline for updated game state
    RenderFrame(canvas);
    //Invalidate previous frame, so that updated pipeline can be
    // rendered
    //Calling invalidate() causes recall of onDraw()
    invalidate();
  }
  else
  {
    //If there is no active game loop
    //Exit the game
    System.exit(0);
  }
}
```

In the current age of Android game development, developers use `SurfaceView` instead of `View`. `SurfaceView` is inherited from `View` and more optimized for games made with Canvas. In this case, a customized view is extended from `SurfaceView` and implements the `SurfaceHolder.Callback` interface. In this scenario, three methods are overridden:

```
/* Called When a surface is changed */
@Override
public void surfaceChanged(SurfaceHolder holder, int format, int
  width, int height)
{
}
/* Called on create of a SurfaceView */
@Override
public void surfaceCreated(SurfaceHolder holder)
{
}
/* Called on destroy of a SurfaceView is destroyed */
@Override
public void surfaceDestroyed(SurfaceHolder holder)
{
}
```

While developing a game, the developer need not change the surface each time. That's the reason the `surfaceChanged` method should have an empty body to function as a basic game loop.

We need to create a customized game thread and override the `run()` method:

```
public class BaseGameThread extends Thread
{
  private boolean isGameRunning;
  private SurfaceHolder currentHolder;
  private MyGameState currentState;
  public void activateGameThread(SurfaceHolder holder, MyGameState
    state)
  {
    currentState = state;
    isGameRunning = true;
    currentHolder = holder;
    this.start();
  }
```

```
@Override
public void run()
{
  Canvas gameCanvas = null;
  while(isGameRunning)
  {
    //clear canvas
    gameCanvas = null;
    try
    {
      //locking the canvas for screen pixel editing
      gameCanvas  = currentHolder.lockCanvas();
      //Update game state
      currentState.update();
      //render game state
      currentState.render(gameCanvas);
    }
    catch(Exception e)
    {
      //Update game state without rendering (Optional)
      currentState.update();
    }
  }
}
```

Now, we are set to start the newly created game loop from the customized `SurfaceView` class:

```
public myGameCanvas extends SurfaceView implements SurfaceHolder
{
  //Declare thread
  private BaseGameThread gameThread;
  private MyGameState gameState;
  @Override
  public void surfaceCreated(SurfaceHolder holder)
  {
    //Initialize game state
    gameState = new MyGameState();
    //Instantiate game thread
```

```
    gameThread = new BaseGameThread();
    //Start game thread
    gameThread. activateGameThread(this.getHolder(),gameState);
}

@Override
public void surfaceChanged(SurfaceHolder holder, int format, int
   width, int height)
{
}

@Override
public void surfaceDestroyed(SurfaceHolder holder)
{
}
}
```

There can be many approaches to implementing a game loop. However, the basic approach follows either of the two ways mentioned here. Some developers prefer to implement the game thread inside the game view. Handling input is another important part of the game loop. We will discuss this topic later in this chapter.

Another part of this game loop is **frames per second (FPS)** management. One of the most common mechanisms is to use `Thread.sleep()` for such a calculated time that the loop executes at a fixed rate. Some developers create two types of update mechanism: one based on FPS and another based on per frame without delay.

Mostly, physics-based games need an update mechanism that follows a real-time interval to function uniformly across all devices.

For small-scale development, few developers in the industry follow the first approach but do not follow typical looping. This system invalidates the current draw based on the required action. In this scenario, the game loop is not dependent on fixed FPS.

# Game life cycle

The Android game life cycle is almost similar to any other application's life cycle, other than the game loop mechanism. Mostly, the application state changes with external interference. States can be manipulated otherwise, where games have algorithms or artificial intelligence that is capable of interfering with the main game cycle.

An Android game is initialized with an activity. The `onCreate()` method is used for initialization. Then, the game thread starts and enters the game loop. The game loop can then be interrupted by an external interrupt.

In the case of game development, it is always a good practice to save the current game state and pause the loop and threads properly. On resuming the game, it should be easy to return to the last state.

# Game update and user interface

We have already covered a few update and interface mechanisms previously. A running game state can be changed by user input or internal AI algorithms:

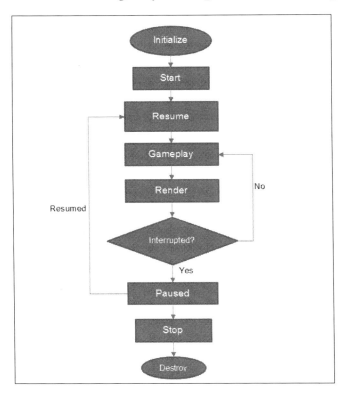

Mostly, game update is called once per frame or once after a fixed time interval. Either way, an algorithm does its job to change the game state. You have learned about user input queues. On each game loop cycle, the input queues are being checked.

For example, a mobile game loop with a touch interface works as follows:

```
/* import proper view and implement touch listener */
public class MyGameView extends View implements
  View.OnTouchListener
/* declare game state */
private MyGameState gameState;
/* set listener */
public MyGameView (Context context)
{
  super(context);
  setOnTouchListener(this);
  setFocusableInTouchMode(true);
  gameState = new MyGameState();
}

/* override onTouch() and call state update on individual touch
  events */
@Override
public boolean onTouch(View v, MotionEvent event)
{
  if(event.getAction() == MotionEvent.ACTION_UP)
  {
    //call changes in current state on touch release
    gameState.handleInputTouchRelease((int)event.getX(),
      (int)event.getY());
    return false;
  }
  else if(event.getAction() == MotionEvent.ACTION_DOWN)
  {
    //call changes in current state on touch begin
    gameState.handleInputTouchEngage((int)event.getX(),
      (int)event.getY());
  }
  else if(event.getAction() == MotionEvent.ACTION_MOVE)
  {
    //call changes in current state on touch drag
    gameState.handleInputTouchDrag((int)event.getX(),
      (int)event.getY());
  }
  return true;
}
```

Now, let's have a look at the input queue system with the same approach:

```java
Point touchBegin = null;
Point touchDragged = null;
Point touchEnd = null;

@Override
public boolean onTouch(View v, MotionEvent event)
{
  if(event.getAction() == MotionEvent.ACTION_UP)
  {
    touchEnd = new Point(int)event.getX(), (int)event.getY());
    return false;
  }
  else if(event.getAction() == MotionEvent.ACTION_DOWN)
  {
    touchBegin = new Point(int)event.getX(), (int)event.getY());

  }
  else if(event.getAction() == MotionEvent.ACTION_MOVE)
  {
    touchDragged = new Point(int)event.getX(), (int)event.getY());

  }
  return true;
}

/* declare checking input mechanism */
private void checkUserInput()
{
  if(touchBegin != null)
  {
    //call changes in current state on touch begin
    gameState. handleInputTouchEngage (touchBegin);
    touchBegin = null;
  }

  if(touchDragged != null)
  {
    //call changes in current state on touch drag
```

```
        gameState. handleInputTouchDrag (touchDragged);
        touchDragged = null;
      }

      if(touchEnd != null)
    {
        //call changes in current state on touch release
        gameState.handleInputTouchRelease (touchEnd);
        touchEnd = null;
      }
    }

    /* finally we need to invoke checking inside game loop */
    @Override
    public void onDraw(Canvas canvas)
    {
      //If the game loop is active then only update and render
      if(gameRunning)
      {
        //check user input
        checkUserInput();
        //update game state
        MainGameUpdate();

        //set rendering pipeline for updated game state
        RenderFrame(canvas);
        //Invalidate previous frame, so that updated pipeline can be
        // rendered
        //Calling invalidate() causes recall of onDraw()
        invalidate();
      }
      else
      {
        //If there is no active game loop
        //Exit the game
        System.exit(0);
      }
    }
```

The same process can be repeated for the `SurfaceView` game loop approach as well.

# Interrupt handling

The game loop is a continuous process. Whenever an interrupt occurs, it is necessary to pause every running thread and save the current state of the game to ensure that it resumes properly.

In Android, any interrupt triggers from `onPause()`:

```
@Override
protected void onPause()
{
  super.onPause();
  // pause and save game loop here
}
// When control is given back to application, then onResume() is //
called.
@Override
protected void onResume()
{
  super.onResume();
  //resume the game loop here
}
```

Now, we need to change the class where the actual game loop is running.

First, declare a Boolean to indicate whether the game is paused or not. Then, put a check in the game loop. After that, create a static method to deal with this variable:

```
private static boolean gamePaused = false;
@Override
public void onDraw(Canvas canvas)
{
  if(gameRunning && ! gamePaused)
  {
    MainGameUpdate();
    RenderFrame(canvas);

    invalidate();
  }
  else if(! gamePaused)
  {
    //If there is no active game loop
    //Exit the game
```

```
      System.exit(0);
    }
  }

  public static void enableGameLoop(boolean enable)
  {
    gamePaused = enable;
    if(!gamePaused)
    {
      //invalidation of previous draw has to be called from static
      // instance of current View class
      this.invalidate();
    }
    else
    {
      //save state
    }
  }
```

# General idea of a game state machine

A game state machine runs within the update cycle of the game loop. A game state machine is the mechanism of binding all the game states together. In old techniques, this was a typical linear control flow. However, in modern development processes, it can be parallel control running in multiple threads. In the old architecture of game development, it was encouraged to have only one game thread. Developers used to avoid parallel processing as it was vulnerable to game loop and timer management. However, even in modern development, many developers still prefer to use a single thread for game development whenever possible. With the help of various tools and advanced scripting language, most game developers now use a virtual parallel processing system.

One of the processes of a simple game state machine is to create a common state interface and override it for each game state. In this way, it becomes easy to manage the state inside the game loop.

Let's see a loop of a simple game state machine manager. This manager should conduct four main functionalities:

- Creating the state
- Updating the state
- Rendering the state
- Changing the state

An example implementation might look like this:

```java
public class MainStateManager
{
  private int currentStateId;
  //setting up state IDs
  public Interface GameStates
  {
    public static final int STATE_1 = 0;
    public static final int STATE_2 = 1;
    public static final int STATE_3 = 2;
    public static final int STATE_4 = 3;
  }

  private void initializeState(int stateId)
  {
    currentStateId = stateId;
    switch(currentStateId)
    {
      case STATE_1:
        // initialize/load state 1
      break;
      case STATE_2:
        // initialize/load state 2
      break;
      case STATE_3:
        // initialize/load state 3
      break;
      case STATE_4:
        // initialize/load state 4
      break;
    }
  }
}
/*
 * update is called in every cycle of game loop.
 * make sure that the state is already initialized before updating
   the state
 */
private void updateState()
{
  switch(currentStateId)
  {
```

```
      case STATE_1:
        // Update state 1
      break;
      case STATE_2:
        // Update state 2
      break;
      case STATE_3:
        // Update state 3
      break;
      case STATE_4:
        // Update state 4
      break;
    }
}
/*
 * render is called in every cycle of game loop.
 * make sure that the state is already initialized before updating
   the state
 */
private void renderState()
{
    switch(currentStateId)
    {
      case STATE_1:
        // Render state 1
      break;
      case STATE_2:
        // Render state 2
      break;
      case STATE_3:
        // Render state 3
      break;
      case STATE_4:
        // Render state 4
      break;
    }
}
/*
 * Change state can be triggered from outside of manager or from
   any other state
 * This should be responsible for destroying previous state and
   free memory and initialize new state
 */
```

```
    public void changeState(int nextState)
{
  switch(currentStateId)
  {
    case STATE_1:
      // Destroy state 1
    break;
    case STATE_2:
      // Destroy state 2
    break;
    case STATE_3:
      // Destroy state 3
    break;
    case STATE_4:
      // Destroy state 4
    break;
  }
  initializeState(nextState);
}
}
```

In some cases, developers pass the input signal to a particular state through the state manager as well.

# The FPS system

In the case of game development and gaming industry, FPS matters a lot. The game quality measurement depends heavily on the FPS count. In simple words, the higher the FPS of the game, the better. The FPS of a game is dependent on the processing time for instructions and rendering.

It takes some time to execute the game loop once. Let's have a look at a sample implementation of FPS management inside a game loop:

```
long startTime;
long endTime;
public final int TARGET_FPS = 60;

@Override
public void onDraw(Canvas canvas)
{
  if(isRunning)
  {
```

```
        startTime = System.currentTimeMillis();
        //update and paint in game cycle
        MainGameUpdate();

        //set rendering pipeline for updated game state
        RenderFrame(canvas);

        endTime = System.currentTimeMillis();
        long delta = endTime - startTime;
        long interval = (1000 - delta)/TARGET_FPS;

        try
        {
          Thread.sleep(interval);
        }
        catch(Exception ex)
        {}
        invalidate();
     }
}
```

In the preceding example, we first noted the time before execution (`startTime`) of the loop and then noted down the time after the execution (`endTime`). We then calculated the time taken for execution (`delta`). We already know the amount of time (`interval`) it should take to maintain a maximum frame rate. So, for the remaining time, we put the game thread to sleep before it executes again. This can be applied to a different game loop system as well.

While using `SurfaceView`, we can declare the FPS system inside the game loop in the `run()` method:

```
long startTime;
long endTime;
public final int TARGET_FPS = 60;
@Override
public void run()
{
  Canvas gameCanvas = null;
  while(isGameRunning)
  {
    startTime = System.currentTimeMillis();
    //clear canvas
```

```
      gameCanvas = null;
      try
      {
        //locking the canvas for screen pixel editing
        gameCanvas  = currentHolder.lockCanvas();
        //Update game state
        currentState.update();
        //render game state
        currentState.render(gameCanvas);
        endTime = System.currentTimeMillis();
        long delta = endTime - startTime;
        long interval = (1000 - delta)/TARGET_FPS;

        try
        {
          Thread.sleep(interval);
        }
        catch(Exception ex)
        {}
      }
      Catch(Exception e)
      {
        //Update game state without rendering (Optional)
        currentState.update();
      }
    }
  }
```

In this process, we capped the FPS count and tried to execute the game loop on the predefined FPS. A major drawback in this system is this mechanism massively depends on hardware configuration. For a slow hardware system, which is incapable of running the loop on the predefined FPS, this system has no effect. This is because the interval time is mostly zero or less than zero, so there is no per frame cycle.

# Hardware dependency

We have discussed earlier that hardware configuration plays a major role in the FPS system. If the hardware is not capable of running a certain set of instructions with a certain frequency, then it is not possible for any developer to run a game on the target FPS.

Let's list the tasks that take most of the processing time for a game:

- Display or rendering
- Memory load/unload operations
- Logical operations

## Display or rendering

Display processing depends mostly on the graphics processor and what all needs to be displayed. When it comes to interaction with the hardware, the process becomes slow. Rendering each and every pixel with shader manipulation and mapping takes time.

There were times when running a game with a frame rate of 12 was difficult. However, in the modern world, a superb display quality game needs to be run on a frame rate of 60. It is only a matter of hardware quality.

A large display requires a good amount of cache memory. So, for example, hardware with a large and dense display and with low cache memory is incapable of maintaining a good display quality.

## Memory load/unload operations

Memory is a hardware component of a system. Again, it takes more time to interact with the memory component. From a developer's perspective, it takes time when we allocate memory, deallocate memory, and read or write an operation.

From the game development perspective, four types of memory are the most important:

- Heap memory
- Stack memory
- Register memory
- ROM

## Heap memory

Heap memory is user-defined manually managed memory. This memory has to be allocated manually and freed manually as well. In the case of Android, the garbage collector is responsible for freeing memory, which is flagged as non-referenced. This memory location is the slowest in the random access memory category.

## Stack memory

This segment of memory is used for elements that are declared inside a method. Allocation and deallocation of this memory segment is automatically done by the program interpreter. This memory segment works only for local members.

## Register memory

Register memory is the fastest of all. Register memory is used to store data for the current process and frequently used data. Game developers can achieve a higher frame rate in the case of devices where the register memory is better and faster.

## ROM

**Read-only memory (ROM)** is permanent memory. Especially in game development, a huge chunk of assets is stored in the ROM. It takes maximum time during the load/unload operation of those assets. A program needs to load the necessary data onto the RAM from the ROM. So, having faster ROM helps achieve better FPS during the load/unload operation.

## Logical operations

Developers should define the instructions in such a way that they can use hardware in the most efficient way. In technical terms, each and every instruction goes in stacks in a binary instruction form. The processor executes one instruction in one clock cycle.

For example, let's have a look at a badly constructed logical instruction:

```
char[] name = "my name is android";
for(int i = 0; i < name.length; i ++)
{
  //some operation
}
```

Calling `length` and using a post increment operator every time increases the instructions to the processor, which eventually increases the execution time. Now, look at this code:

```
char[] name = "my name is android";
int length = name.length;
for(int i = 0; i < length; ++ i)
{
  //some operation
}
```

This code executed the same task; however, the processing overhead is reduced a lot in this approach. The only compromise this code made is blocking memory for one integer variable and saving a lot of nested tasks related to `length`.

Processors with a better clock speed can execute the task faster, which directly implies better FPS. However, managing the task amount depends on the developer, as is shown in the previous example.

Every processor has a mathematical processing unit. The power of the processor varies from one processor to another. So, developers always need to check the mathematical expression to know whether it can be simplified or not.

# Balance between performance and memory

As you learned earlier, memory operation takes a lot time. However, developers always have a limited memory. So, it is extremely necessary to have a balance between performance and memory.

Loading or unloading any asset from ROM to RAM takes time, so it is recommended that you do not do such operations for games that depend on FPS. This operation affects FPS significantly.

Suppose a game requires a lot of assets while running one game state and the target device has a limited heap available. In such a case, the developer should group assets. Small assets can be loaded in the game running the state only in required cases.

Sometimes, many developers preload all the assets and use it from cache. This approach makes the gameplay smoother and faster. However, loading assets in a cache that is not required for that particular game state may crash the game if an interrupt occurs. The Android OS is fully authorized to clear memory occupied by inactive or minimized applications. When an interrupt occurs, the game goes to the minimized state. If a new application requires memory and free memory is not available, then the Android OS kills inactive apps and frees the memory for a new application.

So, it is always a good practice to break the set of assets into parts according to game states.

# Controlling FPS

We have already seen some ways of defining the FPS system. We have already discussed the major drawback of the system as well. So, we can manipulate the game loop according to the real-time FPS generated in the current game loop cycle:

```
long startTime;
long endTime;
public static in ACTUAL_FPS = 0;

@Override
public void onDraw(Canvas canvas)
{
  if(isRunning)
  {
    startTime = System.currentTimeMillis();
    //update and paint in game cycle
    MainGameUpdate();

    //set rendering pipeline for updated game state
    RenderFrame(canvas);

    endTime = System.currentTimeMillis();
    long delta = endTime - startTime;
    ACTUAL_FPS = 1000 / delta;
    invalidate();
  }
}
```

Now, let's have a look at the hybrid FPS system where we cap the maximum FPS to 60. Otherwise, the game can be manipulated through actual FPS:

```
long startTime;
long endTime;
public final int TARGET_FPS = 60;
public static int ACTUAL_FPS = 0;

@Override
public void onDraw(Canvas canvas)
{
  if(isRunning)
  {
    startTime = System.currentTimeMillis();
    //update and paint in game cycle
```

```
      MainGameUpdate();

      //set rendering pipeline for updated game state
      RenderFrame(canvas);

      endTime = System.currentTimeMillis();
      long delta = endTime - startTime;

      //hybrid system begins
      if(delta < 1000)
      {
        long interval = (1000 - delta)/TARGET_FPS;
        ACTUAL_FPS = TARGET_FPS;
        try
        {
          Thread.sleep(interval);
        }
        catch(Exception ex)
        {}
      }
      else
      {
        ACTUAL_FPS = 1000 / delta;
      }
      invalidate();
   }
}
```

## Summary

The game loop is mainly a logical approach for game development. In many cases, developers do not opt for such a mechanism. Some games may be typically interactive and have no algorithm that runs continuously. In such cases, the game loop may not be needed. Game states can be updated as per input given to the gaming system.

However, an exception cannot be an example. That is why it is an industrial approach to follow a game loop to maintain a development standard irrespective of game design.

You learned about the game loop and game state management here. Developers are free to invent and execute game loops in different ways. There are many game engines that have different ways to control game loop and manage game states. The idea and concept of game loop and state management may change as per the game requirement.

However, developers should always keep in mind that the technique they are using should not affect the game performance and FPS. Besides that, developers need to maintain the readability and flexibility of code. Some approaches may consume more memory and run faster and vice versa. Android has various sets of hardware configuration, so there might not be the same processing and memory support on all hardware. Finally, balancing between memory and performance is the key to creating better games.

We will have a deep look at performance and memory management in later chapters. We will try to look at these segments of game development from different perspectives, such as 2D/3D games, VR games, optimization techniques, and more.

# 6
# Improving Performance of 2D/3D Games

Once upon a time, gaming on the mobile platform was limited to black-and-white pixel games, and other mediums of gaming were also heavily dependent on pixel graphics. Times have changed now. 3D games are running on handhelds with ease. However, the requirement of 2D assets has not changed yet. Even in a hardcore 3D game, 2D assets are mandatory. Few games are fully 2D.

We will discuss the performance of 2D and 3D games here with the help of the following topics:

- 2D game development constraints
- 3D game development constraints
- The rendering pipeline in Android
- Rendering through OpenGL
- Optimizing 2D assets
- Optimizing 3D assets
- Common game development mistakes
- 2D/3D performance comparison

## 2D game development constraints

From the perspective of 2D game development, the main constraints are as follows:

- 2D art assets
- 2D rendering system
- 2D mapping
- 2D physics

## 2D art assets

Art asset constraints are mainly limited to graphical or visual assets, which include images, sprites, and fonts. It is not difficult to understand that a larger asset will take more time to process and render than a smaller asset, resulting in less performance quality.

## Sets of 2D art assets

It is not possible to deliver maximum display quality with a single set of assets in Android game development. This is the reason most Android game developers choose high-resolution assets as their base build. This normally performs well for high-configuration hardware platforms, but does not provide quality performance on low-configuration devices. Many developers opt for the option of porting for multiple resolution hardware platforms. This again takes time to complete the project.

## Same asset set for multiple resolutions

Many times, developers choose to ignore a set of hardware platforms. Mostly, in the mobile gaming industry, it is a common practice to choose higher resolution art assets and fit them into lower resolution devices by scaling down. Nowadays, most hardware platforms have better RAM. Hence, this process has become convenient for developers.

## Number of assets drawn on screen

Game performance does not always depend on the asset size; it also depends on the number of assets that are being drawn on screen. The concept of a sprite sheet has evolved to reduce the number of drawing elements on screen.

Generally, the system issues a call for a draw instruction for a single art asset. As the number of assets increases, it takes more such draw instructions to complete the rendering in each game loop cycle. Obviously, this process slows down the processor, and the game performance becomes poor.

A sprite sheet can consist of multiple assets within a single image. So, it takes only one draw instruction to render all the assets of the sprites. However, the physical size of the sprite sheet is restricted. The maximum size varies for different devices with different hardware platforms. Most conveniently, 1024x1024 sprites are the safest option to use, as they are supported by almost all the available devices in the current scenario.

# Use of font files

Almost every game uses custom or special fonts other than the default system font of Android. In those cases, the font source file has to be included in the game build. There are multiple ways to use different fonts. We will discuss three of them here:

- Sprite font
- Bitmap font
- TrueType font

## Sprite font

This is a typical old school technique but is still effective in some cases. The developer creates a sprite sheet that contains all the necessary characters. All the characters are mapped within a data file. This mapping is used to clip each character and form words accordingly.

Here are some advantages of this font:

- Developers have total control of mapping
- Character stylization can be customized as per requirement
- Fast processing speed can be achieved; however, it will depend on development efficiency

Here are some disadvantages of this font:

- They increase development overhead
- The system efficiency entirely depends on the developer's skill set
- It is very difficult to map characters in the case of multi-language support
- Any change takes a lot of iteration to achieve perfection

This style is not usually used nowadays as we have many designer and stylish fonts available.

## Bitmap font

The bitmap font system is inherited from the sprite font. It is updated with a predefined mapping style and a library to support development process. It also uses one or more sprite sheets with one data file. The working principle of bitmap font is the same as sprite font. There are a lot of tools available to create such fonts with a bit of stylization directly from the TrueType font.

Here are some advantages of this font:

- It is compatible with any existing codebase, irrespective of the rendering framework, whether it is OpenGL, DirectX, Direct Draw, or GDI+
- It is easy to integrate
- It can manipulate the style of the existing TrueType font

Here are some disadvantages of this font:

- The same disadvantages of the sprite font are applicable here, only with less development overhead
- Scaling up the bitmap font results in blurry output

## TrueType font

This is the universal format of font that is supported by most platforms, including Android. It is the fastest way to integrate various fonts in games.

Here are some advantages of this font:

- Universal font style
- Maximum platform support
- Easy multi-language implementation
- This is a vector font, so it has no scaling issue
- Easy special character availability

Here are some disadvantages of this font:

- Using this font style may cost a few kilobytes extra to the game
- Not all scripting languages are supported by TTF

# 2D rendering system

Android provides a scope to render 2D assets onto the canvas through an API framework. Canvas can be used with `Drawable` objects in `View` or `SurfaceView`.

Canvas acts as an interface of the actual drawing surface upon which all the graphical objects can be drawn. Draw on the canvas happens within the `onDraw()` callback method. The developer just needs to specify graphical objects along with their position on the canvas.

Canvas itself has a set of default drawing methods to render almost each type of graphical objects. Here are some examples:

- The `drawBitmap()` method is used to draw image objects in the bitmap format. However, images need not be in bitmap format.
- The `drawRect()` and `drawLine()` methods are used to draw primitive shapes on the canvas.
- The `drawText()` method can be used to render text on canvas using a specific font style.

Canvas can be used within a view in the Android architecture.

## 2D mapping

2D mapping is based on a simple 2D coordinate system. The only difference is the opposite *y* axis in comparison with the conventional coordinate system:

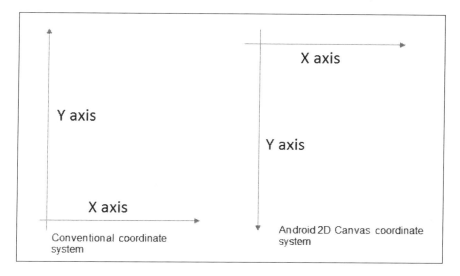

In Android 2D, the origin is located in the top-left corner of the canvas. All the geometrical calculations are based on this mapping. However, it has no direct effect on the performance like the 2D canvas-based application has. Many developers are used to mapping their graphic assets based on the conventional system, and they reverse the vertical axis to render it on the canvas. This requires some additional calculation.

*Improving Performance of 2D/3D Games*

There is one more performance constraint regarding the 2D rendering systems. A common development approach across the world is to have a minimum set of graphic assets and use them as much as possible. Often, this leads to rendering the same pixel multiple times. This affects the processing speed and hence the FPS.

For example, bitmap **A**, bitmap **B**, bitmap **C**, and bitmap **D** are being rendered on a canvas in such a way that **A**, **B**, and **C** overlap each other, and **D** remains separate. The following happens:

- Pixels in the region **R0** where only one bitmap is drawn will be rendered once
- Pixels in region **R1** where two bitmaps are overlapping will be rendered twice
- Pixels in region **R2** where three bitmaps are overlapping will be rendered three times

This is shown here:

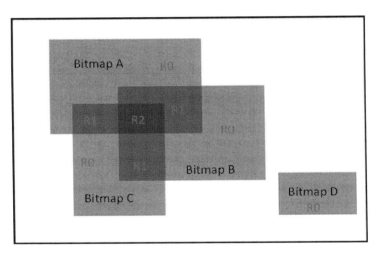

Now, in regions **R1** and **R2**, all the pixels are rendered multiple times. In this system, the pixel data information will append to the previous data, resulting in the final pixel value. In this system, the processing overhead increases. Hence, performance decreases.

Even today, it is a common practice for 2D game programming. The reasons are as follows:

- Transparency blending
- Modular graphical assets

- Low build size
- Easy construction of screens by overlapping multiple assets

Sometimes, there may be a scenario where a device has a very low-performing graphics processor, and rendering the same pixel multiple times has a major impact on performance. In this scenario, the double buffer mechanism helps a lot.

The double buffering system refers to creating a buffered displayable asset in which the display screen is created using graphic assets. Then, this buffered object is drawn on the screen only once. It prevents the following issues:

- Flickering of screen
- Multiple draws of one pixel
- Tearing of assets

# 2D physics

2D physics takes only the $x$-$y$ plane into consideration for all the calculations. There are plenty of 2D physics engines available in market. **Box2D** is the most popular one. A physics engine consists of every mechanism and calculation of real-time physics.

Real-time physics calculation is much complicated than is required in games. Let's discuss a few available physics engines.

# Box2D

Box2D is an open source physics engine based on C++. It consists of almost every aspect of solid physics that can be used in various games. A few of its mentionable features are as follows:

- Dynamic collision detection of rigid bodies
- Collision state callbacks, such as collision enter, exit, stay, and so on
- Polygonal collision
- Vertical, horizontal, and projectile motion
- Friction physics
- Torque and momentum physics
- Gravity effects based on pivot point and joints

## LiquidFun

LiquidFun is a physics engine with all aspects of liquid physics. This engine is actually based on Box2D. Google released this open source physics engine to cover the liquid physics formula and mechanism. LiquidFun can be used for Android, iOS, Windows, and a few other popular platforms. LiquidFun supports every feature of Box2D, along with liquid particle physics. This includes the following:

- Wave simulation
- Liquid fall and particle simulation
- Liquid stir simulation
- Solid and liquid dynamic collision
- Liquid mixing

## Performance impact on games

Collision detection is a costly process. Multi-edge and polygonal collisions increase the process overhead. The number of rigid bodies and collision surfaces have the maximum impact on performance. This is why liquid physics is slower than solid physics.

Let's have a look at the major impacts:

- Each transformation of any rigid body requires a refresh on the collision check of the entire system
- The physics engine is responsible for repetitive transform change, which is responsible for heavy processes

Each and every possible force on the rigid body is calculated in the physics engine. Not all the games require every calculation. Game development does not always required real-time implementation of physics. However, real-time visualization is required for games.

## 2D collision detection

Most games use the box-colliding system to detect most collisions. Rectangular collision detection is the cheapest possible method, which can be used inside games to detect collisions.

Sometimes, triangular and circular collision detection is also used for 2D games for collision detection accuracy. There needs to be a balance of using such methods.

For example, if we need to detect the collision between two circles, we can opt for any of these systems:

- Considering each circle a rectangle and detecting the collision between them
- Considering one circle a rectangle and detecting the collision between the circle and rectangle
- Applying the actual circular collision detection method

Let's consider two circles having origins *O1* and *O2* and diameters *R1* and *R2*:

*O1* is located at *(Ox1, Oy1)*

*O2* is located at *(Ox2, Oy2)*

## Rectangle collision

If we imagine the circles as rectangles on a 2D canvas, then it will look like this:

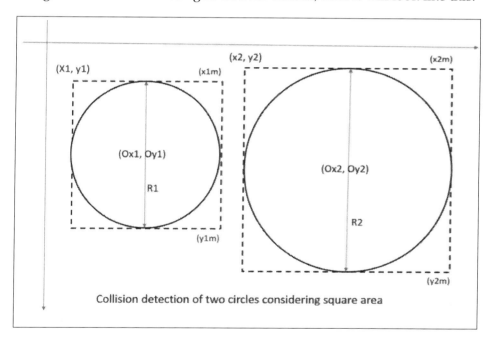

Collision detection of two circles considering square area

Rectangular collision detection refers to this formula.

Input feed will be as follows:

*xMin1 = x1* (minimum co-ordinate on *x* axis of first rectangle)

$yMin1 = y1$ (minimum co-ordinate on $y$ axis of the first rectangle)

$xMax1 = x1m$ (maximum co-ordinate on $x$ axis of the first rectangle)

$yMax1 = y1m$ (maximum co-ordinate on $y$ axis of the first rectangle)

$xMin2 = x2$ (minimum co-ordinate on $x$ axis of the second rectangle)

$yMin2 = y2$ (minimum co-ordinate on $y$ axis of the second rectangle)

$xMax2 = x2m$ (maximum co-ordinate on $x$ axis of the second rectangle)

$yMax2 = y2m$ (maximum co-ordinate on $y$ axis of the second rectangle)

In the given circumstances, we will have the following:

$x1 = Ox1 - (R1/2)$

$y1 = Oy1 - (R1/2)$

$x1m = Ox1 + (R1/2) = x1 + R1$

$y1m = Oy1 + (R1/2) = y1 + R1$

$x2 = Ox2 - (R2/2)$

$y2 = Oy2 - (R2/2)$

$x2m = Ox2 + (R2/2) = x2 + R2$

$y2m = Oy2 + (R2/2) = y2 + R2$

The condition for colliding or not colliding these two rectangles will be as follows:

```
if( x1m < x2 )
{
   // Not Collide
}
else if( y1m < y2 )
{
   // Not collide
}
else if( x1 > x2m )
{
   //Not collide
```

```
}
else if( y1 > y2m )
{
   //Not collide
}
else
{
   //Successfully collide
}
```

## Rectangle and circle collision

Now, considering only the second circle as a rectangle, we will have this:

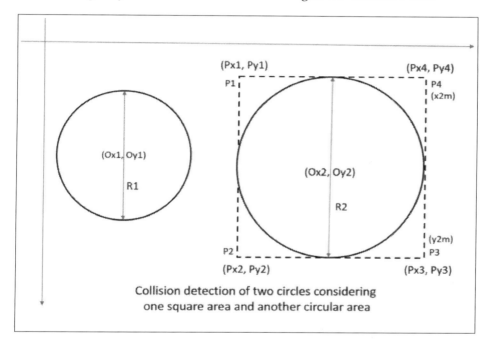

Collision detection of two circles considering one square area and another circular area

As we have already discussed the general idea of the coordinate system for the same system, we can directly derive the values:

$Px1 = Ox2 - (R2/2)$

$Py1 = Oy2 - (R2/2)$

$Px2 = Ox2 - (R2/2)$

$Py2 = Oy2 + (R2/2)$

$Px3 = Ox2 + (R2/2)$

$Py3 = Oy2 + (R2/2)$

$Px4 = Ox2 + (R2/2)$

$Py4 = Oy2 - (R2/2)$

$x2m = Ox2 + (R2/2) = x2 + R2$

$y2m = Oy2 + (R2/2) = y2 + R2$

$radius1 = (R1/2)$

$distanceP1 = squareRoot(((Px1 - Ox1)*(Px1 - Ox1)) + ((Py1 - Oy1)*(Py1 - Oy1)))$

$distanceP2 = squareRoot(((Px2 - Ox1)*(Px2 - Ox1)) + ((Py2 - Oy1)*(Py2 - Oy1)))$

$distanceP3 = squareRoot(((Px3 - Ox1)*(Px3 - Ox1)) + ((Py3 - Oy1)*(Py3 - Oy1)))$

$distanceP4 = squareRoot(((Px4 - Ox1)*(Px4 - Ox1)) + ((Py4 - Oy1)*(Py4 - Oy1)))$

The colliding and non-colliding condition would be as follows:

```
if ( (Ox1 + radius1) < x2 )
{
  //Not collide
}
else if ( Ox1 > x2m )
{
  //Not collide
}
else if ( (Oy1 + radius1) < y2 )
{
  //Not collide
}
else if ( Oy1 > y2m )
{
  //Not collide
}
else
{
if (distanceP1 <= radius1)
{
  //Successfully collide
}
else if (distanceP2 <= radius1)
{
  //Successfully collide
}
```

```
  else if (distanceP3 <= radius1)
  {
    //Successfully collide
  }
  else if (distanceP4 <= radius1)
  {
    //Successfully collide
  }
  else if ( Ox1 >= Px1 && Ox1 <= x2m &&
  (Oy1 + radius1) >= Py1 && (Oy1 <= y2m))
  {
    //Successfully collide
  }
  else if ( Oy1 >= Py1 && Oy1 <= y2m &&
  (Ox1 + radius1) >= Px1 && (Ox1 <= x2m))
  {
    //Successfully collide
  }
  else
  {
    //Not collide
  }
```

# Circle and circle collision

Finally, the actual collision detection system is between the circle and circle collision:

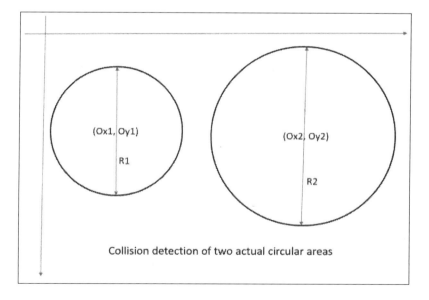

Collision detection of two actual circular areas

Logically, this is the simplest procedure to find out the circular collision.

First, calculate the distance between the two origins of the circles:

*originDistance = squareRoot ( ((Ox2 − Ox1)\* (Ox2 − Ox1)) + ((Ox2 − Ox1)\* (Ox2 − Ox1)))*

Now, we need to check whether the distance is less than or equal to the sum of the radius of the two circles:

```
if (originDistance <= ((R1 + R2) / 2))
{
  //Successfully Collide
}
else
{
  //Not Collide
}
```

## Performance comparison

For the first approach, it will take a minimum clock cycle to execute the checking. However, it is not that accurate. Particularly when developers work with a bigger circle, the lack in accuracy becomes visible.

The third approach is perfectly accurate, but takes more time to process. In the case of many circles colliding in runtime, this process and mathematical calculation may cause performance delay.

The second approach is, overall, the worst possible way to solve this problem. However, this approach may be used in a very specific situation. When a developer wants to detect circle and rectangle collisions accurately, then only this approach can be tried.

Detecting these sorts of collision may have multiple solutions. The approaches and solutions you have learned here are few of the most efficient solutions from the point of view of performance.

When detecting rectangle and circle collisions accurately, there is one more popular approach by creating a bigger round rectangle by increasing the width and height by the diameter of the circle. This procedure is heavier but more accurate.

# 3D game development constraints

3D game development in Android native is very complicated. The Android framework does not support direct 3D game development platforms. 2D game development is directly supported by Android Canvas. The developer requires OpenGL support to develop 3D games for Android.

Development is supported by Android NDK, which is based on C++. We will discuss a few constraints of 3D development for Android with OpenGL support.

Android provides the OpenGL library for development. The developer needs to set up scenes, light, and camera first to start any development process.

## Vertices and triangles

Vertex refers to a point in 3D space. In Android, `Vector3` can be used to define the vertices. A triangle is formed by three such vertices. Any triangle can be projected onto a 2D plane. Any 3D object can be simplified to a collection of triangles surrounding its surface.

For example, a cube surface is a collection of two triangles. Hence, a cube can be formed of 12 triangles as it has six surfaces. The number of triangles has a heavy impact on the rendering time.

## 3D transformation matrix

Each 3D object has its own transformation. `Vector` can be used to indicate its position, scaling, and rotation. Generally, this is referred through a matrix called a transform matrix. A transformation matrix is 4 x 4 in dimension.

Let's assume the matrix to be $T$:

$$[T] = \begin{bmatrix} a & b & c & d \\ e & f & g & h \\ i & j & k & l \\ m & n & o & p \end{bmatrix}$$

Here:

- {a, b, c, e, f, g, i, j, k} represents linear transformation
- {d, h, l} represents perspective transformation
- {m, n, o} represents translations along the x, y, and z axes
- {a, f, k} represents local scaling along the x, y, and z axes
- {p} represents overall scaling
- {f, g, i, k} represents rotation along the x axis where $a = 1$
- {a, c, i, k} represents rotation along the y axis where $f = 1$
- {a, b, e, f} represents rotation along the z axis where $k = 1$

Any 3D object can be translated using this matrix and a respective transform 3D vector. Naturally, matrix calculation is heavier than 2D simple linear calculation. As the number of vertices increases, the number of calculations increases as well. This results in performance drop.

# 3D object and polygon count

Any 3D model or object has surfaces referred to as polygons. Fewer of polygons implies fewer of triangles, which directly decreases the vertices count:

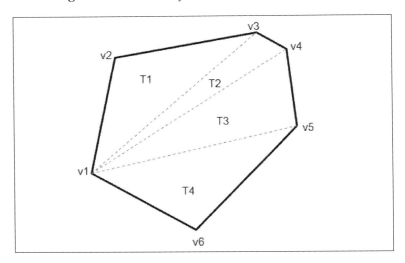

This is a simple example of a polygonal distribution of a 3D object surface. A six-sided polygon has four triangles and six vertices. Each vertex is a 3D vector. Every processor takes time to process each vertex. It is recommended that you keep a check on the total polygon count, which will be drawn in each draw cycle. Many games suffer a significant amount of FPS drop because of a high and unmanaged polygon count.

Android is specifically a mobile OS. Most of the time, it has limited device configuration. Often, managing the poly count of 3D games for Android becomes a problem for developers.

## 3D rendering system

Android uses OpenGL to provide a 3D rendering platform with both framework and NDK. The Android framework provides GLSurfaceView and GLSurfaceView.Renderer to render 3D objects in Android. They are responsible for generating the model on screen. We have already discussed the 3D rendering pipeline through OpenGL.

3D rendering maps all the objects on a 3D world coordinate system following the right-hand thumb system:

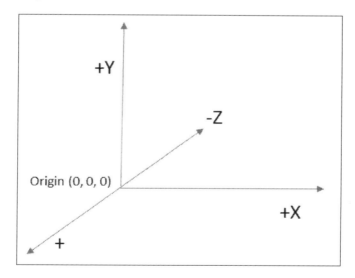

## 3D mesh

A 3D mesh is created with vertices, triangles, and surfaces. A mesh is created to determine the shape of the object. A texture is applied to the mesh to create the complete model.

Creating a mesh is the trickiest part of 3D model creation, as basic optimization can be applied here.

Here is the procedure of creating the mesh:

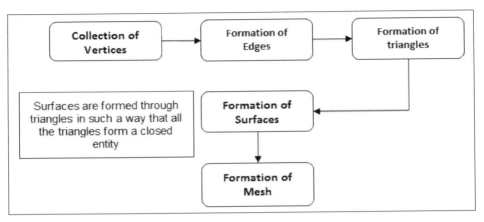

A 3D model can contain more than one mesh, and they may even be interchangeable. A mesh is responsible for the model detailing quality and for the rendering performance of the model. For Android development, it is recommended that you keep a certain limit of vertices and triangles for meshes to render performance.

## Materials, shaders, and textures

After the formation of the model structure through the mesh, the texture is applied on it to create the final model. However, the texture is applied through a material and manipulated by shaders:

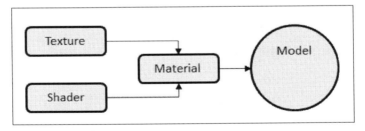

## Textures

Textures are 2D images applied to the model to increase detailing and view the quality of a model. This image is mapped through the surfaces of the mesh so that each surface renders a particular clip of the texture.

## Shaders

Shaders are used to manipulate the quality, color, and other attributes of the texture to make it more realistic. Most of the time, it is not possible to create a texture with all the attributes properly set. A 3D model visibility is dependent on light source, intensity, color, and material type.

## Materials

The material determines the texture attribute and shader property. The material can be termed as a container for the shader and texture before applying it to the mesh to create the model.

## Collision detection

Collision detection for 3D Android games can be categorized into two types:

- Primitive colliders
- Mesh colliders

### Primitive colliders

These colliders consist of basic 3D elements such as cubes, spheres, cylinders, prisms, and so on. This collision detection system follows certain geometric patterns and rules. That's why it is comparatively less complicated than the arbitrary mesh collider.

Most of the time, the developer assigns primitive colliders to many models to increase the performance of the game. This approach is obviously less accurate than actual collider.

### Mesh colliders

Mesh colliders can detect actual arbitrary collision detection. This collision detection technique is process heavy. There are few algorithms to minimize the process overhead. **quadtree**, **kd-tree**, and **AABB tree** are a few examples of such collision detection techniques. However, they do not minimize the CPU overhead significantly.

The oldest but most accurate method is triangle to triangle collision detection for each surface. To simplify this method, each mesh block is converted to boxes. A special AABB tree or quadtree is generated to reduce the vertex check.

This can be further reduced to **octree** vertex mapping by merging two box colliders. In this way, the developer can reduce the collision check to reduce CPU overhead.

## Ray casting

Ray casting is a geometric system to detect the surfaces of 3D graphical objects. This system is used to solve the geometric problems of 3D computer graphics. In the case of 3D games, all 3D objects are projected in a 2D view. It is not possible to determine depth without ray casting in the case of a 2D electronic display:

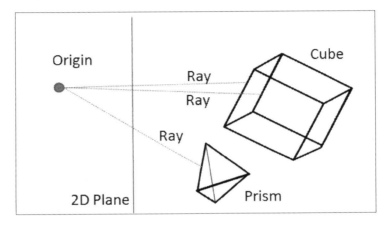

Each ray from the origin projected on different objects can detect the shape of the object, distance from the plane, collision detection, rotation, and scaling of the objects, and so on.

In the case of Android games, ray casting is vastly used to handle touch input on the screen. Most of the games use this method to manipulate the behavior of 3D objects used in the game.

From the point of view of development performance, ray casting is a quite costly system to use in a major scale. This requires a series of geometrical calculation, resulting in a processing overhead. As the number of rays increases, the process gets heavier.

It is always a best practice to keep a control on using multiple rays casting at one point.

# Concept of "world"

The word "world" in 3D games is a real-time simulation of the actual world with a regional limitation. The world is created with 3D models, which refer to actual objects in the real world. The scope of the game world is finite. This world follows a particular scale, position, and rotation with respective cameras.

The concept of camera is a must for simulating such a world. Multiple cameras can be used to render different perspectives of the same world.

In the gaming industry, a game world is created according to requirements. This means that the worlds of different games are different. But a few of the parameters remain the same. These parameters are as follows:

- Finite elements
- Light source
- Camera

## Elements of the game world

A world consists of the elements that are required in game design. Each game may require different elements. However, there are two things that are common across the games: sky and terrain. Most of the elements are usually placed on the terrain, and the light source is in the sky. However, many games offer different light sources at different scopes of the game.

Elements can be divided into two categories: movable objects and static objects. A game's rigid bodies are associated with such elements. Normally, static objects do not support motion physics.

Optimizing objects in the world is necessary for performance. Each object has a certain number of vertices and triangles. We have already discussed the processing overhead of the vertices of 3D objects. Generally, world optimization is basically the optimization of each element in the world.

## Light sources in the game world

A game world must have one or more light sources. Lights are used to expose the elements in the world. Multiple light sources have a great visual impact on the user experience.

The game development process always requires at least one good light artist. Modern games use light maps to amplify the visual quality. The light and shadow play in the game world is entirely dependent on light mapping.

There is no doubt that light is a mandatory element in the game world. However, the consequence of processing light and shadow is a large amount of processing. All the vertices need to be processed according to a light source with a particular shader. Use of extensive light sources results in low performance.

Light sources can be of the following types:

- Area light
- Spot light
- Point light
- Directional light
- Ambient light
- Volume light

## Area light

This kind of light source is used to light a rectangular or circular region. By nature, it is a directional light and lights the area with equal intensity:

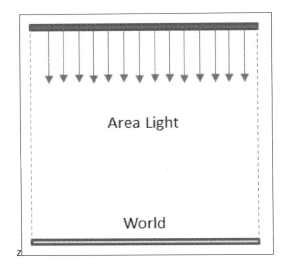

## Spot light

A spot light is used to focus on a particular object in a conical directional shape:

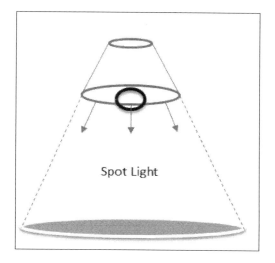

Spot Light

## Point light

A point light illuminates in all directions of the source. A typical example is a bulb illumination:

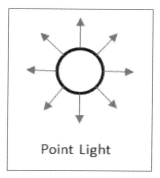

Point Light

## Directional light

A directional light is a set of parallel light beams projected on a place in a 3D world. A typical example is sunlight:

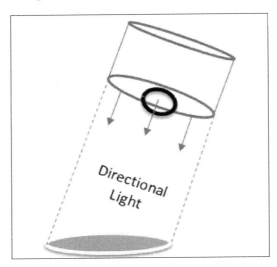

## Ambient light

An ambient light is a set of arbitrary light beams in any direction. Usually, the intensity of this kind of light source is low. As a light beam does not follow a particular direction, and it does not generate any shadows:

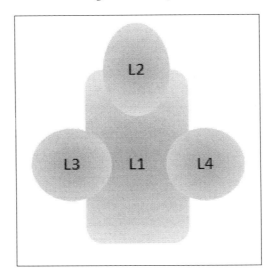

**L1, L2, L3,** and **L4** are ambient light sources here.

**Volume light**

A volume light is a modified type of point light. This kind of light source can be converted into a set of light beams within a defined geometrical shape. Any light beam is a perfect example of such a light source:

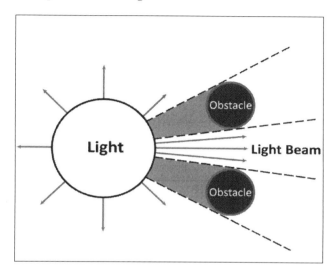

# Cameras in the game world

The camera is the last but the most important element of the game world. A camera is responsible for the rendering of the game screen. It also determines the elements to be added in the rendering pipeline.

There are two types of camera used in a game.

## Perspective camera

This type of camera is typically used to render 3D objects. The visible scale and depth is fully dependent on this type of camera. The developer manipulates the field of view and near/far range to control the rendering pipeline:

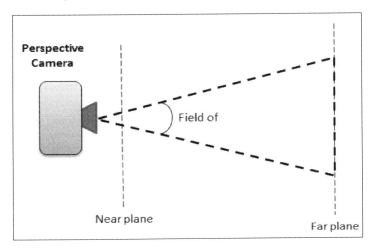

## Orthographic camera

This type of camera is used to render objects from a 2D perspective, irrespective of the objects. An orthographic camera renders objects on the same plane, irrespective of the depth. The developer manipulates effective width and height of the camera to control the 2D rendering pipeline. This camera is typically used for 2D games and to render 2D objects in a 3D game:

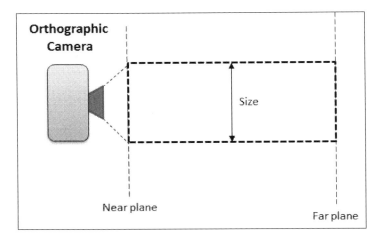

Besides this, the game camera can also be categorized by their nature and purpose. Here are the most common variations.

### Fixed camera

A fixed camera does not rotate, translate, or scale during the execution. Typically, 2D games use such cameras. A fixed camera is the most convenient camera in terms of processing speed. A fixed camera does not have any runtime manipulation.

### Rotating camera

This camera has a rotating feature during runtime. This type of camera is effective in the case of sports simulation or surveillance simulation games.

### Moving camera

A camera can be said to be moving when the translation can be changed during runtime. This type of camera is typically used for an aerial view of the game. A typical use of this sort of camera is for games such as *Age Of Empires*, *Company Of Heroes*, *Clash Of Clans*, and so on.

### Third-person camera

This camera is mainly the part of gameplay design. This is a moving camera, but this camera follows a particular object or character. The character is supposed to be the user character, so all the actions and movements are tracked by this camera including the character and object. Mostly, this camera can be rotated or pushed according to the actions of the player.

### First-person camera

When the player plays as the main character, this camera is used to implement a typical view of the eyes of the player. The camera moves or translates according to the actions of the player.

# The rendering pipeline in Android

Let's now have a look at the types of rendering pipeline in Android.

# The 2D rendering pipeline

In the case of the 2D Android drawing system through Canvas, all the assets are first drawn on the canvas, and the canvas is rendered on screen. The graphic engine maps all the assets within the finite Canvas according to the given position.

Often, developers use small assets separately that cause a mapping instruction to execute for each asset. It is always recommended that you use sprite sheets to merge as many small assets as possible. A single draw call can then be applied to draw every object on the Canvas.

Now, the question is how to create the sprite and what the other consequences are. Previously, Android could not support images or sprites of a size more than 1024 x 1024 pixels. Since Android 2.3, the developer can use a 4096 x 4096 sprite. However, using such sprites can cause permanent memory occupancy during the scopes of all the small assets. Many low-configuration Android devices do not support such large images to be loaded during an application. It is a best practice that developers limit themselves to 2048 x 2048 pixels. This will reduce memory usage peak, as well as significant amounts of draw calls to the canvas.

# The 3D rendering pipeline

Android uses OpenGL to render assets on the screen. So, the rendering pipeline for Android 3D is basically the OpenGL pipeline.

Let's have look at the OpenGL rendering system:

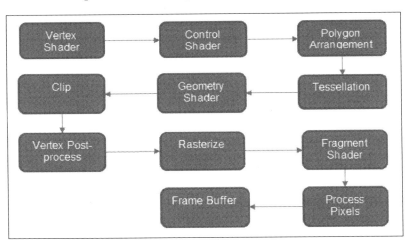

Now, let's have a detailed look at each step of the preceding rendering flow diagram:

1. The **vertex shader** processes individual vertices with vertex data.
2. The **control shader** is responsible for controlling vertex data and patches for the tessellation.

3. The **polygon arrangement** system arranges the polygon with each pair of intersecting lines created by vertices. Thus, it creates the edges without repeating vertices.
4. **Tessellation** is the process of tiling the polygons in a shape without overlap or any gaps.
5. The **geometry shader** is responsible for optimizing the primitive shape. Thus triangles are generated.
6. After constructing the polygons and shapes, the model is **clipped** for optimization.
7. **Vertex post processing** is used to filter out unnecessary data.
8. The mesh is then **rasterized**.
9. The **fragment shader** is used to process fragments generated from rasterization.
10. All the pixels are **mapped** after fragmentation and **processed** with the processed data.
11. The mesh is added to the **frame buffer** for final rendering.

# Optimizing 2D assets

Any digital game cannot be made without 2D art assets. There must be 2D assets in some form inside the game. So, as far as game component optimization is concerned, every 2D asset should also be optimized. Optimization of 2D assets means these three main things.

## Size optimization

Each asset frame should only contain the effective pixels to be used in games. Unnecessary pixels increase the asset size and memory use during runtime.

## Data optimization

Not all images require full data information for pixels. A significant amount of data might be stored in each pixel, depending on the image format. For example, full screen opaque images should never contain transparency data. Similarly, depending on the color set, images must be formatted in 8-bit, 16-bit, or 24-bit format.

Image optimization tools can be used to perform such optimizations.

## Process optimization

The larger the amount of data compressed during optimization, the more time it takes to decompress it and load it to memory. So, image optimization has a direct effect on the processing speed.

From another point of view, creating an image atlas or sprite sheet is another way to reduce the processing time of images.

# Optimizing 3D assets

A 3D art asset has two parts to be optimized. A 2D texture part is to be optimized in the same 2D optimization style. The only thing the developer needs to consider is after optimization, the shader should have the same effect on the structure.

The rest of the 3D asset optimization entirely depends on the number of vertices and the model polygon.

## Limiting the polygon count

It is very obvious that a large number of polygons used to create a mesh can create more details. However, we all know that Android is a mobile OS, and it always has hardware limitations.

The developer should count the number of polygons used in the mesh and the total number of polygons rendered on the screen in a single draw cycle. There is always a limitation depending on the hardware configuration.

So, limiting the polygon and vertex count per mesh is always an advantage in order to achieve a certain frame rate or performance.

## Model optimization

Models are created with more than one mesh. Using a separate mesh in the final model always results in heavy processing. This is a major effort for the game artist. Multiple overlaps can occur if multiple meshes are used. This increases vertex processing.

Rigging is another essential part of finalizing the model. A good rigger defines the skeleton with the minimum possible joints for minimum processing.

# Common game development mistakes

It is not always possible to look into each and every performance aspect at every development stage. It is a very common practice to use assets and write code in a temporary mode and use it in the final game.

This affects the overall performance and future maintenance procedure. Here are few of the most common mistakes made during game development.

## Use of non-optimized images

An artist creates art assets, and the developer directly integrates those into the game for the debug build. However, most of the time, those assets are never optimized, even for the release candidate.

This is the reason there may be plenty of high-bit images where the asset contains limited information. Alpha information may be found in opaque images.

## Use of full utility third-party libraries

The modern day development style does not require each and every development module to be written from scratch. Most of the developers use a predefined third-party library for common utility mechanisms.

Most of the time, these packages come with most of the possible methods, and among them, very few are actually used in games. Developers, most of the time, use these packages without any filtration. A lot of unused data occupies memory during runtime in such cases.

Often, a third-party library comes without an editing facility. In this case, the developer should choose such packages very carefully, depending on their specific requirements.

## Use of unmanaged networking connections

In modern Android games, the use of Internet connectivity is very common. Many games use server-based gameplay. In such cases, the entire game runs on the server with frequent data transfers between the server and the client device. Each data transfer process takes time, and the connectivity drains the battery charge significantly.

Badly managed networking states often freeze the application. A significant amount of data is handled, especially for real-time multiplayer games. In this case, a request and response queue should be created and managed properly. However, the developer often skips this part to save development time.

Another aspect of unmanaged connections is unnecessary packet data transferred between the server and client. So, there is an extra parsing process involved each time data is transferred.

## Using substandard programming

We have already discussed programming styles and standards. The modular programming approach may increase a few extra processes, but the longer management of programming demands modular programming. Otherwise, developers end up repeating code, and this increases process overhead.

Memory management also demands a good programming style. In few cases, the developer allocates memory but often forgets to free the memory. This causes a lot of memory leakage. At times, the application crashes due to insufficient memory.

Substandard programming includes the following mistakes:

- Declaring the same variables multiple times
- Creating many static instances
- Writing non-modular coding
- Improper singleton class creation
- Loading objects at runtime

## Taking a shortcut

This is the funniest fact among ill-practiced development styles. Taking a shortcut during development is very common among game developers.

Making games is mostly about logical development. There may be multiple ways of solving a logical problem. Very often, the developer chooses the most convenient way to solve such problems. For example, the developer mostly uses the bubble sorting method for most of the sorting requirements, despite knowing that it is the most inefficient sorting process.

Using such shortcuts multiple times in a game may cause a visible process delay, which directly affects the frame rate.

# 2D/3D performance comparison

Android game development in 2D and 3D is different. It is a fact that 3D game processing is heavier than 2D games. However, the game scale is always the deciding factor.

## Different look and feel

3D look and feel is way different than 2D. The use of a particle system in 3D games is very common to provide visual effects. In the case of 2D games, sprite animation and other transformations are used to show such effects.

Another difference between 2D and 3D look and feel is dynamic light and shadow. Dynamic light is always a factor for greater visual quality. Nowadays, most 3D games use dynamic lighting, which has a significant effect on game performance. In the case of 2D games, light management is done through assets. So, there is no extra processing in 2D games for light and shadow.

In 2D games, the game screen is rendered on a Canvas. There is only one fixed point of view. So, the concept of camera is limited to a fixed camera. However, in 3D games, it is a different case. Multiple types of camera can be implemented. Multiple cameras can be used together for a better feel of the game. Rendering objects through multiple cameras causes more process overhead. Hence, it decreases the frame rate of the game.

There is a significant performance difference between using 2D physics and 3D physics. A 3D physics engine is far more process heavy than a 2D physics engine.

## 3D processing is way heavier than 2D processing

It is a common practice in the gaming industry to accept less FPS in 3D games in comparison to 2D games. In Android, the standard accepted FPS for 2D games is around 60 FPS, whereas a 3D game is acceptable even if it runs at as low as 40 FPS.

The logical reason behind this is that 3D games are way heavier than 2D games in terms of process. The main reasons are as follows:

- **Vertex processing**: In 3D games, each vertex is processed on the OpenGL layer during rendering. So, increasing the number of vertices leads to heavier processing.
- **Mesh rendering**: A mesh consists of multiple vertices and many polygons. Processing a mesh increases the rendering overhead as well.
- **3D collision system**: A 3D dynamic collision detection system demands each vertex of the collider to be calculated for collision. This calculation is usually done by the GPU.
- **3D physics implementation**: 3D transformation calculation completely depends on matrix manipulation, which is always heavy.
- **Multiple camera use**: Use of multiple cameras and dynamically setting up the rendering pipeline takes more memory and clock cycles.

# Device configuration

Android has a wide range of device configuration options supported by the platform. In the previous chapters, we have already seen such variations. Running the same game on different configurations does not produce the same result.

Performance depends on the following factors.

## Processor

There are many processors used for Android devices in terms of the number of cores and the speed of each core. Speed decides the number of instructions that can be executed in a single cycle. There was a time when Android used to have a single core CPU with speed less than 500 MHz. Now we have multicore CPUs with more than 2 GHz speed on each core.

## RAM

Availability of RAM is another factor that decides performance. Heavy games require a greater amount of RAM during runtime. If RAM is limited, then frequent loading/unloading processes affect performance.

# GPU

GPU decides the rendering speed. It acts as the processing unit for graphical objects. A more powerful processor can process more rendering instructions, resulting in better performance.

# Display quality

Display quality is actually inversely proportional to the performance. Better display quality has to be backed by better GPU, CPU, and RAM, because better displays always consist of bigger resolution, with better dpi and more color support.

We can see various devices with different display quality. Android itself has divided the assets by this feature:

- **LDPI**: Lowest dpi display for Android (~120 dpi)
- **MDPI**: Medium dpi display for Android (~160 dpi)
- **HDPI**: High dpi display for Android (~240 dpi)
- **XHDPI**: Extra high dpi display for Android (~320 dpi)
- **XXHDPI**: Extra extra high dpi display for Android (~480 dpi)
- **XXXHDPI**: Extra extra extra high dpi display for Android (~640 dpi)

It can be easily predicted that the list will include more options in the near future, with the advancement of hardware technology.

# Battery capacity

Battery capacity is an odd factor in the performance of the application. More powerful CPUs, GPUs, and RAM demand more power. If the battery is incapable of delivering power, then processing units cannot run at their peak efficiency.

To summarize these factors, we can easily make a few relational equations with performance:

- CPU is directly proportional to performance
- GPU is directly proportional to performance
- RAM is directly proportional to performance
- Display quality is inversely proportional to performance
- Battery capacity is directly proportional to performance

# Summary

The scope of 3D games is increasing day by day with more quality and performance. However, this requires hardware support for the running Android platform. Old devices are not obsolete yet.

It becomes a serious problem when the same application runs on various devices. This becomes a challenge for developers to run the same application across devices.

There are many technical differences between 2D and 3D games in terms of rendering, processing, and assets. The developer should always use an optimized approach to create assets and write code. One more way of gaining performance is to port the games for different hardware systems for both 2D and 3D games.

We can see a revolutionary upgrade in hardware platforms since the last decade. Accordingly, the nature of games has also changed. However, the scope of 2D games is still there with a large set of possibilities.

There are many frameworks and engines available for developing 2D and 3D games. Support for multiple operating systems has also increased its value for both 2D and 3D games.

Improving performance is more of a logical task than a technical one. There are a few tools available to do the job, but it is the developer's decision to choose them. So, selecting the right tool for the right purpose is necessary, and there should be a different approach to making 2D and 3D games.

We have already discussed the rendering processes in both 2D and 3D development. We will further enhance rendering with the help of shaders in Android and try to explore various techniques of optimizing Android games later in this book.

# 7
# Working with Shaders

Every game's success depends largely on its look and feel. This directly means that the game must have an eye-catching graphical display. It is not always possible to provide maximum quality graphical assets due to space and heap restrictions. So, there has to be a way to create or improvise the graphical assets at runtime for display. This necessity gave birth to the concept of shaders.

Shaders can operate on any visual element and can tweak every pixel of drawable elements before rendering. Mostly, shaders are optimized for a specific graphics processor. However, nowadays, shaders can be written to support multiple processors on multiple platforms.

Android accommodates the option to work with shaders in the Android framework itself. Additionally, OpenGL shaders can also be used and customized with the help of the Android NDK. There are many occasions where exquisite graphical quality is delivered with the help of shaders without excellent raw art assets.

We will have a discussion about shaders in this chapter from the point of view of Android game development through the following topics:

- Introduction to shaders
- How shaders work
- Types of shaders
- Android library shaders
- Writing a custom shader
- Shaders through OpenGL
- Use of shaders in games
- Shaders and game performance

# Introduction to shaders

Many developers develop games on Android, but do not possess much knowledge about shaders. In most cases, developers do not need to work with shaders, or there are some pre-defined shaders inside the game development framework or engines.

In 1988, the animation studio Pixar introduced the modern concept of shaders. However, GPUs were not capable of handling shaders at that point of time. OpenGL and Direct3D are the first two graphic libraries to support shaders. GPU started supporting shaders through pixel shading at the 2D level. Soon, it was enhanced to support vertex shaders. Nowadays, geometry shaders are also supported by OpenGL 3.2 and Direct3D 10 libraries.

Let's now dive a bit deeper into shaders to understand their definition, necessity, and scope for Android games.

## What is a shader?

In simple words, a shader is an instruction set to manipulate the visual display of the input graphic assets.

Let's elaborate the definition a bit. All the instructions are basically done through programming. That's the reason the concept of a shader exists only in computer graphics. Shaders are able to perform a computation based on the instruction and input asset to produce more efficient output-displayable assets.

Typical shaders can process either a vertex or a pixel. Pixel shaders can compute on the color, depth, and alpha properties of an asset. Vertex shaders can compute the position, color, co-ordinates, depth, illuminations, and so on of a vertex. Thus, shaders can be primarily divided into two categories depending on the operational base type:

- 2D shaders
- 3D shaders

## Necessity of shaders

In the normal practice of game development, Android developers do not bother about shaders. But the necessity of shaders is inevitable. Initially, for small-scale games, art assets are used without improvement. Any modification to the assets is managed by the old process of updating the art asset itself.

Shaders can minimize this extra time-consuming effort. The same asset can be manipulated to create different objects on screen. For example, you can blur out the object as it goes out of focus, change the color of the sprites during gameplay to indicate different teams or players, create masks of art assets, and so on.

Shaders have the following benefits:

- When different shaders are applied to the same art asset, it produces different assets, depending on your requirements at runtime. Thus, the shader can save extra art-creation time.
- One-time integration of drawable objects in the game can lead to a different visual experience through different shaders.
- As the art assets are minimized, using shaders can reduce the game build size.
- There will be more visual difference with the same set of assets.
- Animation can be created by shaders with simple art by manipulating the visual content repeatedly.
- Shaders are useful for creating visual effects during runtime.

However, using shaders may lead to some negative consequences:

- Using shaders will increase the processing time due to the manipulation of the visual assets during runtime
- Unoptimized use of shaders may lead to more heap memory consumption as various intermediate instances will be stored in it
- Sometimes, shaders are responsible for the distortion of objects while processing
- Art assets become vulnerable to quality loss using shaders

Only the first two are actual direct consequences of using shaders. The rest of the problems can occur only if the developer uses a badly written shader or faulty shader. Therefore, it is extremely necessary to choose the perfect shader for a specific task.

Sometimes, the shader process takes a long time, resulting in poor FPS output. A few old GPUs do not support all kinds of shaders. Therefore, the developer should check and confirm the hardware platform on which the shader is to perform.

## Scope of shaders

Shaders can be used in a variety of sectors related to computer graphics, such as image processing, photography, digital animation, video/computer/digital games, and so on.

The gaming sector is one of the largest communities that uses shaders. The Android platform is no exception. Android game developers use shaders on a large scale in both 3D and 2D games.

Frankly speaking, 2D games do not have much scope for shaders. Only a pixel shader can manipulate the color, opacity, saturation, and hue of a pixel. This is useful when the same raw assets are used for different visibility.

For example, a 2D cricket game has many teams with different outfits to distinguish between them. The developer creates all the sprite animation assets in one design and applies shaders to manipulate color differently for different teams. Thus, the output sprites have different visibility and are recognized easily by the player.

## How shaders work

We have already discussed that shaders process either vertices or pixels. So, the basic working principle is to change or manipulate data at runtime:

A shader process is a specific set of instructions to process vertices or fragments. Different shader programs can be written for various types of processing.

A vertex shader is used to change the shape of the model; it can also change the surface-formation system.

Pixel/fragment shaders can change the pixel color value along with opacity. Pixel data can be merged, modified, or replaced by a shader program to form a new digital image.

# Types of shaders

There are many shaders used in the gaming industry. They are categorized on the basis of their behavior and features. Some of the shaders are as follows:

- Pixel shaders
- Vertex shaders
- Geometry shaders
- Tessellation shaders

Let's have a detailed look at these types.

## Pixel shaders

Pixel shaders are 2D shaders that work on textures or digital images. Pixel shaders process colors and other attributes of a single pixel. Each single pixel is called a fragment. This is the reason pixel shaders are often called fragment shaders.

## Vertex shaders

A vertex shader mainly operates on the vertices of a mesh or model. Every mesh of a model is made up of multiple vertices. A vertex shader can only be applied to 3D models. So, a vertex shader is a type of 3D shader.

## Geometry shaders

Geometry shaders are used to create new primitive graphic elements. After applying a vertex shader in order to execute a rendering pipeline, geometry shaders are used to create points, lines, and triangles to form a surface.

## Tessellation shaders

This is a typical 3D shader used to simplify and improve 3D mesh during tessellation. It is subdivided into two shaders:

- Hull shaders or tessellation control shaders
- Domain shaders or tessellation evolution shaders

These two shaders are used together to reduce mesh bandwidth.

Tessellation shaders have the power to improve 3D models in such a way that the drawable vertex count is reduced significantly. Thus, rendering becomes faster.

*Working with Shaders*

# Android library shaders

Android provides the shader option in its framework in the `android.graphics` package. A few well-known and widely used shaders are also in the Android library. Some of them are as follows:

- `BitmapShader`: This can be used to draw a bitmap in the texture format. It also supports tiling or mirroring of the bitmap. It is very useful for creating terrain with tiling.
- `ComposeShader`: This is used to merge two shaders. So, it is very useful for masking or merging colors for two different shaders.
- `LinearGradient`: This is used to create a gradient along with the given line segment with a defined color set.
- `RadialGradient`: This is used to create a gradient along with the given circle segment with a defined color set. A radial origin and radius are provided to create the gradient.
- `SweepGradient`: This is used to create a sweep gradient color around a point with the given radius.

Here is an example:

```
@Override
protected void onDraw ( Canvas c)
{
  float px = 100.0f;
  float py = 100.0f;
  float radius = 50.0f;

  int startColor = Color.GREEN;
  int targetColor = Color.RED;

  Paint shaderPaint = new Paint();
  shaderPaint.setStyle(Paint.Style.FILL);

  //LinearGradient Example to a circular region
  LinearGradient lgs = new LinearGradient( px, py, px + radius, py + radius,
      startColor, targetColor, Shader.TileMode.MIRROR);
  shaderPaint.setShader(lgs);
  c.drawCircle( px, py, radius, shaderPaint);

  //RadialGradient Example to a circular region
  px = 200.0f;
```

```
    py = 200.0f;
    RadialGradient rgs = new LinearGradient( px, py, radius,
      startColor, targetColor, Shader.TileMode.MIRROR);
    shaderPaint.setShader(rgs);
    c.drawCircle( px, py, radius, shaderPaint);

    //SweepGradient Example to a circular region
    px = 300.0f;
    py = 300.0f;
    shaderPaint.setShader(new SweepGradient(px, py, startColor,
 targetColor));
    c.drawCircle( px, py, radius, shaderPaint);
}
```

Here is what it looks like:

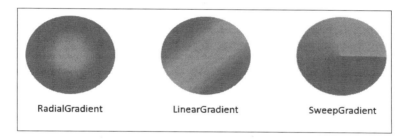

These options are really good for creating different objects with different styles of the same primitive object.

## Writing custom shaders

A developer has the option to write a customized shader as per their requirements. Android provides the `android.graphics.Shader` class. It is easy to create your own shader class using the primitive shaders provided.

The custom shader may not include only one shader. It can be a combination of various shaders. For example, consider masking an image with a circular view port with a motion-touch event:

```
    private float touchX;
    private float touchY;
```

## Working with Shaders

```java
private boolean shouldMask = false;

private final float viewRadius;
private Paint customPaint;

@Override
public boolean onTouchEvent(MotionEvent motionEvent)
{
  int pointerAction = motionEvent.getAction();
  if ( pointerAction == MotionEvent.ACTION_DOWN ||
  pointerAction == MotionEvent.ACTION_MOVE )
    shouldMask = true;
  else
    shouldMask = false;

  touchX = motionEvent.getX();
  touchY = motionEvent.getY();
  invalidate();
  return true;
}

@Override
protected void onDraw(Canvas canvas)
{
  if (customPaint == null)
  {
    Bitmap source = Bitmap.createBitmap( getWidth(), getHeight(),
      Bitmap.Config.ARGB_8888);
    Canvas baseCanvas = new Canvas(source);
    super.onDraw(baseCanvas);

    Shader customShader = new BitmapShader(source,
      Shader.TileMode.CLAMP, Shader.TileMode.CLAMP);

    customPaint = new Paint();
    customPaint.setShader(customShader);
  }

  canvas.drawColor(Color.RED);
  if (shouldMask)
  {
    canvas.drawCircle( touchX, touchY - viewRadius, viewRadius,
      customPaint);
  }
}
```

This example is one of the most commonly used shader styles in picture-based games. You can also implement such shaders to create hidden object games.

Another use case is highlighting a specific object on the screen. The same viewable circle can be used to show only the highlighted object. In this case, color can be semitransparent to show a dull background.

# Shaders through OpenGL

In Android, OpenGL supports implementing shaders for Android 3D games. OpenGL ES 2.0 is the supporting platform in Android for shaders. It has two functional segments while manually creating the shader:

- Shader
- Program

The shader is converted into intermediate code to support the program to run on GPU. In the compiling stage, the shaders are converted. This is the reason why shaders need to be recompiled before the program execution.

We will work with GLSurfaceView of the android.opengl package in our example.

For 3D games, an Android developer can use this package to play with shaders on the Android SDK. This package provides the API to create and use an OpenGL shader with Java.

We will use GLSurfaceView instead of the normal Android View or SurfaceView. The implementation will look like this:

```
import android.opengl.GLSurfaceView;
import android.content.Context;

public class MyGLExampleView extends GLSurfaceView
{
  private final GLRenderer mRenderer;

  public MyGLExampleView (Context context)
  {
    super(context);

// Set OpenGL version 2.0 as we will be working with that particular library
    this.setEGLContextClientVersion(2);

// Set the Renderer for drawing on the GLSurfaceView
```

## Working with Shaders

```
      MyOpenGLRendererExample = new MyOpenGLRendererExample
        (context);
      setRenderer(mRenderer);

// Render the view only when there is a change in the //drawing data
      setRenderMode(GLSurfaceView.RENDERMODE_CONTINUOUSLY);
    }

    @Override
    public void onPause()
    {
      super.onPause();
    }

    @Override
    public void onResume()
    {
      super.onResume();
    }
}
```

We need to create a renderer for the view to draw objects through OpenGL:

```
import java.nio.ByteBuffer;
import java.nio.ByteOrder;
import java.nio.FloatBuffer;
import java.nio.ShortBuffer;

import android.content.Context;
import android.opengl.GLES20;
import android.opengl.GLSurfaceView.Renderer;
import android.opengl.Matrix;
import android.util.Log;

import javax.microedition.khronos.egl.EGLConfig;
import javax.microedition.khronos.opengles.GL10;

public class MyOpenGLRendererExample implements Renderer
{

  // Declare matrices
  private float[] matatrixProjection = new float[32];
  private float[] matrixView = new float[32];
  private float[] matatrixProjectionOnView = new float[32];
```

```java
// Declare Co-ordinate attributes
private float vertexList[];
private short indicxList[];
private FloatBuffer vertexBuffer;
private ShortBuffer drawBuffer;

private final String vertexShader =
        "uniform     mat4       uMVPMatrix;" +
        "attribute   vec4       vPosition;" +
        "void main() {" +
        "  gl_Position = uMVPMatrix * vPosition;" +
        "}";

private final String pixelShader =
        "precision mediump float;" +
        "void main() {" +
        "  gl_FragColor = vec4(0.5,0,0,1);" +
        "}";

// Declare Screen Width and Height HD display
float ScreenWidth = 1280.0f;
float ScreenHeight = 800.0f;

private int programIndex = 1;

public MyOpenGLRendererExample (Context context)
{

}

@Override
public void onDrawFrame(GL10 param)
{
   renderView(matatrixProjectionOnView);
}

@Override
public void onSurfaceChanged(GL10 objGL, int width,
int height)
{
   ScreenWidth = (float)width;
   ScreenHeight = (float)height;

   GLES20.glViewport(0, 0, (int)ScreenWidth,
```

```java
            (int)ScreenHeight);

    //reset matrices
    for( int i = 0; i < 32 ; ++ i )
    {
      matatrixProjection[i] = 0.0f;
      matrixView[i] = 0.0f;
      matatrixProjectionOnView[i] = 0.0f;
    }

    Matrix.orthoM(matatrixProjection, 0, 0f, ScreenWidth,
0.0f, ScreenHeight, 0, 50);

    Matrix.setLookAtM(matrixView, 0, 0f, 0f, 1f, 0f, 0f,
0f, 0f, 1.0f, 0.0f);

    Matrix.multiplyMM(matatrixProjectionOnView, 0,
matatrixProjection, 0, matrixView, 0);
  }

  @Override
  public void onSurfaceCreated(GL10 gl, EGLConfig config)
  {
    //create any object
    //Eg. Triangle:: simplest possible closed region

    createTriangle();

    // Set the color to black
    GLES20.glClearColor(0.0f, 0.0f, 0.0f, 1);

    // Create the shaders
    int vertexShaderTmp =
loadShader(GLES20.GL_VERTEX_SHADER, vertexShader);

    int pixelShaderTmp =
loadShader(GLES20.GL_FRAGMENT_SHADER, pixelShader);

    int programIndexTmp = GLES20.glCreateProgram();

    GLES20.glAttachShader(programIndexTmp,
vertexShaderTmp);

    GLES20.glAttachShader(programIndexTmp,
```

```
    pixelShaderTmp);

      GLES20.glLinkProgram(programIndexTmp);

      // Set shader program
      GLES20.glUseProgram(programIndexTmp);
    }

    void renderView(float[] matrixParam)
    {
      int positionHandler =
    GLES20.glGetAttribLocation(programIndex, "vPosition");

      GLES20.glEnableVertexAttribArray(positionHandler);
      GLES20.glVertexAttribPointer(positionHandler, 3,
    GLES20.GL_FLOAT, false, 0, vertexBuffer);

      int mtrxhandle =
    GLES20.glGetUniformLocation(programIndex, "uMVPMatrix");

      GLES20.glUniformMatrix4fv(mtrxhandle, 1,
     false, matrixParam, 0);

      GLES20.glDrawElements(GLES20.GL_TRIANGLES,
    indicxList.length, GLES20.GL_UNSIGNED_SHORT, drawBuffer);

      GLES20.glDisableVertexAttribArray(positionHandler);
    }

    void createTriangle()
    {
      // We have to create the vertexList of our triangle.
      vertexList = new float[]
      {
        20.0f, 200f, 0.0f,
        20.0f, 300f, 0.0f,
        200f, 150f, 0.0f,
      };

      //setting up the vertex list in order
      indicxList = new short[] {0, 1, 2};

      ByteBuffer bytebufVertex =
```

```java
        ByteBuffer.allocateDirect(vertexList.length * 4);

    bytebufVertex.order(ByteOrder.nativeOrder());
    vertexBuffer = bytebufVertex.asFloatBuffer();
    vertexBuffer.put(vertexList);
    vertexBuffer.position(0);


    ByteBuffer bytebufindex =
ByteBuffer.allocateDirect(indicxList.length * 2);

    bytebufindex.order(ByteOrder.nativeOrder());
    drawBuffer = bytebufindex.asShortBuffer();
    drawBuffer.put(indicxList);
    drawBuffer.position(0);

    int vertexShaderTmp =
loadShader(GLES20.GL_VERTEX_SHADER, vertexShader);

    int pixelShaderTmp =
loadShader(GLES20.GL_FRAGMENT_SHADER, pixelShader);

    int program = GLES20.glCreateProgram();
    if (program != 0)
    {
      GLES20.glAttachShader(program, vertexShaderTmp);
      GLES20.glAttachShader(program, pixelShaderTmp);
      GLES20.glLinkProgram(program);

      int[] linkStatus = new int[1];

      GLES20.glGetProgramiv(program,
GLES20.GL_LINK_STATUS, linkStatus, 0);

      if (linkStatus[0] != GLES20.GL_TRUE)
      {
        Log.e("TAG_EXAMPLE_OPENGL", "Linking Failed !!
Error:: " + GLES20.glGetProgramInfoLog(program));

        GLES20.glDeleteProgram(program);
        program = 0;
      }
    }
  }
```

```
// method to create shader
    int loadShader(int type, String shaderCode)
    {
        int shader = GLES20.glCreateShader(type);

        GLES20.glShaderSource(shader, shaderCode);
        GLES20.glCompileShader(shader);

        return shader;
    }
}
```

The vertex shader code (`String vs_SolidColor`) has two parameters that it needs. The `uMVPMatrix` parameter is of the type `mat4`, which holds in the transformation matrix that can be used to translate the position. The `uMVPMatrix` parameter is a uniform matrix. The `vPosition` parameter is of type `vec4`, which holds the positions of vertex.

This system can be applied for a triangular surface.

# Use of shaders in games

Shaders are vastly used in games and animation, especially when creating dynamic lighting, changing tints, and making dynamic visual improvements. Sometimes, the world environment is created with shaders.

## Shaders in a 2D game space

Only pixel shaders can be used in 2D games. Each pixel of a digital image is considered a fragment. This is the reason why pixel shaders are also called fragment shaders. Pixel shaders can only perform color changes, tiling, and masking.

`BitmapShader`, `ComposeShader`, `LinearGradient`, `RadialGradient`, and `SweepGradient` are the variants of Android 2D shaders.

A 2D game world is created with images. Developers often choose to create different assets to give the same object a different look and feel. In this process, developers end up making a bigger APK with almost the same use set.

Sprites can also be a field where shaders can hold a significant role. When using the same sprite to create different objects, the colors of certain fragments need to change dynamically. Pixel shaders can be very useful here.

Shaders in a 2D space are used to change color, blur segments, change brightness, change opacity, tint images, and so on.

# Shaders in a 3D game space

The most common use of shaders in 3D games is for dynamic shadow. In modern game development, a shadow is an inevitable element to improve the game experience. 3D models look real after applying a texture.

In Android, a 3D shader is applied through OpenGL. We have already discussed an example:

A raw model with only vertex information

This is a simple model without any lightening or shaders. Let's apply some shaders to give it a solid 3D look:

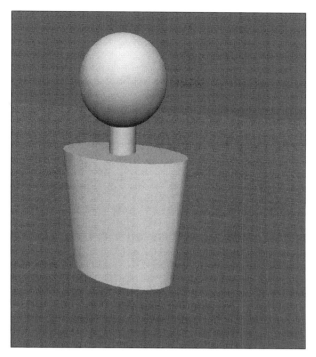

A simple flat shader applied

Now, the developer can apply any texture or color to give it a different feel. In this part, the developer can choose to restrict this with color or texture. Generally, textures are used in this kind of scenarios in order to make the model visually real. However, this costs more than just color manipulation.

We will see a color and lighting change here to get a completely different feel of the same object. There are different procedures to handle different scenario requirements for the game.

This example, however, is just a visual representation of how shaders can manipulate 3D models for a different look and feel:

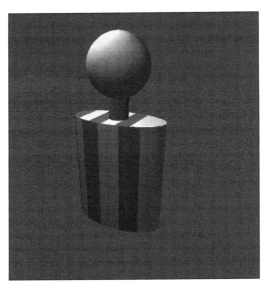

Shaders and game performance

Shaders are usually process-heavy. A fragment shader processes each fragment of a texture and manipulates its data. A large texture may lead to a visible delay in the game loop.

We can see shaders from different perspectives to create an idea of performance. Large textures decrease performance, and many small textures also affect performance. There has to be a balance between them to have a feasible real-time use of shaders.

Creating shadows is one of the extensive uses of shaders. However, the quality of shadow processing is inversely proportionate to performance. In high-quality games, we can experience real-time shadow. Shaders map the object vertices and process it according to the light direction. It is then projected on the X-Z plane to create shadow. Shadows are merged with objects on the plane and with other shadows.

Shaders can be used to improve world visibility with different lights, materials, and colors.

Here are some pros of using shaders in games:

- Complete flexibility when rendering assets
- Fewer asset packages and increased reusability
- Dynamic visual effects
- Dynamic lighting and shadow
- Sprite manipulation on the fly

There are few disadvantages of using shaders:

- Comparatively low frame rate
- Performance drop
- Required supported hardware platforms and graphic drivers

In spite of the few disadvantages, shaders have proved enough to be an intrinsic part of game development. Any performance drop is handled by upgrading the hardware and graphic drivers.

Nowadays, shaders are being optimized for embedded devices with limited resources. This even opens up the chance to increase the use of shaders on almost every platform, without affecting the performance significantly.

# Summary

Since Android API level 15, the framework supports OpenGL ES 2.0. This gave immense flexibility to graphic programmers to implement shaders in Android games.

Almost every hardware configuration supports shaders to run on GPU. However, the scale of using shaders determines the performance. In modern day, this is not actually an issue.

Shaders are being used widely in games. In every aspect of graphical programming, shaders have already proven their place. All the famous and successful game developers have acknowledged the importance of shaders. Graphic artists need not worry about everything visual in the game, which reduces the development time significantly.

Shaders are, therefore, widely used in games. Newer shaders are coming up with additional features now. The upgrading cycle of shaders has become less. However, hardware is also being upgraded with newer technology to support the graphical updates.

It feels like magic to see a simple cube turn into anything that has the same orientation. This magic will keep happening on a larger scale in the future.

Just developing a game is not enough. Shaders help a lot in reducing memory usage, but they increase processing overhead. We will try to explore various optimization techniques of storage and processing in the next chapter.

# 8
# Performance and Memory Optimization

Optimization is one of the most important tasks of any development cycle. It is inevitable, especially for games. Game optimization enhances performance significantly. Through optimization, more hardware platforms can be targeted.

You have already learned that Android supports a range of hardware platforms. Each platform has a separate configuration. By optimizing the use of hardware resources, a game can be run on more hardware platforms. This technique can be applied to visual quality as well. Not all devices have the same quality display, so optimizing the assets for low resolution saves a lot of storage space as well as heap memory during runtime.

In programming, the developer often writes intermediate code and forgets to optimize it later. This may cause a significant amount of performance loss or even cause the game to crash.

We will discuss the scope of various optimizations in Android game development through the following topics:

- Fields of optimization in Android games
- Relationship between performance and memory management
- Memory management in Android
- Processing segments in Android
- Different memory segments
- Importance of memory optimization
- Optimizing performance
- Increasing the frame rate

- Importance of performance optimization
- Common optimization mistakes
- Best optimization practices

# Fields of optimization in Android games

We all know the requirement of optimization in any development project. In the case of game development, this fact remains the same. In a game development project, the process starts with limited resources and design. After development, the game is expected to be run on maximum possible devices with maximum quality. To achieve that, memory and performance optimization becomes mandatory. So, let's discuss the following four segments of optimization:

- Resource optimization
- Design optimization
- Memory optimization
- Performance optimization

## Resource optimization

Resource optimization is basically optimizing the art, sound, and data files.

### Art optimization

We have already discussed many optimization techniques and tools. Here, we will discuss the necessity of art optimization.

Art is visually the most important part in games. Improving the art with bigger and better display quality increases processing and storage costs.

Large textures occupy a large amount of memory. However, scaling up art to fit a bigger resolution screen affects visual quality. So, a balance must be met. Also, various Android devices support various limitations on texture size. Moreover, it takes more time for a shader to work on a larger texture.

One common mistake that developers make is using alpha information for a completely opaque texture. This data increases the texture size significantly.

Art assets can be optimized on the art style. Many developers use flat-colored texture over gradient. Flat color information can be accommodated within 8-bit pixel data. This again saves disk space and processing time.

In spite of these optimization scopes, the developer might not use all of them to increase flexibility in order to create quality visual art without spending much time on optimization.

## Sound optimization

Sound is another vital resource for games. Audio may be compressed to save space and effort. A common practice in the Android game industry is to use a compressed format for long audio files.

It takes time to compress and decompress files during runtime. So, using SFX dynamically can be a problem if it is compressed. It can trigger a significant and visible stutter. Developers like to use an uncompressed format for SFX and a compressed format for long and continuous playing sounds such as background music.

## Data file optimization

Sometimes, game developers use separate data files to create a flexible project structure to interact with external tools or for better data interface. Such files are commonly in text, XML, JSON, or binary formats. Developers may create their own data format in a binary model.

Binary data can be processed quickly if the correct algorithm is used. There is not much technicality in data optimization. However, developers always need to keep a check on the amount of data and the total file size.

## Design optimization

Design optimization is used to increase the scalability, quality experience, flexibility, and durability of the game. The main method is to restructure or modify the game parameters around the core game concept.

Let's divide this section into two parts from the point of view of functionality:

- Game design optimization
- Technical design optimization

## Game design optimization

A game can be completely different from the initial idea during the game design optimization phase. Design optimization is done based on certain tasks. The developer needs to find different ways to communicate the basic game idea. Then, they can choose the best one, following some analysis.

Game design should be flexible enough to accommodate runtime changes to improve the overall experience and increase user count. A highly optimized game design can be efficient enough to predict user behavior, game performance on various devices, and even monetization.

The game control system design has to be optimized enough to carry out all the tasks easily. Game controls should be easy to spot and understand. For Android touch devices, the placement of controls is also very important.

## Technical design optimization

Technical design optimization is limited to the development cycle. It sets the project structure, program structure, development platform dependency, and so on.

The technical design document also specifies the scope and scale of the game. Such specifications help run the game smoothly on a device, because the hardware platform is already covered within the technical design document.

This is a pre-development process. A few assumptions need to be taken care of in this document. These assumptions should be optimized enough to evolve when a real-time situation occurs.

Technical design can also take care of the following tasks during development. By optimizing these tasks, it is much easier to implement and execute:

- Program architecture
- System architecture
- System characteristics
- Defined dependencies
- Impacts
- Risk analysis
- Assumptions

All these tasks can be optimized for a better development cycle with less effort, and the game will be more polished and will have a higher performance rate.

## Memory optimization

Memory optimization is mandatory for any software development procedure. Memory has its physical limitation based on the hardware configuration, but games and applications cannot be made separately for each device.

In a technical design, the range of memory use for the game across all targeted hardware platforms should be mentioned. Now, it is a very common scenario that games take more memory than predicted, which eventually results in the game crashing. The developer is awarded with a memory overflow exception.

To avoid this scenario, there are two main things to be taken care of:

- Keep memory peak within the defined range
- Don't keep data loaded in memory unnecessarily

Android uses paging and mapping to manage memory usage. Unfortunately, it does not offer memory swapping. Android knows where to find the paged data and loads accordingly.

Here are some tricks to optimize memory in Android gaming.

## Don't create unnecessary objects during runtime

Often, the developer creates an intermediate data object inside a loop. It leaves memory footprints for the garbage collector to collect. Here is an example:

```
//Let's have an integer array list and fill some data
List<int> intListFull = new ArrayList<int>();
//Fill data
for( int i = 0; i < 10; ++ i)
{
  intListFull.add(i);
}

// No we can have two different approach to print all
// values as debug log.
// Approach 1: not optimized code
for ( int i = 0; i < intListFull.size() ; ++ i)
{
  int temp = intListFull.get(i);
  Log.d("EXAMPLE CODE", "value at " + i + " is " + temp);
}
// List size will be calculated in each cycle, temp works
//as auto variable and create one memory footprint in each
//loop. Garbage collector will have to clear the memory.

// Approach 2: optimized code
int dataCount = intListFull.size();
int temp;
for ( int i = 0; i < dataCount ; ++ i)
```

```
  {
    temp = intListFull.get(i);
    Log.d("EXAMPLE CODE", "value at " + i + " is " + temp);
  }
  // only two temporary variable introduced to reduce a foot
  //print in each loop cycle.
```

## Use primitive data types as far as possible

User-defined data types take more memory space than primitive data types. Declaring an integer takes less space than embedding an integer in a class. In Android, if the developer uses the `Integer` class instead of `int`, the data size increases four times.

For Android compilers (32 bit), `int` consumes 4 bytes (32 bit), and `Integer` consumes 16 bytes (128 bit).

With full respect to modern age Android devices, limited use of this data type may cause no significant harm to memory. However, extensive use of non-primitive data types may cause a significant amount of memory block until the developer or garbage collector frees the memory.

So, the developer should avoid `enum` and use static final `int` or `byte` instead. `enum`, being a user-defined data type, takes more memory than a primitive data type.

## Don't use unmanaged static objects

In older Android versions, it is a common issue that a static object does not get destroyed automatically. Developers used to manage static objects manually. This issue is no longer there in newer versions of Android. However, creating many static objects in games is not a good idea as the life span of static objects is equal to the game life. They directly block memory for a longer period.

Using too many static objects may lead to memory exceptions, eventually crashing the game.

## Don't create unnecessary classes or interfaces

Each class or interface has some extra binding space in its instance. The modular programming approach demands maximum possible breakage in the coding structure. This is directly proportional to the number of classes or interfaces. This is considered to be a good programming practice.

However, this has a consequence on memory usage. More classes consume more memory space for the same amount of data.

## Use the minimum possible abstraction

Many developers use abstraction in multiple layers for a better programming structure. It is very useful to restrict a certain part of a custom library and provide only selective APIs. When it comes to game development, if the developer works on games only, then use of abstraction is not very necessary.

Abstraction results in more instructions, which directly leads to more processing time and more memory use. So, even if abstraction may be convenient sometimes, the developer should always think twice before using abstraction while developing games.

For example, a game may have a set of various enemies. In such a case, creating a single enemy interface and implementing it for different enemy objects helps create a simple and convenient program hierarchy. However, there may be completely different attributes for different enemies. So, the use of abstraction will depend on the game design. Whatever the case is, if developers use abstraction, then it will always increase the set of instructions to be processed at runtime.

## Keep a check on services

Services are useful for the completion of one task in the background, but they are very costly in terms of both process and memory. A developer should never keep a service running unless required. The best way to automatically manage the service life cycle is to use `IntentService`, which will finish once its work is done. For other services, it is the developer's responsibility to make sure that `stopService` or `stopSelf` are being called after the task is done.

This process proves to be very efficient for game development, as it actively supports dynamic communication between the user and developer.

## Optimize bitmaps

Bitmaps are the heaviest assets for a game. In game development, most of the heap memory is used by bitmaps. So, optimizing bitmaps can significantly optimize the use of heap memory during runtime.

Usually, the memory required for a bitmap to be loaded in memory is given by this formula:

*BitmapSize = BitmapWidth * BitmapHeight * bytePerPixel*

For example, if a 480 x 800 size bitmap is being loaded in the `ARGB_8888` format (4 bytes), the memory will be as follows:

*BitmapSize = 480 x 800 x 4 = 1536000 bytes ~ 1.5mb*

The format can be of the following types in Android:

- `ARGB_8888` (4 bytes)
- `RGB_565` (2 bytes)
- `ARGB_4444` (2 bytes) (deprecated in API level 13)
- `ALPHA_8` (1 byte)

Each bitmap will occupy memory according to the preceding formula. So, it is recommended that you load a bitmap in memory as per requirement to avoid unnecessary heap usage.

## Release unnecessary memory blocks

As we have discussed earlier for freeing memory, the same can be applied on any object. After the task is finished, the instance should be set to null so that the garbage collector can identify and free the allocated memory.

In a game state machine, the class structure should provide an interface to free the memory of instantiated objects. There may be a scenario where a few of the member objects are done with their tasks and a few are still in use, so it would be a bad idea to wait for the entire class instance to be freed. The developer should selectively free the memory of unused objects without deleting the class instance.

## Use external tools such as zipalign and ProGuard

The ProGuard tool is efficient at shrinking, optimizing, and obfuscating the code by removing unused code and renaming classes, fields, and methods with a secured and encoded naming structure. ProGuard can make the code more compact, which directly impacts RAM usage.

In game development, developers often use many multiple third-party libraries, which may be pre-compiled with ProGuard. In those cases, the developer must configure ProGuard to exclude those libraries. It is also a good idea to protect the codebase from getting stolen.

zipalign can be used to realign the released APK. This optimizes the APK further to use less space and have a more compact size. Normally, most of the APK building frameworks provide zipalign automatically. However, the developer might need to use it manually for few cases.

# Performance optimization

Performance means how smoothly the game will run on the target platform and maintain a decent FPS throughout the gameplay session. In the case of Android gaming, we already know about the wide range of hardware configurations. Maintaining the same performance across all devices is practically impossible. This is the reason developers choose target hardware and minimum hardware configuration to ensure that the game is performing well enough to be published. However, the expectation also varies from device to device.

In real development constraints, performance optimization is limited to the targeting set of hardware. Thus, memory has its own optimizing space in the development process.

Technically, from the programming point of view, performance optimization can be done by paying more attention to writing and structuring code:

- Using minimum objects possible per task
- Using minimum floating points
- Using fewer abstraction layers
- Using enhanced loops wherever possible
- Avoiding getters/setters of variables for internal use
- Using static final for constants
- Using minimum possible inner classes

## Using minimum objects possible per task

Creating unnecessary objects increases processing overhead as they have to be initialized in a new memory segment. Using the same object for the same task multiple times is much faster. Here is an example:

```
public class Example
{
  public int a;
  public int b;

  public int getSum()
  {
    return (a + b);
  }
}
//Lets have a look on un-optimized code
// Here one object of Example class is instantiating per loop //cycle
```

```java
// Same is freed and re-instantiated
public class ExecuterExample
{
  public ExecuterExample()
  {
    for ( int i = 0; i < 10; ++ i)
    {
      Example test = new Example();
      test.a = i;
      test.b = i + 1;
      Log.d("EXAMPLE", "Loop Sum: " + test.getSum());
    }
  }
}
// Optimized Code would look like this
// Here only one instance will be created for entire loop
public class ExecuterExample
{
  public ExecuterExample()
  {
    Example test = new Example();
    for ( int i = 0; i < 10; ++ i)
    {
      test.a = i;
      test.b = i + 1;
      Log.d("EXAMPLE", "Loop Sum: " + test.getSum());
    }
  }
}
```

## Using minimum floating points

In machine-level language, there is nothing like an integer or float. It is always a bit indicating true or false (0 and 1 in technical language). So, an integer can be directly represented by a set of bits, but floating points requires extra processing overhead.

Until a point of time, there was no use of floating points in programming languages. Later, the conversion came, and floating point was introduced with extra processing requirements.

## Using fewer abstraction layers

It is very obvious that abstraction demands extra processing per layer. So, as we increase the abstraction layers, the process becomes slower.

## Using enhanced loops wherever possible

In the case of array and list parsing, an enhanced `for` loop works way faster than the usual conventional `for` loop as it has no iterating variable system, and each array or list element can be accessed directly.

Here is an example of a non-enhanced loop:

```
int[] testArray = new int[] {0, 1, 2, 3, 5};
for (int i = 0; i < testArray.length; ++ i)
{
  Log.d("EXAMPLE", "value is " + testArray[i]);
}
```

Here is an example of an enhanced loop:

```
int[] testArray = new int[] {0, 1, 2, 3, 5};
for (int value : testArray)
{
  Log.d("EXAMPLE", "value is " + value);
}
```

## Avoid getter/setters of variables for internal use

Getters and setters are used to access or change the state of any internal element of an object from outside the object. In high-level reasoning, it does not follow the basic concept of data encapsulation. However, getters and setters are used widely in Android game development.

In many cases, developers use getters and setters from inside the class object. This unnecessarily increases processing time, resulting in degraded performance. So, developers should use getters and setters as little as possible and make sure they are not being used internally.

## Use static final for constants

Constants are not meant to be changed during runtime. In the case of global constants, the data is directly associated with the class object. Hence, we're required to parse the class object in order to access it.

Using static is an excellent idea to get rid of this extra process. Element accessibility increases significantly when using static for constants. However, the developer needs to keep a check on memory usage as well.

## Using minimum possible inner classes

Each inner class adds an extra layer to processing. Sometimes, it is good to have inner classes in order to structure the codebase in an efficient and readable way. However, it comes with the cost of processing overhead. So, the developer should use the fewest possible inner classes in order to optimize performance.

# Relationship between performance and memory management

In Android game development, performance and memory optimization often conflict with each other. To maintain the visual quality of the game, better art assets are mandatory, which eventually increases memory overhead and performance lag.

Optimizing memory needs to do frequent memory operations, resulting in performance drop. To increase performance, objects have to be readily available for smooth processing. Clearly, both cannot be applied at their extreme levels.

Balancing between them is the only way out to optimize the full game to run smoothly without exhausting memory.

# Memory management in Android

Let's discuss the memory management system in Android. It has a direct effect on the game development process. Games are treated like applications in Android. Very often, developers face memory issues in both the runtime and minimized states of the game. There are three main topics to discuss to understand the working principles:

- Shared application memory
- Memory allocation and deallocation
- Application memory distribution

# Shared application memory

Android uses the Linux kernel, and Linux uses "shared" pages to share the same memory segment within running processes or services. For example, Android often shares the "code" memory within processes. Very often, external libraries and JVM's executable code memory can be safely shared across processes without creating a deadlock. Data pages could be shared temporarily between processes, until a process modifies the shared memory.

Android allocates dedicated memory for each application or process. This is called private memory. The same process may also use shared memory. Android automatically sets a cap, depending on the total of both, to determine when the process or application will be killed, especially if it is in the background. This cap is called **Proportionate Set Size (PSS)**:

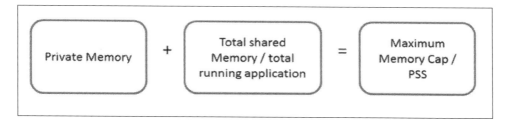

If an application's PSS is high, then there is a very high chance that the process might be killed by Android. This scenario can be handled programmatically to keep memory usage in check, especially if the application is relying on some background activities or services to carry out some task. The developer has to make sure that the game uses minimum possible memory at any point in time, especially when the application goes into the background. It may be a good idea to free memory and objects that you no longer need in the background, and disconnect from any shared memory that you no longer need when you go into the background. This will reduce the chances of your application getting unexpectedly killed by the Android system.

# Memory allocation and deallocation

The Android memory management system defines a virtual cap for each application, which is the logical heap size. It can be increased if necessary, but only if there is free memory available. However, this logical heap size is not the actual allocated memory for the application. Calculated PSS is the actual physical cap that may vary during runtime and shared memory dependency.

Application memory cannot use more physical memory than PSS. So, after reaching this limit, if the application tries to allocate more memory, then it will receive `OutOfMemoryError` thrown by the system. Android might kill other empty or background processes to accommodate memory for the running application in a critical situation. Application memory will be deallocated in these scenarios:

- If the application quits
- If the process becomes inactive and some other process requires the memory
- If the application crashes for any reason

## Application memory distribution

Android sets a hard limit on the heap size for each app to maintain a multitasking environment. The exact heap size limit varies between hardware configurations based on the capacity of RAM of the device. If the application reaches the heap capacity and tries to allocate more memory, it will receive `OutOfMemoryError`, and the application will be killed by Android.

The developer needs to check the amount of memory available on the device and then determine an average target memory use. The developer can query the operating system for this amount of memory by calling `getMemoryClass()`. This returns an integer indicating the number of MBs available for the application's heap.

## Processing segments in Android

A game is basically an application in terms of functionality. Multiple applications or games can run on an Android platform. However, for games, only one game is active at one point of time, but rest of the applications run in the background.

Let's have a look at how Android processes its applications.

## Application priority

Android sets the priority of the running applications, and it can kill a running application of low priority depending on the requirement.

Each application uses some memory and processing bandwidth. There may be a situation where multiple applications are running together. If a new application wants to run, then Android allocates memory and process bandwidth for the new application. If there is not enough bandwidth or process available, then Android kills one or more than one running application with low priority.

Android sets priority by the following status:

- Active process
- Visible process
- Active services
- Background process
- Void process

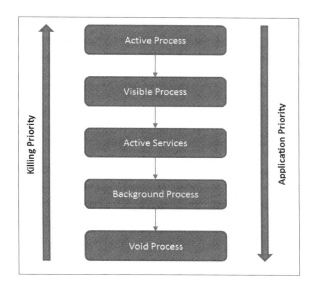

## Active process

An active process is basically a process that communicates with the platform very frequently and runs in the foreground. This process is the last one to be killed by Android, when necessary.

An active process fulfils the following criteria:

- It runs in the foreground
- It is visible
- At least one Android activity is running
- It interacts actively with the user interface
- All event handlers are in the active state

## Visible process

This process is basically an active process that is not in the foreground and does not interact with the user interface. It is the second highest priority for the Android platform.

The criteria for this process are as follows:

- It runs in the background
- It has visible activity
- It does not interact with the user interface
- UI event handlers are not active
- Process event handlers are active

## Active services

Active services are services that support an ongoing process without a visible interface. Android will kill such services first and then the actual active process.

This service follows the following criteria:

- It has no visible interface
- It supports or works for respective active processes
- It runs in the background

## Background process

Background processes are basically minimized or inactive processes. These processes are not visible on the screen. The process thread does not run for these processes, but the application state is saved in the memory. These are vulnerable to being killed by the processor. These processes can be resumed after interruption.

These are inactive/minimized processes. They remain in memory. The application stays in the paused state.

## Void process

Void processes are also called empty processes. A void process is literally empty. It holds no application data or state in memory. This process has the highest priority in order to get killed by the operating system.

# Application services

Android application services are parts of the actual application process. These services may run within and outside the parent process.

Let's clear two very common misconceptions about services:

- A service is not a separate process
- A service is not a thread

The fact is, services are part of an application process and not separate processes. Services are not threads. They are part of the process that runs in the background, and they keep running even if the main application is in a suspended state.

Services are meant to carry out a single task and do not call back the parent application. This is why they can run even after the application is closed.

## Service life cycle

Services are started by the parent application process, as follows:

```
Context.startService();
```

After being started, the service starts carrying out a single task in the background. The service can stop itself after the task is done. For example, a simple file download service will stop after a successful downloading task. Many game developers use such features in their games to improve the user experience.

These services can be bound with one or more processes for interactivity. The application can send request and get response from a bound service, which creates a server-client architecture. But these bound services have a limited lifetime until the last application component is bound with the service.

# Resource processing

Android has its own resource process structure. It has some predefined resource types:

- Drawable resources
- Layout resources
- Color resources
- Menu resources
- Tween animation resources
- Other resources

## Drawable resources

All drawable resources fall in this category, including frame animation. Android provides the `res/drawable/` project path dedicated to all drawable resources. All bitmaps, various XML, and predetermined frame animations can be placed here.

These can be accessed through the `R.drawable` class.

## Layout resources

All defined layouts fall in this category. Android provides the `res/layout/` project path dedicated to all layout files. Layout is useful to define the application UI.

These can be accessed through the `R.layout` class.

## Color resources

Color resources are basically a list of colors that are due to change upon changing the view of the applicable object. Android stores this in the `res/color/` folder in the hierarchy.

These can be accessed through the `R.color` class.

## Menu resources

All menu contents can be defined here. Android provides the `res/menu/` project path dedicated to all **drawable** resources.

These can be accessed through the `R.menu` class.

## Tween animation resources

All tween animation resources fall in this category. Android provides the `res/anim/` project path dedicated to all tween animation resources.

These can be accessed through the `R.anim` class.

## Other resources

All other resources are places in the `res/values/` folder. Many developers define the string under this category with styles.

These can be accessed through the `R.values` class.

# Different memory segments

During the runtime of an application, three main kinds of memory segments are used depending on the behavior:

- Stack memory
- Heap memory
- Register memory

## Stack memory

All auto variables and runtime allocation during processing will be stored in the stack memory segment. The garbage collector deallocates the memory after use. So, there is no manual memory management process associated with the stack memory.

However, extensive use of auto variables also may cause memory errors. This is the reason we have already discussed why minimizing unnecessary auto variable declarations is necessary.

Stack memory is also used to execute program instructions. Each instruction is broken down into a single operation and put into a stack by the interpreter. Then, a recursive procedure is used to execute all the instruction stacks and return the result.

Let's have a look at how stack memory works for objects and primitives:

```
public class ExampleClass
{
  public ExampleClass()
  {
    int bitMapCount = 0;   // primitive type
    Bitmap testBmp = BitmapFactory.decodeFile("bitmap path");
      // Object loading
    bitMapCount = 1;
  }
}
```

In this example, `bitMapCount` is an `int` local variable and gets stored in the stack directly. The memory used for this variable will be freed just after the scope.

However, `testBmp` is a bitmap object, which will be allocated in the heap, but the reference will be stored in the stack. When the program pointer comes out of the scope, the reference will be automatically deleted, and the garbage collector can identify the heap memory allocated for `testBmp` as having zero reference and will free this memory segment.

# Heap memory

Heap memory is the segment where all the instances of classes and arrays are stored. JVM allocates this memory while instantiating any object.

The garbage collector does not operate automatically on this memory segment during application runtime. It is the developer's responsibility to free the memory after use. In the case of Android, the garbage collector will only free the memory when there is no reference for the memory segment in the running application.

Game assets are the major elements that are stored in this memory segment. Art is the most significant asset among them. So, optimizing bitmaps has a direct impact on heap memory uses. Very often, the developer allocates memory for assets and does not break the reference. This causes the memory block to be occupied during the entire runtime.

Here is an example:

```
// create a bitmap in a class constructor having global
// scope with public access
public class ExampleClass
{
  public Bitmap testBmp;
  public ExampleClass()
  {
    testBmp = BitmapFactory.decodeFile("bitmap path");
  }
}
```

In this example, the memory for the bitmap will be occupied even after the use, until the `ExampleClass` instance is there in memory. The interpreter has no standing instruction to free the memory segment, because `testBmp` still has the reference to the memory allocated to the bitmap.

We can optimize this in the following way with a bit of modification:

```
public class ExampleClass
{
  public Bitmap testBmp;
  public ExampleClass()
  {
    testBmp = BitmapFactory.decodeFile("bitmap path");
  }
  // create a method to free memory allocated for the
  // bitmap after use
  public void unloadBitmap()
  {
```

```
    testBmp = null;
  }
}
```

In this case, by calling `unloadBitmap()` after the use of the bitmap will remove the reference of the loaded bitmap from `testBmp`. So, the garbage collector will find this memory location as zero-referenced memory and free it to be used for other allocations.

## Register memory

In the case of Android development, the developer must not worry about register memory. Registers are directly associated with the processor, and the processor stores the most significant and frequently used data in this memory segment.

Register memory is the fastest memory segment used for any application runtime.

## Importance of memory optimization

No matter how the game is, how good it looks, or how well it is designed, if the game does not run on the target platform, then it cannot be successful. We already know that Android has various sets of hardware configurations.

The main variations of hardware are specific to the processor and memory. In the case of processors, it depends on their speed and quality. In case of memory or RAM, it is only the volume.

Even today, RAM can vary from 512 MB to 4 GB in Android devices. Memory optimization should always have a minimum target of RAM as per design. So, memory optimization is immensely important in order to run a game on the minimum available RAM.

Sometimes, the developer fits the peak usage within the target limit of memory. However, they perform on a testing device, which does not project a real-time scenario most of the time. There is always an error margin. So, it is not always true that if the game runs on a certain limit of RAM, it will always be provided with the same memory. This is the place when memory optimization plays a major role. It helps a lot in creating the buffer range for the game to run in a real-time scenario.

There could be a scenario where the application runs out of memory, even when it does not require the amount of RAM it demands. This clearly indicates that the application is suffering from memory leakage. Memory leakage is one of the most common problems in game development. Optimizing memory properly helps get rid of this problem.

Another aspect of memory optimization is to increase the probability of the game to stay in the background. When an application goes into the background, Android might kill the application if it needs to free memory space for other foreground applications. Memory optimization makes sure that the application occupies the minimum possible memory while running. So, it is possible to save the data of the state in the cache for a longer period of time for applications that use less memory.

Many games use game services at the backend. If the application is not active, then there is a good chance that the service may also get killed by the operating system.

## Optimizing overall performance

Earlier, we discussed performance optimization from only the programming point of view. Let's discuss other scopes of optimizing the performance of Android games.

The developer can optimize performance from the time of design to development through the following points:

- Choosing the base resolution
- Defining the portability range
- Program structure
- Managing the database
- Managing the network connection

## Choosing the base resolution

From the point of view of game development on Android, choosing the base resolution is probably the most significant design decision. Base resolution defines the scale of the graphical or visual element. The larger the resolution that the developer chooses to work upon, the more storage and process time it takes. Base resolution is also responsible for the quality and color information to be stored with bitmaps. Comparatively lower resolution does not demand many details in the visible asset, which can optimize bitmap data. However, as the resolution increases, it requires more data to preserve detailing. Eventually, this has a significant influence on processing.

With the advancement of technology, Android device resolutions are getting bigger and better. So developers now choose a bigger resolution to support higher range devices.

# Defining the portability range

This is also a design phase optimization. In this stage, the developer needs to decide the range of hardware platform to support. This includes various configurations. We already know that the Android device range includes a large set of variations in terms of memory, processing speed, graphics quality, and so on.

If the range supports the range of portability of a similar device, then optimization becomes easier. However, this is not the case for most cases of game development. Usually, the developer should divide the optimization into three segments:

- Low-performing devices
- Average-performing devices
- High-performing devices

So, ideally, there should be three layers of optimization to properly define the portability range.

# Program structure

The program structure is another very important technical design decision for both performance and memory optimization. This includes all the parameters for programming optimization, which we have already discussed.

Additionally, program hierarchy also matters for performance. Often, the developer creates unnecessary intermediate calls to parse through several layers. A few singleton classes help here to optimize performance significantly. Proper game state machine design also helps optimize performance.

# Managing the database

There are many games that are mainly data driven. In such cases, a database needs to be managed properly.

For example, a quiz game must have a question bank maintained in the database at some server to avoid frequent update of the game build. Database queries take time to execute as there is also a network layer in between. So, the game layer sends a query to the database. Then, the database fetches the data, binds it accordingly, and sends it back to the game. Then, the game has to unbind the received data in order to use it. Using the minimum query calls is the only way to minimize the performance overhead. Using a faster database also helps the game to perform well.

## Managing the network connection

Modern day gaming has enhanced to multiplayer and server-controlled mechanisms, which reduces the job of frequent updates of the game build. In both cases, network connection needs to be implemented in a proper way. There are mainly two types of multiplayer architecture currently being followed:

- Turn-based multiplayer
- Real-time multiplayer

It's comparatively easy to manage a turn-based multiplayer system than real-time multiplayer. There is another model of multiplayer called asynchronous multiplayer.

Each network call results in a lag in performance, as the game is dependent on the data from the server. So, the client-server architecture needs to be optimized in order to achieve the following goals:

- Less lag time
- Less layer processing
- Less number of pings to the server

## Increasing the frame rate

The ultimate target for performance optimization is to increase the frame rate. A high frame rate automatically delivers smooth gameplay. However, the developer has to make sure that the frame rate effect is visible in the game in terms of smoothness and effect.

For the current mobile gaming industry, an average FPS of 60 for a 2D game or mid-scaled 3D game is considered high performance. On the other hand, massive 3D games might consider an average FPS of 30-35 as good performance.

High-performing games with higher FPS open a door for further visual effects to improve the user experience. This has a direct impact on monetization.

## Importance of performance optimization

As we have just discussed, performance optimization directly influences the frame rate, which again directly impacts the gameplay experience. However, performance optimization has other importance too:

- Games might crash or go in a not-responding state due to a non-optimized program
- Performance optimization has a direct impact on memory as well
- Performance optimization can enlarge the range of supported hardware platforms

# Common optimization mistakes

The gaming industry is now one of the fastest growing industries. To keep up with the speed and to stand in the market, many companies plan a shorter development period with limited optimization. In this scenario, the developer often commits the following mistakes knowingly or unknowingly:

- Programming mistakes
- Design mistakes
- Wrong data structure
- Using game services incorrectly

## Programming mistakes

Programming is a manual process, and to err is human. So, it is obvious that there is no bug-free and completely optimized programming for games. However, there are few ways in which a programmer can minimize mistakes to have an optimized game code base. Let's discuss the major mistakes a programmer commits while developing a game in Android.

Programmers often create many temporary variables and forget to keep track of them. Often, these variables occupy unnecessary memory and increase processing calls.

Sorting is widely used in game development for many purposes. There are several sorting algorithms. Most of the time, the developer chooses convenient techniques rather than efficient ones. For large arrays or lists, this may cause a serious lag in process flow.

Using too many static instances for accessibility ease is another bad practice. Using static may help in faster processing, but is not a good idea to make many static instances, as it blocks a lot of memory space during its lifetime. Many programmers even forget to manually free this memory.

Creating abstract layers and using them extensively makes the process slower. However, it is a good programming practice generally, but for game programming, it only helps in limited cases.

Convenient loop use is another bad programming practice for games. There are several ways to work with loops. A programmer should first determine what goes best with the algorithm.

Game programming is mostly about logical development than technical. It may take time to build up the perfect logic for certain tasks. Many game programmers do not consider multiple ways of doing one task. Most of the time, it leaves a great scope of optimization unexplored.

## Design mistakes

Designers often make mistakes when defining the hardware range and the game scope. Both are very important factors to create an optimized game design.

Another mistake is to target the wrong target resolution. The target resolution has a direct effect on the art asset size. Targeting the wrong resolution leads to unnecessary scaling, causing extra processing overhead.

## Wrong game data structure

Data structure is an inevitable part of game programming. Android supports dynamic array initialization. Yet, many developers prefer lists to store data. Lists are much slower than arrays. Lists should only be used when it is absolutely necessary.

It is the developer's responsibility to figure out the perfect data structure for data-driven games. Proper technical design should include a data structure model and its use.

## Using game services incorrectly

Services are very useful at times. In the modern day gaming industry, services are used for download/upload of data, for push notifications, for deep linking in games, or for server connectivity. However, services come at a huge cost of processing and memory consumption. Running services causes significant amount of power consumption as well.

So, using services should be mandatory only when there is no other way around.

# Best optimization practices

Some defined and logical optimization techniques are available. We will discuss the major scopes and fields that are related to Android game development:

- Game design constraints
- Game development optimization
- Game data structure model
- Using game assets
- Handling cache data

## Design constraints

It is always a best practice to define the target hardware platforms and acknowledge the limitation. Technical design can structure the development constraints according to it.

The scalability and portability should also be decided at the time of designing the game. This should give the developer a tentative platform limitation along with other constraints. We have already discussed design optimization. All those segments should be evaluated before going into development.

Targeting screen size and resolution has to be fixed when designing the game along with creating layouts, which will fit in multiple resolutions. This is because Android has many screen sizes as discussed earlier.

Selecting the minimum Android version and the target Android version gives the developer an advantage when structuring the development project, as supported API levels and platform features are already defined.

## Development optimization

This is one of the most important segments of optimization. Here are some tips to carry out the development process successfully with optimization:

- Using as many as possible folder structures provided by Android for project scalability.
- Using resource formats according to the dpi list provided by Android.
- The developer should avoid scaling images. This effectively reduces memory and processing overhead.
- Using sprites for multiple purposes is also a good practice to create animations.

- The tiling technique is very useful in terms of reducing memory consumption.
- Overriding the `onDraw()` method is always a good practice to flush the old rendering pipeline and to use a systematic draw order with absolute requirement.
- Use XML-based layout wherever possible; however, games have very limited scope for this Android feature.

## Data structure model

Data structures are one of the inevitable parts of game program design since the beginning, irrespective of the scale of the game. Each game always processes data for various purposes such as sorting, searching, storing, and so on.

There are many data structure models available for various operations. Each operation has its own advantages and disadvantages. The developer must choose the most efficient one depending on the requirement.

Let's take an example of data storing comparison between an array and a linked list. Effectively, linked lists are more flexible and dynamic in nature than arrays. However, this feature comes at a cost of slow processing and higher memory consumption.

The developer might not always require to store dynamic data. For example, if cricket team data needs to be stored, then an array is sufficient, because there will always be 11 players on each side, and that cannot be modified during gameplay. It will make the process much faster and more efficient than using a linked list in this particular case.

In another case, for a shooting game, the developer cannot predict the number of bullets the user may fire during gameplay. So, a queue data structure will be most efficient in order to process all the fired bullets.

Similarly, stacks and tree structures can be chosen whenever they fit the purpose. The same approach may be taken for sort and search algorithms.

## Asset-using techniques

We have already categorized assets for games. Let's discuss them from the perspective of optimization techniques and best practices.

## Art assets

A separate optimization technique can be applied to a set of art assets. Art assets are the face of games. So, it is necessary that the visuals are attractive enough to start gameplay.

As we have discussed already, better art assets cost memory and performance. However, this can be minimized to a certain level. There are several tools for art asset optimization. However, using inappropriate tools can cause data loss, which eventually results in poor visual quality.

Art should never compromise from the perspective of visual quality. Often, artists develop assets that do not reflect perfectly in games because of inappropriate optimization.

We have already discussed how art assets should be made. Now, let's assume that some art is using only 8-bit data space as raw format, but the same is exported in a 24-bit format. Then, the developer can use tools to optimize the asset to a typical 8-bit format without affecting the visual quality.

This rule also applies for complete opaque assets. The developer can get rid of the transparency information in order to have optimized art assets.

## Audio assets

Audio assets are standalone assets too. Audio has become a very important asset for extended user experience. Audio configuration can vary with a wide range of frequency, bit depth, and compression techniques. Each variation in configuration has a different level of processing and memory consumption.

So, audio optimization is also a very important part of the optimization process. Regular practice in the Android game development industry is to choose two different formats of audio for SFX and music files.

One thing that developers generally ignore is audio information data. Few Android devices have a certain frequency cap, but sounds are usually good when more frequencies are used. So, it is a technical design level step to determine the cap for Android game sounds. So, every sound should be made within the proximity.

Sound designers need to keep up the quality within the limit. In this way, audio assets can be optimized at the time of development.

## Other assets

Besides art and audio, there may be other data assets used in games. The data format can be anything, such as binary, text, XML, JSON, or custom. Custom formats are basically the same as binary format, with some encryption.

It is a common practice in game development to use data sets separately. A separate data set helps structure the project and give flexibility to use the same code for a different output. Often, the developer updates data source to update the complete game experience without creating a new APK. This reduces development time in the longer run in order to maintain the game and do easy updates.

From the optimization point of view, these data sources should be optimized enough to get processed quickly and not consume too much memory. However, reading and writing an external file takes time. Normally, binary files are the fastest to be processed and smallest in size. However, after reading the binary data, it has to be parsed to be used in games, which eventually increases processing.

The most commonly used data formats are XML and JSON. The Android library has support for both of them, which includes a generic parser. The developer can have readily available data without making extra processing effort. However, the data can be manipulated during gameplay, depending on the game's requirements.

## Handling cache data

A cache is a memory segment that is similar to RAM from a functionality point of view, but acts faster than conventional RAM. The processor can access this segment much faster. So, logically, a cache should only store data that is being used frequently.

The best possible way to handle cache data is to keep a check on the application memory usage. Generally, there should be at least 10 % of free memory available for the operating system. It is tested that an application can use an average of 2% of the total free memory.

However, the developer cannot control the cache technically. They can only make sure that the most commonly used elements are optimized in a perfect way so that the executer automatically uses cache memory for them.

# Summary

Optimization is one of the most important tasks in any software development, especially in games, where logical programming dominates technical programming. There are plenty of optimization tools and techniques available for technical programming as it has the most common algorithms to implement. However, in the case of game programming, each gameplay indicates a different set of algorithms. In many cases, an artificial intelligence algorithm is also made separately. So, there is a very high probability that the programmer has to find out an efficient way to optimize freshly written algorithms.

We have discussed all the possible scopes of optimization in Android game development. Technical optimization is mandatory as it has fixed guidelines to follow. However, logical development will depend on the game algorithm and its requirements. So, it is an extra effort for the game developer to optimize Android games.

Sometimes, developers over-optimize games. This is not recommended. Over-optimization usually downgrades the quality of the game. So, at the time of technical design, optimization cases should be declared.

Most large-scale development processes have a separately defined task set for optimization. Some developers choose to develop a dynamic optimization process. This means that the developer optimizes the game in different stages on different scales. Both the processes are effective, but the first one is logically more sensible, because defining a separate task will always give an idea about the tentative time duration for overall optimization. This helps manage the entire game development process in a better way.

All optimization processes are validated through a testing phase. All design, engineering, and art work is tested in this segment of game development. We will have a deeper look at testing in the next chapter of this book.

# 9
# Testing Code and Debugging

"A bug free product is a myth" is a common phrase in the development industry. A problem-free and issue-free application or any other product is rationally not possible. However, the developer can always minimize the number of bugs and issues so that the game can run with the fewest possible problems and support the most platforms with the maximum possible efficiency.

We will discuss the scope of various debugging aspects in Android game development through the following topics:

- Android AVDs
- Android DDMS
- Android device debugging
- Monitoring the memory footprint
- Strategic placement of different debug statements
- Exception handling in Android games
- Debugging for Android while working with cross-platform engines
- Best testing practices

## Android AVDs

AVDs are the most significant and important part of debugging Android games. In the initial stages, the concept started with an emulator. There are a few predefined emulators that can be used to run the build on a development PC. An Android emulator provides an interface of a real-time-like device.

*Testing Code and Debugging*

AVDs have a few features that virtually provide the device RAM, Android version, screen size, display dpi, keyboard, and different visual skins. Older AVDs mostly looked the same.

In the current version of Android Studio, most of the Android device categories are provided. Developers can create AVDs as per the target development platform.

The categories are as follows:

- Android mobile phones
- Android tablets
- Android TVs
- Android wearables

AVDs can be created or manipulated by the AVD manager tool provided within the Android SDK. Each and every attribute of AVD can be managed by the AVD manager. This tool can also help the developer to create a custom AVD.

Let's have a look at the attribute factors for each different AVD:

- Name
- Resolution
- Display size
- Android version API level
- Android target version
- CPU architecture
- RAM amount
- Hardware input options
- Other options
- Extended AVD settings and creation

## Name of the AVD

The name is only to identify the AVD. Anything can assigned to it, and it can be changed later. Predefined AVD names can also be changed at the time of creation.

## AVD resolution

AVD resolution is one of the most important factors for visibility. There are some predefined resolution standards, but they can also be changed. Nowadays, mostly, developers pick resolutions that are widely used on an actual hardware platform.

One more use of resolution is to check and verify the display portability of games. Mostly, games are made in a target base resolution. Then, the game can be tested on various resolutions to check the compatibility.

Normally, multiple resolutions would create any issues if the aspect ratio is the same. However, in the case of Android, we can find multiple aspect ratios for different devices. The resolution factor of AVD helps fit the game and check its compatibility for multiple aspect ratios as well.

## AVD display size

This is the visible space or visible display area on an AVD. One high-resolution AVD can have a small display area. It directly implies that the AVD has a high dpi value, which means a higher display quality.

This section of AVD helps ensure the visual quality of the game. However, it is not always possible to set the actual display region in the development system as the development system has its own display limit.

## Android version API level

While developing an Android game, the developer needs to limit the API usage to a certain version. The API version can be deprecated in future versions of Android or even discontinued. To check this factor, the developer can set an API version for AVD.

## Android target version

This is the Android version that will be used to run the AVD. This can verify the manifest target Android version and minimum version range.

## CPU architecture

Android devices mainly use three types of CPU architecture: armeabi, armeabi-v7, and x86. This does not have a direct impact on games. However, the processing speed and quality varies with CPU architecture.

The developer should keep in mind that actual game performance on a real device with a different CPU architecture will always perform differently than an AVD. So, it may give the developer an idea of performance, but it needs to be tested on a real device.

## RAM amount

RAM amount specifies the total amount of memory that the AVD has, which can be used to check the memory consumption of the game at various levels.

It is best to predict the memory overflow issue for various devices. By running multiple apps at a time, a real-time clone can be created with the AVD. The default value is set to 66 MB. The developer can set any value according to the requirement.

External storage can be also defined as an SD card for a virtual device.

# Hardware input options

In Android devices, there can be many types of hardware input distributed within a wide range of hardwires. The most common variations are as follows:

- Touch screen
- Touch pad
- Key pad
- Custom controller
- Hardware buttons

Many hardware platforms have opted for a combination of these variants. An AVD creates a virtual system for all of these input systems.

## Other options

There are a few other options that are readily available for manipulation. If the development system has a camera attached to it, then the AVD can also use a camera, both front and back.

Additionally, virtual accelerometers, sensors, and so on can be associated with an AVD.

## Extended AVD settings

A custom AVD can be made through a modern AVD manager tool. A developer can design a virtual device with a custom look and feel, and with complete custom hardware configuration.

# Android DDMS

DDMS can be used to analyze a running application for all run-time details such as memory consumption, process calls, and so on.

The main functions of Android DDMS are port providing, screen capture on a device, thread details, heap details, and Logcat processing. This service can be used for spoofing calls and messaging.

# Testing Code and Debugging

Android DDMS is widely used for device debugging. Particularly in the game development procedure, it is often used as a line-by-line debugging system. This is very useful to identify unwanted loaded objects and assets, and to track runtime exceptions:

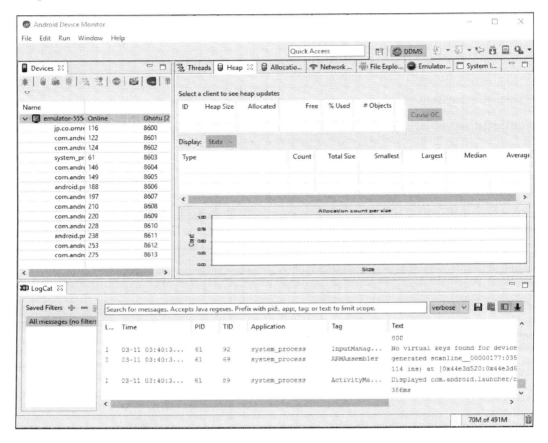

Android DDMS can be used to carry out the following activities.

## Connecting an Android device filesystem

DDMS can connect to a device filesystem and provide a file browser-based operation to copy, modify, or delete any file on the device through a PC. This method or feature, however, is not very important for Android game development.

# Profiling methods

Another interesting DDMS feature is profiling or tracing matrices of certain methods. It gives information on the following topics:

- Execution time
- Number of operations
- Number of cells
- Memory use during execution

Extending this feature, the developer can even gain control over profiling the data of a method by calling `startMethodTracing()` and `stopMethodTracing()`.

The developer needs to keep an eye on two things:

- Up to Android 2.1, it is mandatory to have an SD card installed on the device with the application's permission to read/write on it
- From Android 2.2 onward, the device can stream profiling data directly to the development PC

# Thread information monitoring

DDMS provides details on each thread running for each process on a selected device. However, games mostly run on a single thread. As devices are getting better each day, games are also using the multithreading feature to support various operations such as rendering, processing, file I/O, and networking.

# Heap information monitoring

DDMS provides heap usage at runtime for a running process. It is very useful for game developers to track the game process heap during execution.

# Tracking memory allocation

This is very useful for tracking each and every memory allocation of runtime objects. This gives every detail on each specific object of each class. This means the developer can find out which class is taking exactly how much memory. This helps achieve memory optimization in a much more efficient way.

## Monitoring and managing network traffic

From Android 4.0 onwards, DDMS features a **Detailed Network Usage** tab to track when a game makes network requests. Using this feature, the developer can monitor network data transfer. This option can be very useful to optimize network development. It can distinguish between different traffic types by applying a "tag" to network sockets before use.

## Tracking log information using Logcat

Logs are the most useful debugging technique for tracking almost anything. It is a good practice to use logs properly to check the data or value of certain objects during runtime. It is very useful for logic development for games.

In game development, logical requirements will be different for different games. So, there must be a good amount of code that is written for the first time. Predefined test cases are not available. This deficiency can be overcome using Logcat from DDMS.

Logcat provides log information in the following types:

- Verbose
- Debug
- Error
- Warning
- Information

## Emulating device operations

As we discussed Android virtual devices earlier, DDMS can work upon AVDs as well. So, it becomes much easier to emulate a real-time scenario to debug the game being developed.

The most commonly used emulations are as follows:

- Emulating an incoming phone call
- Emulating an incoming message
- Emulating network state change during runtime

These three are the most common scenarios at runtime. So, these situations can be checked without a physical device. Interruption handling has been difficult for Android devices since the beginning. As a matter of fact, this can be a nightmare for a programmer if interrupts are not handled properly.

There are some common problems of crashing/freezing/restarting the game after an interrupt. Many times, some unnecessary services or processes can be interrupts, and they may change the game state during the interruption period. Emulating every possible interrupt on an AVD is always an added advantage to speed up the debugging or interrupt handling procedure.

# Android device testing and debugging

Android device debugging is the most important part for any Android game development process. Let's divide this topic into two sections:

- Device testing
- Device debugging

## Device testing

The main challenge for a game developer is to run the game on a large number of different devices. These different devices include different displays, different resolutions, different Android operating system versions, different processors, and different memory capacities. Due to these reasons, Android device testing is important and has to be carried out with great effort and planning.

Normally, in a game development cycle, first-point testing is carried out by the developer. This process makes sure that the game is running on devices.

Then, the tester or a group of testers test the game on different devices from various aspects. This is the main part of device testing.

Generally, the main testing phases are divided into four parts according to game development stages:

- Prototype test
- Full or complete test
- Regression test
- Release test or run test

In other words, a similar kind of distribution in each category is termed as follows:

- Pre-alpha test
- Alpha test
- Beta test
- Release candidate test

There are many other testing procedures that may follow typical software testing. However, in game development, usually, these approaches are followed. Let's describe these stages in brief.

## Prototype testing

The developer and designer together develop a playable stage of the basic game idea with an initial set of game rules. These rules and gameplay are tested during the phase of prototype testing.

Ideally, core gameplay is tested in this phase to analyze the feasibility, potential, and scope for the game concept.

Prototype testing is probably the most important part of the game development process. This phase determines the future of the game concept and also helps in developing a meta game and monetization model for the concept.

## Full or complete testing

Usually, whenever the first few builds are submitted to testing in each phase, full testing is conducted. This reveals each and every possible issue with the game, including crashing, freezing, visual issues, playability, game rules, and design faults.

Most of the issues are usually reported during this phase, which eventually implies the possible completion time and effort for that game build.

## Regression testing

Regression testing comes after full testing. Developers, designers, and producers take a call on each and every issue reported during full test. They select issues for resolving, and after the issues are resolved, they are submitted back to the testing team for regression test.

In regression testing, a tester usually picks the issue and specifically checks whether it is actually solved or not. If the issue occurs in a fixed build, then the testers reopen the issue for the next regression cycle. This cycle continues until all the reported issues are addressed.

## Release testing or run testing

This is probably the most mechanical testing phase of game testing. In this phase, the tester runs the regression test passed builds on various target devices, just to check whether the game is running on that hardware or not. This is the reason this phase is often called a "run test".

As many physical devices as possible are used for this segment of testing for a compatibility check. The final device support list is created after this testing phase. It is almost impossible to arrange all the available devices and perform a run test on them. So, the developer groups the devices according to their configuration and performance. Devices that behave in a similar manner are put in the same category, and only one or two devices are actually arranged for run testing for the whole group.

## Device debugging

We have already seen that device testing is mainly the job of a tester. Now, we will see that device debugging is basically the job of a developer. However, commonly, it is done by both developers and testers.

In the game industry, device debugging is mainly used to find out runtime crashes, freezes, memory issues, networking issues, and performance issues. Through device debugging, the developer gathers the following information:

- Runtime maximum heap consumption
- Average FPS on various devices or multiple set of devices
- Unnecessary loaded objects
- Hardware button behavior
- Network request and response

### Use of breakpoints

Breakpoints are very useful and handy in the case of device debugging. The game thread is paused at breakpoint, and the state info can be achieved through DDMS. Game programming is mostly about customized algorithms, which might produce some unusual behavior during runtime. Breakpoints come handy in this situation. The developer can debug the logic line by line after a breakpoint so that the root cause of the behavior is found and fixed.

## Monitoring the memory footprint

Memory footprints are the signs and ways of using memory during runtime. From the point of game memory usage optimization, monitoring the memory footprint is very important:

- Checking log messages
- Checking heap updates

- Tracking memory allocation
- Checking overall memory usage
- Tracking memory leaks

## Checking log messages

Using log messages has been the most effective and immediate debugging technique. Message logs are very useful for tracking the program control flow and runtime object tracking.

## Dalvik message log

The Dalvik message log is useful for tracking memory. Whenever garbage collection happens, the garbage collector can print the following information through Dalvik log messaging:

- **Garbage collection reason**: This info reveals the reason for triggering garbage collection. The reasons can be GC_CONCURRENT, GC_FOR_MALLOC, GC_HPROF_DUMP_HEAP, GC_EXPLICIT, or GC_EXTERNAL_ALLOC.
- **Amount of memory freed**: This section states the amount of memory freed by the garbage collector in KB.
- **Current heap memory status**: This shows the percentage of heap memory used and live objects memory/total heap.
- **External memory status**: There may be some operations that allocate memory externally. This section shows the allocated memory/garbage collection limit.
- **Garbage collector pause time**: Pause time is triggered twice, at the beginning of garbage collection and at its end. Normally, the pause time is higher in the case of a large heap.

## ART message log

The ART message log is also capable of showing or tracking memory footprints. However, it is not triggered unless explicitly requested.

If the garbage collector pause time exceeds 5 ms or the garbage collector takes more than 100 ms to execute, then garbage collector logs are printed. In the case of ART, the following information can be shown as logs:

- **Garbage collection reason**: In ART log messages, the developer can have `Concurrent`, `Alloc`, `Explicit`, `NativeAlloc`, `CollectorTransition`, `HomogeneousSpaceCompact`, `DisableMovingGc`, or `HeapTrim` as the reason for collection.
- **Name of garbage collector**: ART has few different garbage collectors that can be involved in a collection process. The name can be known by the field of the collection log. ART has these collectors: **Concurrent Mark Sweep (CMS)**, **Concurrent Partial Mark Sweep (CPMS)**, **Concurrent Sticky Mark Sweep (CSMS)**, and Marksweep plus Semispace.
- **Count of objects freed**: This shows the total number of objects freed from memory by the garbage collector.
- **Amount of memory freed**: This shows the total amount of memory freed by the garbage collector.
- **Count of large objects freed**: This shows the number of objects freed from the large object scope. These objects are freed by the collector.
- **Memory amount freed from large objects**: This shows the amount of memory freed from the large object scope. This memory is freed by the collector.
- **Current heap memory status**: This is the same as the one for Dalvik logs—live objects count/total heap memory.
- **GC pause time**: In the ART pause time section, this is directly proportional to the number of object references modified by the running garbage collector. Unlike Dalvik, the ART CMS garbage collector has only one pause time during the end of the collection process.

# Checking heap updates

The developer can check the heap usage per update. It gives a clear picture of the memory footprint. Heaps can be monitored with the help of several tools. There are plenty of device memory monitors available in the market. DDMS device monitor is one of them. It is a powerful tool that observes heap usage during the game's runtime.

The Android SDK comes with an inbuilt device monitor at `<sdk>/tools/monitor`.

*Testing Code and Debugging*

The memory monitor in Android Studio is useful for Android Studio users. Monitors can interact with the Android application to watch heap update with each garbage collection. Through this, the Android developer can know about exact memory usage for each segment of an application.

Sometimes, developers switch on/off methods to check exact heap usage. Thus, it becomes easier to optimize it further.

# Tracking memory allocation

This is helpful for memory optimization. Memory allocation can be monitored through an **allocation tracker**.

Memory allocation tracking is required after a certain stage of memory optimization. This helps identify each and every object's memory allocation. Often, many useless objects stay back in memory. The developer can identify these objects and remove them for greater memory optimization.

Memory allocation tracker is available with both Device Monitor in Android SDK and Allocation Tracker in Android Studio.

However, it's not necessary to remove all allocations from performance-critical code paths; yet, the allocation tracker can help developers identify important issues in code. For instance, some apps might create a new `Paint` object on every draw. Moving this object into a global member is a simple fix that helps improve performance:

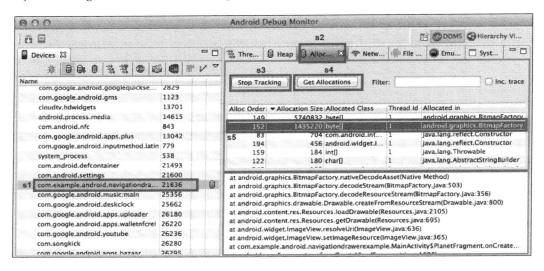

Let's have a quick look at the allocation information obtained:

- **s1**: This is the object package currently being tracked
- **s2**: This shows the **Allocation** tab is selected
- **s3**: This is used to start/stop tracking of the object
- **s4**: This updates the package allocation
- **s5**: This shows the allocation details

In game development, the number of objects in memory is immense, so it is very difficult to keep track of allocation and deallocation of objects manually. This monitoring tool helps find out the hidden spots that could have been easily ignored during the optimization process.

# Checking overall memory usage

Overall memory usage of an Android game is distributed in different segments in RAM. This creates a general idea about application performance and memory security.

Basically, there are two types of allocation.

## Private RAM

This is the dedicated memory portion used by the game during runtime. The Android operating system allocates this memory to the application. Private RAM is distributed in two segments:

- Clean RAM
- Dirty RAM

Private dirty RAM is the most expensive one as it can only be used by specific applications (in our case, it is an Android game).

## Proportional set size (PSS)

This segment of RAM is used by multiple processes. It is basically shared memory. Any RAM pages that are unique to the application process directly contribute to its PSS, while pages that are shared with other processes contribute to the PSS value only in proportion to the amount of sharing.

## Tracking memory leaks

Memory leakage is a serious threat to software development. So, it is absolute necessary to track memory leakage and resolve it. When a process allocates memory and loses the reference pointer, then it is impossible to free the memory within the process.

There are few debug tools that can do this job to track down memory leakage. However, there is another free and more effective solution. The developer can always monitor memory consumption at any given point of time. A game runs within an update loop. So, it is possible to track the memory peaks of different game cycles. If the peak keeps increasing, it means there are leaks in the allocation/deallocation of memory. Now, the developer can check the size of each object and hunt down the leakage. Another benefit of this process is finding unnecessary objects in memory alongside memory leakage.

# Strategic placement of different debug statements

A debug statement is the most important part of any development process. Anything and everything can be tracked and traced through debug statements. However, being a system printing call, each debug statement comes with a cost on performance, which has a direct effect on runtime FPS. This is why a strategy on the placement of debug statements is absolutely necessary.

Let's have a look at the strategies related to following categories:

- Memory allocation
- Tracking the object state
- Checking the program flow
- Tracking object values

## Memory allocation

In a game development object cycle, an object should be allocated once per initialization and deallocated on destruction. However, due to manual programming mistakes, developers forget to free the memory. In this case, the garbage collector cleans the memory when it is invoked by the system automatically. This way, a lag in performance is observed.

Now, as a strategic placement to trace such mistakes, two debug messages should be placed at the constructor and destructor.

Also, a debug statement after initializing each object ensures a successful initialization of the object. This can reveal the amount of memory it consumes.

## Tracking the object state at runtime

An object can be initialized at any time during gameplay. Now, any external dependency in the initialization process can cause failure of allocation. So, the object goes into null state and might cause an exception if not handled properly.

A successful debug statement and a failed debug statement (with reason) helps the developer rectify the issue.

Many times, a wrong deallocation also changes the state of the object. So, the debug statement identifies the spot. The developer can solve the issue with the help of debug statements both for objects and program flow.

## Checking the program flow

A debug statement in every method clearly shows the call hierarchy and program flow. A modular program can be tested with this system. Then, the module set can be tested with one debug statement in each module start.

Any wrong or unnecessary calls can be removed or rectified through this process. Proper program flow ensures a certain frame rate during runtime. So, this approach can be used to optimize performance.

## Tracking object values

Even after a successful initialization of the object, the content may not be correct. So, putting a debug statement to check the loaded/initialized content is necessary to avoid future conflicts.

This is very useful when loading data from an external source. Debug statements are used to verify the loaded data after initialization. Any program module can be designed using an object-tracking method, resulting in a better programming structure.

# Exception handling in Android games

Exception handling may not be a part of debugging, but it helps reduce the number of exceptions and unnecessary application crashes.

Exception handling in Android is the same as Java exception handling.

## Syntax

Standard Java syntax for exception handling is as follows:

```
try
{
  // Handled code here
}
catch (Exception e)
{
  // Put debug statement with exception reason
}
finally
{
  // Default instruction if any
}
```

The suspicious code should be put inside a `try` block, and the exception should be handled in a `catch` block. If the module requires some default task to execute, then put it in the `finally` block. The `catch` and `finally` blocks might not be defined always in exception handling. However, it is recommended that you process the exception in each `try` block failure, which is a good programming practice. This process requires you to analyze the module to find out any vulnerable chunk of code.

Here is a simple example of handling exception along with other vulnerable default tasks.

This is the initial program design:

```
try
{
  // Task 1 which might throw exception
}
catch ( Exception e)
{
  // Handles exception
```

```
}
finally
{
  // Task 2 which might throw exception
}
```

The program should be written in this way:

```
void func1()
{
  try
  {
    funcTask();
  }
  catch ( Exception e)
  {
    // Handles exception
  }
}

void funcTask()
{
  try
  {
    // Task 1
  }
  finally
  {
    // Task 2
  }
}
```

The developer should remember the following points:

- A `try` block can be used only with a `catch` block
- A `try` block can be used only with a `finally` block
- A `try` block can be used with both `catch` and `finally` blocks in sequence
- A `try` block cannot be used alone anywhere
- Nested `try...catch` is possible but not recommended as a good programming practice

# Scope

There are plenty of predefined exception scopes depending on the exception type and cause. However, the major exceptions handled in a game development process are as follows:

- Null pointer exceptions
- Index out of bound exceptions
- Arithmetic exceptions
- Input/output exceptions
- Network exceptions
- Custom exceptions

## Null pointer exceptions

This is one of the most encountered exceptions in the case of game development. `NullPointerException` is thrown when any null object is referred to in the code. The developer should track the initialization and use of the object to rectify this issue.

Here is an example:

```
class A
{
  public int num;
  public A()
  {
    num = 10;
  }
}
// some method in other class which is called during runtime.
void testFunc()
{
  A objA = null;
  Log.d("TAG", "num = " + objA.num);
}
```

This will throw an exception as `objA` has been initialized with null. Hence, this object is nowhere located in the memory, and a reference pointer does not exist. A modern smart compiler can detect this obvious exception during compile time, but the code might be like this, where we defined another class containing the `testFunc()` method:

```
class RootClass
{
  public A objA;
  public RootClass()
  {
    objA = null;
    testFunc();
  }

  void testFunc()
  {
    Log.d("TAG", "num = " + objA.num);
  }
}
```

In this case, most of the smart compilers cannot detect the upcoming exception. To handle this, the developer should add few more lines of code to the `testFunc()` method:

```
void testFunc()
{
  try
  {
    Log.d("TAG", "num = " + objA.num);
  }
  catch (NullPointerException e)
  {
    Log.d("TAG", "Exception:: " + e);
  }
}
```

# Index out of bound exceptions

This exception is thrown when accessing an indexed address, which is supposed be a part of contiguous memory allocation, but is not. The most common one is `ArrayIndexOutOfBoundsException` in the case of game development.

For example, if an array contains five fields and the program tries to access more than five fields, this exception will be thrown. Let's consider this piece of code:

```
int[] arrayNum = new int[5];
for ( int i = 0; i < 5; ++ i)
  arrayNum[i] = i;

Log.d("TAG", "arrayNum[5] is " + arrayNum[5]);
```

Here, the exception will occur in the log statement, as `arrayNum[5]` means the sixth element in the array, which does not exist.

## Arithmetic exceptions

A mathematical expression can signify an undefined value, but in the programming aspect, "undefined" cannot be defined. Hence, `ArithmeticException` is thrown.

For example, if an interpreter tries to divide any value by zero, then the result becomes undefined, which is thrown as an exception. The same result can be seen when calculating the value of tan 90°.

A simple case might look like this:

```
void divideFunct(int num, int deno)
{
  try
  {
    Log.d("TAG", "Division Result = " + (num / deno));
  }
  catch (ArithmeticException ae)
  {
    Log.d("TAG", "number cannot divided by zero");
  }
}
```

## Input/output exceptions

The input/output functionality of a computing system depends on its hardware. However, in the case of gaming, an input/output exception occurs during a read/write operation. Most games are data driven. The basic principal is to feed data to the game software to control the elements in the game. This data is usually stored in a separate binary, text, XML, or JSON file.

Being separate files located at a particular path, these files can go missing, especially when those data files are downloaded from some other location, because there may be a connection interruption and the file may not get saved. In this case, when the game software tries to load such files, then `IOException` is thrown.

Let's look at a quick example:

```
try
{
  File dir = Environment.getExternalStorageDirectory();
  File objFile = new File(dir, "tmpPath/myfile.txt");
}
catch (IOException e)
{
  Log.d("TAG", "Error reading file :: " + e);
}
```

## Network exceptions

This is the age of multiplayer gaming, which requires a mandatory network connection. An application thus depends on the quality and connectivity of the existing network connection. However, the mobile network connection state may change at any point in time. Often, game developers ignore network errors, which causes crashing, freezing, or some malfunctioning in the running of the game.

Commonly handled exceptions are `HttpRetryException`, `UnresolvedAddressException`, and `NetworkErrorException`. If any HTTP request cannot be retired automatically, then `HttpRetryException` is thrown. If an application wants to connect to a certain address and the address is not found, then `UnresolvedAddressException` is thrown. `NetworkErrorException` is used to handle any sort of network mishap such as network lost/dropped, a network using the wrong protocol, and so on.

## Custom exceptions

This is typically used for two purposes:

- Gameplay exception handling
- Game support tool exception handling

Gameplay might create a logical exception during runtime. However, there is small scope for this exception in game development. This is not practiced by most Android developers.

# Debugging for Android while working with cross-platform engines

Modern day game programming does not generally target a single platform. Most games are cross-platform. A cross-platform game engine is very useful for this kind of development.

Most engines come with a built-in profiler and provide some features to debug the game. However, the profiler feature is completely dependent on the manufacturer of the specific game engine.

All native platforms provide complete debug information. Game engines create a wrapper to automatically switch from one platform configuration to another and display profiler details within a common user interface.

However, these cross-platform debug tools cost some extra processing and memory. In a way, they limit game resource consumption to a certain level with an error margin.

# Best testing practices

There are many standards used in the Android game development industry for testing. Testing ensures correctness, stability, functional behavior, and durability after an application is published. The most common approach for Android game testing is manual testing.

However, this process is definitely not the best. As an Android developer, a unit test is always a best practice to save time and get accurate test results.

# Tools and APIs

There are several tools and Android APIs that can be used to carry out the testing procedure. Some of them are inbuilt, such as Android Test Support Library, Dumpsys, Monkeyrunner, and so on.

Most of these testing tools can be triggered through the command line and run through Android Debug Bridge.

The Monkey tools create a virtual environment to populate user actions such as click, touch, swipe and so on to determine real-time result. Monkey can be run with the following command:

```
adb shell monkey -p <Game Package Name> <Event Count>
```

Dumpsys provides status of the system during the runtime of an Android application. This can be triggered through the following command:

```
adb shell dumpsys <option>
```

Dumpsys is able to provide information on running services, input system, network status, RAM uses, and more.

## Testing techniques

Mostly, two types of testing techniques are used in the game industry: automated testing and manual testing. We have already discussed the manual testing procedure in brief. Let's have a look at automated testing.

Automated testing requires tools and extra programming effort. Game UI, memory consumption, network connectivity, and input system testing can be automated. A separate test runs on a simulator or on an actual device to determine the test result, and it is saved at a given location of the development system.

Unit test code can be written to verify the logic of an individual module of a game. A unit test can be used for testing the smallest possible component of the application program, such as elements, classes, and methods. Unit tests are further categorized into two stages:

- Local test
- Instrumented test

## Local test

This type of unit test works on a local machine and runs on the JVM. This saves a lot of testing time. A local test has either no dependency on the Android framework or limited dependency that can be satisfied with dummy objects.

## Instrumented test

Instrumented tests have full dependency on the Android framework and must run on an Android emulator or on an Android device. This testing technique is used to test the runtime behavior of an Android game. It can provide all system and debug information of the running application. However, this technique cannot be used easily with dummy objects. The developer needs to define the testing object data before it can run the test in an Android environment.

# Summary

Any development process is incomplete without quality and performance assurance. Testing is the phase of development where the game needs to be verified technically and logically to see whether it can perform in the real market.

The phases of testing, debugging, and profiling the game ensures the best possible quality of the game for the targeted Android platform range. Often, an Android game works on few Android devices but not on all targeted devices. The developer can identify and resolve the issues for some specific devices through a detailed testing procedure.

# 10
# Scope for Android in VR Games

From a simple point of view, "virtual" and "reality" are two opposite words. So, a natural question is how they can mean something together. The phrase portrays an experience about an imaginary or real environment with a digital computing system.

Game environments are also imaginary or real time. However, the environments do not portray real time experience with touch, smell, sound, and sight. So, gaming has a new scope for exploration with the help of **virtual reality** (**VR**).

Let's explore the concept and scope for VR in Android games through the following topics:

- Understanding VR
- VR in games
- Future of Android in VR
- Game development for VR devices
- Introduction to the Cardboard SDK
- Basic guide to developing games with the Cardboard SDK
- VR game development through Google VR
- Android VR development best practices
- Challenges with the Android VR game market
- Expanded VR gaming concepts and development

# Understanding VR

In the digital computing world, VR means a real-time environment created by digital computing. It means that the environment does not exist on Earth, but can be experienced with digital computing. However, it is not always necessary that VR always replicates a real environment. It has the ability to replicate an imaginary world or environment, which can be displayed on a computer screen or a VR headset (head-mounted display) device (image source: `https://lh3.ggpht.com/uv8mx61-jsrbcu-EPNw1wIi4BCXg7338alepVlr7xKbKJf7eZ9EXT2U3roA8SWx1RC8=h900-rw`):

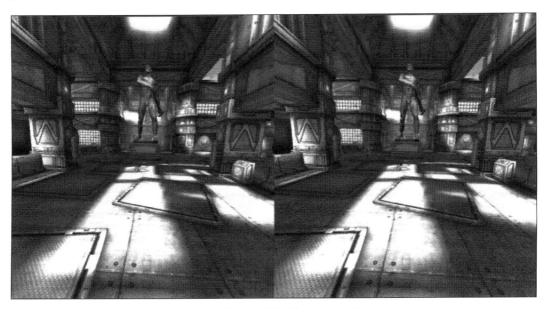

Actual screen display of the Shadowgun VR game

# Evolution of VR

The VR concept seems to represent modern technology, but the fact is that the VR concept was introduced around the second quarter of the twentieth century. In 1935, Stanley G. Weinbaum wrote a short science fiction story *Pygmalion's Spectacles* in which a description of a goggle is found. The goggle described a holographic recording of fictional experience with touch and smell. Technically, it defined virtual reality.

In the mid-twentieth century, the concept was improvised with sight, smell, touch, and sound virtualization. Eventually, in 1968, Ivan Sutherland and his student Bob Sproull created the world's first VR head-mounted display device.

# Modern VR systems

Modern day VR devices evolved after 1990. They were lighter, with better display and computing equipment. Sega developed Sega VR in 1991 for arcade games and consoles. This device was equipped with an LCD display, stereo headphones, and inertial sensors.

Later, after the year 2000, VR devices were improved in many ways. Many technical companies took a lot of interest in developing better VR systems. Nowadays, VR devices are commercially available in the market. VR is now integrated in the latest mobile devices with input controller systems.

There are many companies developing applications that run on VR devices for several purposes. Many more uses of VR technology are being introduced and improvised with each passing day.

# Use of VR

VR is spreading each day in many sectors of the modern world. Let's have a quick look at the fields of VR usability:

- Video games
- Education and learning
- Architectural design
- Fine arts
- Urban design
- Motion picture
- Medical therapy

# Video games

Video games are technically composed of display, sound, and various types of interaction systems. VR devices have proved to have all the necessary components for running a game application. Gamification of VR started in the late twentieth century. Since then, VR has been used in the gaming industry.

A game is basically an interactive entertainment system. VR is just an environment to support the video gaming system. The VR system can take the user inside the game world to interact with the elements.

We will look into the details of the role of VR in gaming later in this chapter.

## Education and learning

Field trips and visualization of educational subjects have a great impact on the learning process. Many times, it is not possible to provide a practical lesson on each subject. VR helps create a virtual, practical, and visual impact on many educational topics. Many institutes and trainers use this method for better teaching.

Training is another major aspect of VR education. For example, VR is used to train pilots to fly fighter jets in developed countries. It reduces the chances of accidents, and trainee candidates can experience the real-time feel of flying a jet.

It is widely used in training medical students for various field treatments.

## Architectural design

VR has been used widely in architectural design. It can navigate through a proposed design without implementing it in reality. Many architectural firms use VR to demonstrate a design.

There are many VR software that can build a VR application from a digital copy of the architectural design.

## Fine arts

This is a lesser known and lesser explored use of VR. However, many fine artists have used VR to create a navigable virtual world of art. A few art museums can be visited virtually through VR technology.

## Urban design

In the modern world, urban design and planning use VR to simulate and validate a design. Urban design is also used to find loopholes and faults in a design. Urban design becomes easier with VR technology in the case of city/town rebuilding, transport planning, landscape design, and so on.

## Motion pictures

We can find some motion pictures that use the concept of VR technology. The motion picture *Avatar* is a great example of this. The whole concept lies within VR technology. The concept portrays a virtual life and activity with the help of technology so that the character can experience a virtual world without being present there in reality.

Motion pictures have gone multi-dimensional with the help of VR simulation. Today, spectator experience has been increased through VR.

## Medical therapy

**Virtual reality therapy** (**VRT**) is quite popular in medical science, especially in psychological treatment. It is recorded that the success rate of VRT is greater than 90% worldwide.

VRT is used mainly to treat people who fear height, flying, insects, motion, public talking, and so on, to create a controlled virtual environment.

# VR in Android games

Before the latest release of Android N, there was no direct support for VR in Android. Google has realized that VR is the future of applications. Previously, Google released the Cardboard SDK to develop VR applications on Android. This SDK is still out there in the market and is being used widely.

There are already many games in the market targeting Android VR headsets. The number of VR headsets is increasing day by day. VR was not part of mainstream Android game development, but it is believed that it will become mainstream very soon as Android has now included a special setting for VR.

## History of Android VR games

In the late 70s, the VR system started evolving at a rapid speed with better equipment. The result is the inclusion of VR in the mainstream Android SDK in 2016. The latest Android devices are VR capable. It is believed that most of the upcoming devices will support VR headsets.

Previously, a high-end PC or console was required to operate VR headsets. But now, VR headsets are being designed to support mobile devices. VR headsets are considered a part of Android wearable devices having a high configuration.

## Technical specifications

Technically, the VR system was lagging with a serious issue of latency. However, with improving technology, the latency is decreasing and the experience is getting better. Some famous VR headsets are Oculus Rift, HTC Vive, Samsung Gear VR, and so on.

Let's have a look at the VR devices that are directly compatible with Android devices. Previously, there was an integrated display in VR devices. However, now, Android devices can be directly associated with VR headsets with multiple input handlers. Here is a limitation that VR headsets are facing. Such VR headsets are only compatible with defined mobile handsets due to their own physical size and hardware specifications. VR headsets are designed to fit certain screen sizes. However, there are a few VR kits available in the market that support multiple screen sizes.

## Current Android VR game industry

The Android VR game industry is growing big rapidly. Almost all the new handsets support VR applications. Many device manufacturers are providing external VR kits specially designed for a particular handset.

Previously, there used to be separate devices to experience VR, such as Oculus VR sets. However, with the help of Android VR development, most mobile devices are capable of running a VR application and they can be experienced with an external VR kit.

## Future of Android in VR

It is a known fact that VR games are taking over the gaming market. Android is growing day by day. The latest release of Android N has a new dimension of VR support. This clearly shows that Android has an immense potential for VR games. Google is potentially working on a future VR-specific platform.

There are more devices coming to market that are VR compatible. So, there is a bright future for VR games on the Android platform.

## Google Daydream

Google Daydream is the next generation VR development platform. It is said to be the successor to Google Cardboard. The latest Android N will include support for Google Daydream, and it has been decided that the handsets will be announced as "Daydream-ready phones".

Google Daydream and Android N will take VR gaming on Android to new heights in the digital gaming world. The experience and the quality of the game is going to be better, smoother, and more realistic.

# Game development for VR devices

There is a large space for VR in the mobile game industry. Based on Android and Google VR platforms, developers are now targeting games for VR. VR gaming is different in nature than other games. It takes users into the game world. Certainly, game design and planning are also different from other mobile games.

## VR game design

VR does not fulfil the criteria for every genre. Hence, VR game design needs to done accordingly. VR games are suitable when there is a character in the game, most preferably a first person shooter or in some RPG or racing games.

The designer needs to keep in mind that the whole game world must be experienced by users through the game. Hence, the game experience is the most important factor for any VR games.

Generally, a game designer starts designing a game from an idea. Then, corresponding controls, environment, and experience are thought of. However, in the case of VR games, the developer or designer already has a defined set of features on which they execute an idea through design.

## VR target audience

There are several billions of handsets out in the world. However, very few of them are actually VR compatible and can run a VR game smoothly. As time passes by, more and more devices are being launched with VR capability.

It is not just a handset that is required to play a VR game on Android, it requires a supported VR headset too. Not every user will go and buy extra equipment to play VR games. That is why casual players are not the main target audience for VR games. Rather, typical gamers and game enthusiasts are the actual target audience for now.

The use of VR is vast. A major section of the use is simulation, which includes education. Gamification of the education process opens up a huge target audience of students. Another major target audience is youths who are energetic and curious about new things.

## VR game development constraints

VR game development does not require extraordinary skills. The developer should be aware and well-versed in Android, and efficient enough to understand VR specifications and platform limitations. Here are a few constraints when developing games for VR on the Android platform:

- Limited handsets to support
- Limited and specific target audience
- Limited controls
- Limited graphical quality with maximum experience

## Introduction to the Cardboard SDK

Google Cardboard is a VR platform developed and released by Google in 2014 for use with a head-mounted device for a smartphone. This platform targets a low-cost project to encourage VR application development on a massive scale, which has proven to be fruitful till date. Google declared Daydream to be the next step for this platform on May 18, 2016.

The name "Cardboard" came from the concept of a VR device made with cardboard, which makes the device significantly cheaper. However, many third-party companies are following the same build architecture with various materials to increase its style and build quality.

Currently, Google Cardboard can be used to create VR applications only for Android and iOS. This has changed the VR development concept, which was limited to typical device and hardware specifications:

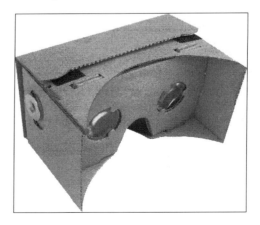

## Cardboard headset components

A typical Google Cardboard headset contains the following parts:

- A piece of cardboard cut into a precise shape
- 45 mm focal length lenses
- Magnets or capacitive tape
- A hook and loop fastener
- A rubber band
- An optional near-field communication tag

Each part of the cardboard device is either pre-fitted or has a mechanical slot to fit in. It is easy and fast to assemble the full gear. The rubber band is fitted last to wear the headset. However, holding the assembled VR headset by any means serves the purpose of a VR experience.

After assembling the kit, a compatible smartphone is inserted into the device slot of the VR headset and held in place by the corresponding components.

## Cardboard application working principle

A Google Cardboard-compatible app splits the smartphone display image into two, one for each eye. The image can be seen through each 45mm lens. It applies barrel distortion to each display segment to counter pincushion distortion from the lenses. Thus, a complete wide 3D world is created.

Initial Cardboard headsets could fit phones with screens up to 5.7 inches (140 mm) and used magnets as input buttons, which also required a compass sensor in the smartphone device. Later, the button was replaced by a conductive lever.

## Upgrades and variations

Google updated the design and released the next Cardboard VR headset in 2016, which works with phones up to 6 inches (150 mm) display. It also updated the input button with a conductive lever that triggers a touch event on the smartphone's screen for better compatibility across devices.

Google allows several vendors and manufacturers to build Cardboard-compatible headsets with different materials and styles. Today, we can observe a lot of variants of this product.

# Basic guide to develop games with the Cardboard SDK

Developing games for the Cardboard SDK or any other VR component is not similar to other Android games. Let's have a quick look at the basics of Cardboard development styles and standards through these points:

- Launching and exiting the VR game
- VR device adaptation
- Display properties
- In-game components
- Game controls
- Game audio setup
- User focus assistance
- Ultimate VR experience

## Launching and exiting the VR game

Normally, after launching an Android game, it performs a few automated tasks and takes the user to the menu to choose an action. In the case of VR games, it takes time to mount the Android device to a VR headset properly, so the developer does not perform any automated task just after launching the game. The game should wait for the user to start it after it is in the perfect situation for running.

For better and common experience, the game should prompt the user with a VR sign or button to start the VR game.

There are two possible exits for a standard VR game:

- Hitting the Back button
- Hitting the Home button

## Hitting the Back button

If the VR has a 2D interface to show popups for exiting, then using the Back button is the best idea. While playing an Android VR game, there is no chance of hitting the back button accidentally as the device is mounted in the VR headset. It is very common to use a single hit on the back button to exit the game, because of the mentioned criteria. Otherwise, an exit popup can serve the purpose, similarly to a non-VR game.

## Hitting the Home button

Generally, hitting the Home button pushes the Android application to the background without killing the application, in the case of a VR game.

## VR device adaptation

A VR game for Android using the Cardboard SDK should adapt the physical characteristics of the VR headset. The Google Cardboard SDK has a feature to carry out this job automatically. The developer can rely on the SDK to adjust application settings and configuration according to the VR headset. The Cardboard SDK itself contains adjustment settings for few specific Cardboard devices. The SDK can configure stereo settings and correct distortion for few specific lenses of a VR headset.

It is recommended that the developers use the Cardboard SDK feature to support the maximum possible VR headsets with a single game to provide users with the best possible VR experience without any hassle.

## Display properties

In many Android devices, there is a feature called Lights Out. In those devices, the Home, Menu, and Back controls are hidden under the Lights Out feature. VR games use a slip-screen technology to generate a 3D experience through VR headset lenses. That is why it is extremely necessary to run the VR games in full-screen mode. System controls or a status bar may actually appear in the user's peripheral vision, blocking or distracting them from the actual VR experience.

## In-game components

Normally, the VR game experience lies within the environment through the device screen. It is very unlikely to trigger any popups and other unwanted components on the screen during gameplay.

Developers must not call any API that will trigger any popup or any unwanted interruption during gameplay. Android currently does not support any 2D component rendering. Forcefully rendered 2D elements may cause disorientation of the VR display. Even if it does not, the user needs to take the device out from the VR headset and then perform the desired action to get rid of the popup, which is not at all convenient.

# Game controls

An Android VR headset contains only one button. That's why control design in VR games does not follow the conventional way. Let's take a look at the control scheme of VR games.

## Control concepts

UI controls generally appear at the launch of the game. Developers should place the UI controls in the initial field of view so that users can locate them to start the gameplay. If the controls are not in the visible range, then users might get confused. In that case, they might look around for the controls or simply leave the game. In both cases, users may lose interest in the game.

While playing the game, if there is any user interface, those controls need to move along with the field of view. Otherwise, users might have to go back to the place where the UI element was.

### Types of controls

Although the headset device has only one control unit, there might be several ways to use the button and a few other options as well. The most popular types of controls are as follows:

- Fuse button
- Visual countdown

### Fuse button

A Cardboard VR headset has only one button on the side of the device. It can be used to click on targets. One of the uses of this button is to trigger a virtual button in the VR world which will fuse. This means a corresponding task will trigger after some time of focusing on the virtual fusing button. However, it may be frustrating, as the user needs to wait for that amount of time. To overcome this problem, the developer should give an option to click on that virtual button immediately wherever possible:

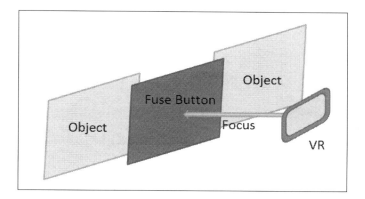

## Visual countdown

While using a fuse button with a timer, there is a fair chance that the user might focus on the button unknowingly, and after a certain amount of time, it changes the game state. In this case, the user might get confused and not be able to continue the same game experience. The developer should indicate the countdown visually to show the user that something is going to happen within a certain amount of time:

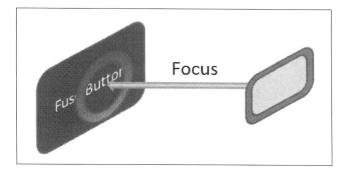

## Fuse button indication

We already know that 2D UI buttons are not supported by VR games. So, developers use fuse buttons. A fuse button can be any element inside the gameplay. There must be an indication to direct the user to focus on a particular fuse button. Then, the action can be performed on countdown or by click.

For example, developers often use some glow, shine, shake, or other dynamic mechanism to make the object visible for clicking. The respective task or action is defined by the surroundings to indicate the task.

### Control placement

It is always a good practice to activate the fuse button when the element is large enough to focus on. It can save the user a lot of confusion. Moreover, there should not be adjacent fuse buttons in the scene that are difficult to locate and might create confusion.

## VR game development through Google VR

Google has released a VR development kit for Android through Google VR, featuring both Android SDK and Android NDK. These SDKs supports both the Cardboard and Daydream VR platforms.

The developer can jump into VR game development through the following tasks:

- Head-tracking system
- Spatial audio
- Dynamic rendering
- UI handling
- 3D calibration
- Lens distortion correction
- Stereo geometry configuration

Let's have a look at the Android SDKs for VR game development:

- Google VR using the Android SDK
- Google VR using the Android NDK

## Google VR using the Android SDK

We will have a look at VR development with the help of the Android SDK. A VR application build can be made with the help of Gradle. Gradle can be used independently or with Android Studio.

The developer can use other tools instead of Android Studio, but it is strongly recommended to use Android Studio for Android builds. It is the most convenient method for VR application development on the Android platform.

The developer is required to check the following factors in order to create a VR application build for Android:

- Android Studio version 1.0 or higher
- Android SDK version 23 or higher
- Gradle version 23.0.1 or higher

Using Android Studio can save users from configuring Gradle settings to build application packages. It also helps the developer identify and update Gradle if required.

The developer can choose Gradle to build an Android application project. In that case, the developer needs to manually edit each `build.gradle` file of every module to include `.AAR` declarations for the Gradle build.

The modification has to be done this way:

```
dependencies
{
  compile(name:'audio', ext:'aar')
  compile(name:'common', ext:'aar')
  compile(name:'core', ext:'aar')
}

repositories
{
  flatDir
  {
    dirs 'libs'
  }
}
```

Android Studio automatically makes these changes and declares dependencies for each module. This will tell Gradle to look in the `libs` subdirectory of the corresponding module for the three `.AAR` declarations. If there is no subdirectory called `libs`, then the developer needs to create a `libs` subdirectory inside the module's directory and copy the required `.AAR` files manually.

## Google VR using Android NDK

VR application development using Android NDK is not very different to SDK development. It requires the following components:

- Android Studio version 1.0 or higher
- Android NDK
- Google VR SDK for Android

It is recommended that you use the Android NDK with the Daydream development platform. So, the developer needs to set up the development environment for the Daydream SDK.

The Google VR development kit started supporting NDK development from version v0.8.0 with beta release. From version v0.8.1, it included a native head-tracking system to power up the development.

Android SDK is sufficient to develop VR games with Cardboard, but a few developers like to use native languages such as C++ to develop games. Having a better understanding of technology, a few choose to develop VR games with C++ and OpenGL. In this way, the VR game can be portable to other VR platforms as well.

## Android VR development best practices

Developers need to have experience of coding regular games for Android before they start building a VR experience with Cardboard. Here are a few areas that developers need to keep an eye on while developing VR games for Google Cardboard:

- Draw call limitations
- Triangle count limitations
- Keeping a steady FPS
- Overcoming overheating problems
- Aiming for a better audio experience
- Setting up proper project settings
- Using a proper test environment

## Draw call limitations

VR games are obviously 3D games with an extensive rendering process. It is always a good practice to minimize the draw calls to limit the rendering time and reduce GPU overhead.

In general terms, based on the list of currently available devices, the developer should keep a rendering call limitation of 100 per frame. In the current industry, most of the developers are trying to keep the draw calls between 50 and 100.

## Triangle count limitations

We have already discussed the functionality of a vertex and triangle in 3D games. The same logic applies to VR games. However, it is more difficult to maintain performance in VR games than normal 3D games. That is why VR games usually use triangle counts within 100k.

Currently, the average triangle count of a decently performing VR game is around 50k to 80k. Developers need to simplify all of its 3D objects and optimize them in the minimum possible triangles and vertices to achieve a decent FPS at runtime.

## Keeping a steady FPS

For any Android game, keeping a steady and decent FPS is necessary. VR games for Android are not an exception. Through the above mentioned limitations, the developer can reduce rendering time to gain performance.

VR games work with a split-screen technology, which is a heavy process. So, the developer should decide and use the minimum possible game objects or elements to keep the FPS steady.

It is a big challenge for VR game developers to provide better visuals with limited resources. Designing and creating art assets is a major part. Using low-poly models with minimum triangles produces poor visual quality. However, this quality can be improved with the help of excellent texturing support for the model and strategic light mapping in the virtual reality world.

## Overcoming overheating problems

Overheating is a common problem for Android VR games. The device heats up while running a VR application due to the extensive use of CPU and GPU. There is not much a developer can do to overcome the problem completely. However, developers can optimize the VR game to reduce processor use. The game should have limited network use and other device components to minimize battery consumption.

## Better audio experience

Android VR games are played with the support of extra VR devices, such as Google Cardboard or similar. We have already discussed the devices in this chapter. Such devices do not have audio support; VR games use device speakers by default.

A virtual reality experience cannot be complete without proper audio experience. It is always good practice to use 3D environment audio in the game and suggest that users wear headsets while playing the VR game.

## Setting up proper project settings

Setting VR project settings right early on can save the developer from headaches in the future. To get better project performance in particular, it is very important to set the quality settings properly at the beginning of the project. The entire project and performance planning cannot be fruitful without a prior project configuration.

## Using a proper test environment

Setting up your test environment is extremely important for the success of any game, especially for large-scale games such as VR. The developer must know the status of each development stage so that they can take future decisions to make the game better. In this way, the development process can run smoothly.

It is always recommended that you run the VR game for testing from outside the VR device. It is also recommended that you use the **adb** to check each debug condition and statement. It is very difficult to use a normal debug bridge for VR games as the game must be tested with a VR device. The developer needs to set up a wireless debug bridge to overcome this problem. The debug bridge can also be used to run and stop the game from outside the VR device. This way, the developer can save a lot of time, which can be used to improve the game.

# Challenges with the Android VR game market

We have already understood the technical challenges for developing VR games on the Android platform. Now, let's have a look at the other challenges that a developer might face while developing or monetizing VR games for Android:

- Low target audience
- Limited game genres

- Long game sessions
- Limited device support
- Real-time constraints

## Low target audience

There are very few Android users who are familiar with the VR concept and technology. Mostly, users are the common handset holders who do not have VR headsets. So, there is already a major section of the audience who are out of scope of VR gaming. This is why the VR gaming market is limited to the audience with VR headsets.

## Limited game genres

We have already looked at the possible game genres in VR gaming. VR games cannot support all the game genres released to date and possibly will not be able to do so in the near future. This limitation is a serious challenge for the Android VR gaming market in securing a profitable position and design monetization aspects.

## Long game sessions

Android VR games must be played with a VR headset fitted with an Android handset. Usually, the game sessions are longer, and it takes time and effort to set up a playable environment.

Android game users are usually addicted to quick and flexible game sessions. Most of the games can be immediately paused and resumed for convenient gameplay. However, VR games cannot be paused or resumed immediately. Users prefer to play VR games when they have a long period of free time.

## Limited device support

Android VR games require high-level hardware configuration to run the game. The hardware platform must have enough power to process the game, and the rendering unit must render the game with the maximum possible quality in the minimum possible time.

There are many cheap and low-configuration handsets available in the market. Millions of Android users use those handsets. However, most of them are incapable of running a VR game with a steady and acceptable FPS. Developers of Android VR games are bound to exclude those devices. This limitation reduces the number of supported devices significantly.

## Real-time constraints

Most of the VR game players are gamers or game enthusiasts. However, they also have some real-time constraints while playing VR games. Users or players must choose a gameplay situation where there is least chance of possible interruptions.

Gamers usually prefer to sit at a location or be in a spacious place to avoid any accidents while playing the game. Their eyes are covered with the VR headset, so users need to take these safety measures. These issues cannot be resolved and this affects the VR gaming market and leads to low session count and time.

## Expanded VR gaming concepts and development

We have talked about only a few of the VR gaming aspects of Android. These ideas have been implemented or are currently being implemented. However, there is a broader concept of virtual gaming.

Game developers are now trying to produce real-time experiences with VR technology. There are a few real-time games that are similar to digital gaming, such as *Paint Ball*, *Laser Tag*, and so on. With the help of VR technology, these experiences can reach the next level. Using a VR headset in a predefined arena that is physically synced with the VR application environment can take the user into the game. This concept of gaming has already started taking shape. A few test arenas for VR games have already been created with the support of various other physical gears and sensors. These gears and sensors track the user's movement in real time and duplicate it within the virtual world through the VR headset display.

Simple actions such as walking, crouching, touching something in the virtual world, and shooting a virtual enemy have already been implemented. Developers and researchers are making it better day by day. However, the Android platform is yet to take a step into this kind of VR development for the following reasons:

- Android is a mobile OS that works best on portable devices.
- Most Android devices are mobile handsets or tablets.
- It is difficult to manage a dedicated hardware platform with a large physical setup through Android. **Real-time operating systems** (**RTOS**) can perform much better than Android for such systems.
- There are low market prospects for such Android setups, and the costing may be huge.

In spite of having these issues in setting up Android VR gaming on a large scale, it is believed that Android will become part of such systems soon.

# Summary

This is the era of technology. VR technology has taken the gaming experience to the next level. Android is now the most progressive platform for gaming. Joining two leading platforms can surely take the mobile gaming experience to the next level.

In VR games, the user gets the chance to be inside the game environment. However, there are a lot of limitations in developing games for Android with the VR feature. Google has already announced its upcoming VR development platform, Daydream, which includes extended controls with a separate controller.

The VR gaming industry is growing rapidly. It has its own set of advantages and disadvantages. However, there is no doubt that the gameplay experience is far better than the conventional gameplay system. So, it will not be a wrong assumption that the future of the Android VR gaming industry is bright.

# 11
# Android Game Development Using C++ and OpenGL

We have already seen the differences between an Android application and an Android game. The Android SDK is very capable of taking care of both. Certainly, the question that arises is "What is the requirement of a separate development toolset in native languages such as C and C++?" Compared to Java, C and C++ are much more difficult to manage and write code in. The answer lies in the question itself. The Java architecture runs on JVM, which is associated with the Android operating system. This creates an extra latency, which has a performance lag. The scale of the lag depends on the scale of the application.

A highly CPU-intensive application may cause a significant amount of visible lag in Java architecture. Native language code can be processed faster. Moreover, native code can be varied depending on the CPU/platform architecture, which is not possible in the case of the Java architecture used by the Android SDK.

Android uses the OpenGL rendering system. So, an application made in OpenGL can also choose Android as the target platform. Native code helps directly structure the application using OpenGL.

We will have a detailed look at these aspects in this chapter through the following topics:

- Introduction to the 3Android NDK
- C++ for games — pros and cons
- Native code performance
- Introduction to OpenGL
- Rendering using OpenGL
- Different CPU architecture support

# Introduction to the Android NDK

Android is actually based on the Java architecture. However, part of an Android application can be developed using native languages such as C and C++. This is where the Android NDK comes into the picture.

The Android NDK is a toolset used to develop a module of an application that will interact with hardware much faster. It is a well-known fact that C and C++ have the ability to interact with a native component directly, which reduces the latency between the application and hardware.

## How the NDK works

An Android native code segment interacts with main application through the **Java Native Interface (JNI)**. The Android NDK comes with a build script that converts native code into binary and includes it in the main Android application.

This binary is basically a native code library that can be used in any Android application as per requirement. An NDK build script creates `.so` files and adds them to the application path.

The Android build process creates Dalvik Executable files (`.dex`) to run on the Dalvik Virtual Machine (or ART) of the Android OS. The Java executable recognizes the native library and loads the implemented methods. The native methods are declared with the `native` keyword:

```
public native void testFunc (int param);
```

The method always has public access, because the native library is always treated as an external source. Here, the developer should always keep in mind that there should never be multiple definitions of a method for the same declaration collectively for all the included native libraries. This will always create a compilation error.

The native building process can build the native project into two types of libraries:

- Native shared library
- Native static library

## Native shared library

The native build script creates `.so` files from C++ files, which is termed as the native shared library. However, it is not always shared between applications in the true sense. An Android application is a Java application, but a native application can be triggered through a native shared library.

For game development, if the game is written in a native language, then the game code is included in the shared library.

## Native static library

Native static libraries are basically collections of compiled objects and represented by .a files. These libraries are included in other libraries. A compiler can remove unused code during compilation.

## Build dependency

Android SDK is capable of building and packaging an Android application project into an APK file with the support of Java. However, the NDK is not sufficient to build and package APK files. Here are the dependencies for creating an Android application APK other than the NDK:

- Android SDK
- C++ compiler
- Python
- Gradle
- Cygwin
- Java

## Android SDK

Android applications are basically Java applications. Hence, it is absolute necessary to have Android SDK in order to create an Android application package.

## C++ compiler

A native Android application is written in C++, so a C++ compiler is required to compile the code base on the development platform. C++ compilers are platform dependent, so it may not be the same C++ compiler on each platform.

For example, on a Windows machine, the C++11 compiler is used currently in the development industry, whereas the GC++ compiler is used on Linux machines.

These may create different code bases for the actual development project in terms of syntax and API calls.

## Python

Python is a separate development language. It can be used to create applications for Android and can support multiple platforms by converting the source into native language. In the case of Android NDK development, Python is used for the conversion of C++ code to native binary.

## Gradle

Gradle is used by the build script and the Android native build tool to convert native code to a shared library. It also provides a virtual Unix environment to make application packages.

## Cygwin

Android requires a Unix environment to build an NDK application project. The Windows system does not have a Unix environment. Cygwin is required to provide a virtual Unix environment to support the building platform.

## Java

Last but not least is the requirement of Java to create an Android application package. However, Java is always required for any type of Android development.

# Native project build configuration

An Android project needs the following configurations in order to create an application package from native source code. A native project build depends on the configuration defined in these two files:

- `Android.mk`
- `Application.mk`

## Android.mk configuration

### Location

The `Android.mk` file can be located at `<Application Project Path>/jni/`.

**Configuration options**:

The `Android.mk` file contains the following options to create an application package:

- `CLEAR_VARS`: This clears the local and user-defined variables. This option is invoked by the `include $(CLEAR_VARS)` syntax.

- BUILD_SHARED_LIBRARY: This includes all local files, defined in LOCAL_MODULE and LOCAL_SRC_FILES, in a shared library. It is invoked by the `include $(BUILD_SHARED_LIBRARY)` syntax.
- BUILD_STATIC_LIBRARY: This specifies static libraries to create .a files used by the shared libraries. It is invoked by the `include $(BUILD_STATIC_LIBRARY)` syntax.
- PREBUILT_SHARED_LIBRARY: This indicates a prebuilt shared library at a specific path to build a dependent shared library from local includes. It is invoked by the `include $(PREBUILT_SHARED_LIBRARY)` syntax.
- PREBUILT_STATIC_LIBRARY: This indicates a prebuild static library at a specific path to build a dependent shared library from local includes. It is invoked by the `include $(PREBUILT_STATIC_LIBRARY)` syntax.
- TARGET_ARCH: This indicates the basic type of processor architecture family such as ARM, x86, and so on.
- TARGET_PLATFORM: This defines the target Android platform. The mentioned platform must be installed in the development system through the Android SDK manager. It indicates the Android API level in order to create the application package.
- TARGET_ARCH_ABI: This indicates the specific ABI for target processor architecture, such as armeabi, armeabi-v7, x86, and so on.
- LOCAL_PATH: This points to the current file directory. This variable does not get cleared by the CLEAR_VARS command. It is invoked by the `LOCAL_PATH := $ (call my-dir)` syntax.
- LOCAL_MODULE: This indicates all the unique local module names. It is invoked by the `LOCAL_MODULE := "<module name>"` syntax.
- LOCAL_MODULE_FILENAME: This indicates the library name that contains the defined LOCAL_MODULE. It is invoked by the `LOCAL_MODULE_FILENAME := "<module library file name>"` syntax.
- LOCAL_SRC_FILES: This indicates all the native source code file paths to be compiled into a shared library. It is invoked by the `LOCAL_SRC_FILES := <Local source file path>` syntax.

There are other optional configurations that can be set in this file, such as LOCAL_C_INCLUDES, LOCAL_CFLAGS, LOCAL_CPP_EXTENSION, LOCAL_CPP_FEATURES, LOCAL_SHARED_LIBRARIES, LOCAL_STATIC_LIBRARIES, and LOCAL_EXPORT_CFLAGS.

# Application.mk configuration

## Location

The `Application.mk` file can be located at `<Application Project Path>/jni/`.

## Configuration options

The `Application.mk` file contains the following options to create an application package:

- `APP_PROJECT_PATH`: This is the absolute path to the project root directory.
- `APP_OPTIM`: This indicates the optional setting to create the build package as release or debug.
- `APP_CFLAGS`: This defines a set of C-compiler flags for the build instead of changing in the `Android.mk` file.
- `APP_CPPFLAGS`: This defines a set of C++-compiler flags for the build instead of changing in the `Android.mk` file.
- `APP_BUILD_SCRIPT`: This is an optional setting to specify a build script other than the default `jni/Android.mk` script.
- `APP_ABI`: This option specifies the set of ABIs to be optimized for the Android application package. Here is the complete list and keywords for each ABI support:
    - ARMv5: `armeabi`
    - ARMv7: `armeabi-v7a`
    - ARMv8: `arm64-v8a`
    - Intel 32-bit: `x86`
    - Intel 64-bit: `x86_64`
    - MIPS 32-bit: `mips`
    - MIPS 64-bit: `mips64`
    - ALL-SET: `all`
- `APP_PLATFORM`: This option specifies the target Android platform.
- `NDK_TOOLCHAIN_VERSION`: This option specifies the version of the GCC compiler. By default, versions 4.9 and 4.8 are used for compilation in 64 bit and 32 bit, respectively.
- `APP_STL`: This is an optional configuration to link alternative C++ implementations.
- `APP_LDFLAGS`: In the case of building a shared library and executables, this option is used to link flags to the build system to link the application.

# C++ for games – pros and cons

There is a never-ending debate between C++ and Java. However, we will not go into the controversy and will try to look at them from the perspective of game development. C++ has a slight performance edge over Java, and Java is known for its simplicity.

There may be many programmers who are more comfortable in C++ than Java, or vice versa. In game development, personal choice of programming language does not matter. Hence, using NDK or SDK has to be determined depending on the requirements. It is always recommended that you use the Android SDK to develop an application rather than using the NDK.

Let's discuss the advantages and disadvantages of using native language for game programming.

## Advantages of using C++

Let's first have a look at the positive side of using C++ for game programming through the following points:

- Universal game programming language
- Cross platform portability
- Faster execution
- CPU architecture support

### Universal game programming language

In the case of game development, C++ is widely used for many platforms, especially for consoles and PC game development. This is the reason many game engines opted for C++ as the primary programming language.

Sometimes, it is difficult to learn many programming languages to work on different platforms with different architecture. C++ provides a most common solution to this problem, as most of the programmers are familiar with C++ library and API use.

### Cross-platform portability

The same C++ code is compiled into a library targeting a specific operating platform. Thus, the same project can be compiled for different platforms. Hence, it is super easy to port a game to various platforms if it is written in C++.

For example, the famous and effective cross-platform game engine Cocos2d-x uses C++ as the development language. Hence, the same game is easily ported for many platforms such as Android, iOS, Mac OS, and Windows.

## Faster execution

C++ is well capable of interacting with platform hardware, and writing games in C++ helps boost their performance. However, in the case of Android, the performance boost is hardly noticeable if the game is not CPU intensive.

## CPU architecture support

C++ code can be compiled for specific target CPU architectures such as x86, ARM, Neon, or MIPS. This specification indicates better performance on that particular processor.

Compiler configuration for CPU architecture in Android NDK ensures the best possible result in each platform. However, it is not always necessary to define each and every platform to avoid extra compilation.

## Disadvantages of using C++

Now, let's discuss the other side of the coin through these points:

- High program complexity
- Platform-dependent compiler
- Manual memory management

## High program complexity

C++ comes with extra program complexity. In the case of Java programming, JVM takes care of memory completely and follows the OOP concept. C++ lags in providing this feature. Thus, it becomes extra overhead for the developer to take care of every programming aspect.

C++ itself has a complex architecture compared to Java. The chances of facing exceptions and errors increases if C++ is used.

## Platform-dependent compiler

Going cross platform is easy when using C++. However, configuring the build script can be a pain in most of the cases. It is a very common scenario that the same game fails to run on a ported platform due to the wrong configuration. Moreover, it becomes difficult to find out the issue as the game is successfully running on some other platform.

Most of the time, different platforms use different C++ compilers. So, it requires an extra effort to identify platform-specific code and find out an alternative for each platform, if required.

## Manual memory management

Java does not require memory management to be implemented by the developer, and the memory is efficiently managed by JVM (DVM in the case of Android). So, there is no chance of facing memory leakage or fragmentation. JVM runs the garbage collector to free the unused memory automatically. However, garbage collector invocation costs a bit of performance, and frequent garbage collector calls can cause a severe drop in performance.

The developer should use optimum memory, because the garbage collector cannot identify unused memory block if there is any active reference in the code.

# Conclusion

C++ has its own advantages. However, when it comes to game programming for Android, it does not help much in the technical sense. So, if we compare the amount of effort and risk taken by opting for C++ than coding in Java for Android, Java should always be preferred for Android. DVM runs Java code efficiently enough to achieve reasonable performance on Android devices. Moreover, the Android NDK library is not actually designed to develop a standalone Android application. Even though it has native activity support, which acts as a middle layer between DVM and native application written in C++, it does not help much.

If the developer chooses not to go for cross platform and keeps the game scope within Android only, then it is recommended that you use Android SDK rather Android NDK. It will decrease the development hustle and complexity with a negligible amount of performance loss.

# Native code performance

As we already know, native code can run faster with better processing speed. This can be further optimized for a specific CPU architecture. The main reason behind this performance boost is the use of pointers in memory operations. However, it depends on the developer and the coding style.

Let's look at a simple example where we can have a better understanding of performance gain in native language.

Consider this Java code:

```
int[] testArray = new int[1000];
for ( int i = 0; i < 1000; ++ i)
{
   testArray[i] = i;
}
```

In this case, the address of 1000 fields in the array is handled by JVM (DVM in the case of an Android Dalvik system). So, the interpreter parses to the $i^{th}$ position and performs an assignment operation each time, which takes a lot of time.

Now, let's implement the same functionality using native C/C++ language and use pointers:

```
int testArray[1000];
int *ptrArray = testArray;
for ( int i = 0; i < 1000; ++ i)
{
  *ptrArray = i;
  ptrArray += i * sizeof(int);
}
```

In this example, the interpreter does not need to parse to the target memory location. The address of the location is pointed out by `ptrArray`. Hence, the value can be directly assigned to the memory location.

Especially for multi-dimensional arrays, a significant performance gain can be observed in the case of properly written native code for the same functionality. Other important use of native code is binary data processing and image processing, where a huge amount of data is processed at a time.

# Rendering using OpenGL

Android uses OpenGL for rendering. Android SDK libraries include the OpenGL libraries, specially optimized for Android. Android started supporting OpenGL from API level 4 and then increased its support as the level increased. Currently, the maximum supported version of OpenGL is OpenGL ES 3.1 from API level 21.

## OpenGL versions

Different OpenGL versions have a different set of features. Versions 1.0 and 2.0 have a lot of differences in terms of coding style, API convenience, functionality, and feature support. Let's discuss the following OpenGL ES versions that are significant to Android development:

- OpenGL ES 1.x
- OpenGL ES 2.0
- OpenGL ES 3.0
- OpenGL ES 3.1

## OpenGL 1.x

OpenGL version 1.x has been supported from Android API level 4 with a shared OpenGL ES 1.x library, `libGLESv1.so`. The headers `gl.h` and `glext.h` contain all the necessary APIs for OpenGL functionality.

## OpenGL 2.0

In the current industry, a developer prefers to use OpenGL ES 2.0 for games, because almost every device supports this OpenGL version, and it provides vertex and fragment shaders useful for games. OpenGL ES 2.0 can be used in Android native development projects by including the `libGLESv2.so` shared library in the project, as follows:

```
LOCAL_LDLIBS := -lGLESv2
```

The headers are `gl2.h` and `gl2ext.h`. OpenGL ES 2.0 is supported from Android API level 5.

## OpenGL 3.0

From Android API level 21, OpenGL ES 3.0 is supported. The developer can include `libGLESv3.so` to use OpenGL 3.1, as follows:

```
LOCAL_LDLIBS := -lGLESv3
```

The headers are `gl3.h` and `gl3ext.h`.

## OpenGL 3.1

From Android API level 21, OpenGL ES 3.1 is supported. The developer can include `libGLESv3.so` to use OpenGL 3.1, as follows:

```
LOCAL_LDLIBS := -lGLESv3
```

The headers are `gl31.h` and `gl3ext.h`.

OpenGL ES 3.0 and OpenGL ES 3.1 are not supported by many Android devices. If a developer intends to use them, then there should be an OpenGL version check before using the version. Also, proper version of OpenGL ES must be used to run the game on that particular device. The latest Android N has support for OpenGL ES 3.2.

## Detecting and setting the OpenGL version

This piece of Android Java code can be used to implement proper OpenGL ES support for an Android game:

```
private GLSurfaceView glSurfaceView;
void setOpenGLVersion()
{
  final boolean supportOpenGLEs3 =
    configurationInfo.reqGlEsVersion >= 0x30000;

  if (supportOpenGLEs3)
  {
    glSurfaceView = new GLSurfaceView(this);
    glSurfaceView.setEGLContextClientVersion(3);
    glSurfaceView.setRenderer(new RendererWrapper());
    setContentView(glSurfaceView);
  }
  else
  {
  final boolean supportOpenGLEs2 =
    configurationInfo.reqGlEsVersion >= 0x20000;

  if (supportsOpenGLEs2)
```

```
    {
      glSurfaceView = new GLSurfaceView(this);
      glSurfaceView.setEGLContextClientVersion(2);
      glSurfaceView.setRenderer(new RendererWrapper());
      setContentView(glSurfaceView);
    }
    else
    {
      glSurfaceView = new GLSurfaceView(this);
      glSurfaceView.setEGLContextClientVersion(1);
      glSurfaceView.setRenderer(new RendererWrapper());
      setContentView(glSurfaceView);
    }
  }
}
```

# Texture compression and OpenGL

Texture compression has a significant effect on the rendering process handled by OpenGL. It can increase or decrease performance for different types of texture compression. Let's have a quick look at some of the important texture compression formats:

- ATC
- PVRTC
- DXTC

## ATC

ATI texture compression is often called ATITC. This compression supports RGB with and without an alpha channel. This is the most common and widely used compression technique for Android.

## PVRTC

Power VR texture compression uses 2-bit and 4-bit pixel compression with or without an alpha channel. This is used by many game developers across the globe.

## DXTC

DXTC is also called S3 texture compression, which is also used for OpenGL. This uses a 4-bit or 8-bit ARGB channel.

# OpenGL manifest configuration

Android requires the version definition of OpenGL used in the application, along with other required options.

Here is the version declaration syntax for OpenGL ES:

```
<uses-feature android:glEsVersion=<Target version goes here>
  android:required="true" />
```

Here are the target version options:

- `0x00010000` for version 1.0
- `0x00010001` for version 1.1
- `0x00020000` for version 2.0
- `0x00030000` for version 3.0
- `0x00030001` for version 3.1
- `0x00030002` for version 3.2

Here is the optional setting for texture compression declaration:

```
<supports-gl-texture android:name=<Compression support type goes
  here> />
```

These are the compression type options:

- `GL_OES_compressed_ETC1_RGB8_texture`
- `GL_OES_compressed_paletted_texture`
- `GL_EXT_texture_compression_s3tc`
- `GL_IMG_texture_compression_pvrtc`
- `GL_EXT_texture_compression_dxt1`
- `GL_EXT_texture_compression_dxt2`
- `GL_EXT_texture_compression_dxt3`
- `GL_EXT_texture_compression_dxt4`
- `GL_EXT_texture_compression_dxt5`
- `GL_AMD_compressed_3DC_texture`
- `GL_EXT_texture_compression_latc`
- `GL_AMD_compressed_ATC_texture`
- `GL_ATI_texture_compression_atitc`

However, not all texture compressions are supported by every device. The developer should always choose the target texture compression depending on the hardware and Android version requirement.

 Google does the filtration process of devices automatically if the target device does not support the declared texture format or formats.

## Choosing the target OpenGL ES version

As you have already learned, not all devices support all OpenGL versions. So, it is very important to choose the correct OpenGL version before developing the game. Here are a few factors that should be evaluated while choosing the OpenGL version:

- Performance
- Texture support
- Device support
- Rendering feature
- Programming comfort

### Performance

It is noticed that OpenGL version 3.x is faster than OpenGL version 2.x, which is way faster than OpenGL 1.x. So, it is always better to use the latest possible version in the game.

### Texture support

Texture compression support varies with OpenGL versions. Older versions support older texture compression factors. Also, Android version support is not universal for all OpenGL versions. Again, it is better to use the latest possible version for texture support.

### Device support

This constraint keeps a developer's feet on the ground. The latest versions of OpenGL are not supported by all devices. So, in order to target a bigger range of devices, the user should change the OpenGL version to 2.0 as most devices support this version.

## Rendering feature

As the version of OpenGL increases, the feature list becomes an important factor while choosing the OpenGL version. The developer must know the support required for developing the application and accordingly, they must choose the version.

## Programming comfort

There is a huge coding style and API change among the versions of OpenGL. The developer should choose the version if it can actually be developed in the company with ease.

# Different CPU architecture support

The developer has the opportunity to optimize an Android application for a separate processor architecture. At a high-level point of view, it is a great feature. However, this feature comes at a significant cost. Let's have a look at the details of this feature.

## Available CPU architectures

Here are the architectures currently supported by the NDK build:

- ARM
- x86
- Neon
- MIPS

## ARM

**ARM** stands for **Acorn RISC Machine**. This is a **RISC (Reduced Instruction Set Computing)** based processor, mainly targeting embedded or mobile computing. As the base says, it is highly efficient for an operating system such as Android.

Currently, most used processors of the Android platform are from the ARM family. It can be further sub-categorized as follows:

- ARMv5TE
- ARMv7
- ARMv8

## x86

Intel introduced the **x86** architecture for processors. At first, these processors were mainly used for desktop/laptop PCs. However, they were optimized to be used in mobile devices in the form of Celeron or Atom processors.

Two types of x86 architecture can be set for the Android NDK build:

- i686
- x86-64

## Neon

The **Neon** architecture is based on ARM technology to optimize it further for mobile computation. The Android build also can be optimized for this specific architecture. All Cortex processors are basically Neon-based processors.

## MIPS

**MIPS** stands for **Microprocessor without Interlocked Pipeline Stages**. There is a variation of 32- and 64-bit processors in this category. As the name says, this architecture is used in microprocessors in embedded devices for small-scale computation. Later, it was introduced to Android with a 64-bit architecture. However, this type of processor is rarely used in Android systems today.

# Advantages and disadvantages of integrating multiple architecture support

Android mobile devices have different configurations in terms of memory and processing capacity. Including separate architecture support may increase the performance that comes with greater build size.

The native build tool builds a separate shared library for each target processor and includes it in the build package.

Here are some advantages and disadvantages of providing separate processor architecture support.

Let's see the advantages first:

- **Faster operation**: Separate architecture for a separate processor results in a faster processing speed of game instructions. If the processor architecture is supported by the Android application, then the processor does not need to perform any conversions and can run the instructions at a faster speed.

- **Optimum use of processor**: The operating system always looks for the specific architecture for an integrated processor. The same architecture makes optimum use of the processor.
- **Minimum power consumption**: Optimum processing directly implies optimum and minimum power usage for processing.
- **Optimum memory usage**: The processor does not need to use extra runtime memory to execute instructions if the same processor architecture is supported by the Android application.

Let's see the disadvantages now:

- **Larger build size**: Using a separate shared library for a separate architecture increases the build package size significantly. The entire native instruction code is rewritten in a separate shared library with different processor optimization.
- **Reduced target device count**: If the size of the APK is large, it creates more problems to accommodate it for a low storage device. Hence, device support becomes less.

# Summary

We looked at Android NDK briefly in this chapter and cleared a few doubts on native development. There are many developers who think that developing games in a native language gives enormous processing power. This is, however, not always true. Processing and performance depend on the development style and standard. In most common scenarios, the difference between native development and SDK development is negligible.

OpenGL works with Android in any scenario. The backend rendering is based on OpenGL for both NDK and SDK. We have already discussed all the technical aspects of OpenGL. Here, you learned which version of OpenGL works with Android and what we should use. Clearly, OpenGL ES 2.0 is a good choice as most Android devices support it. On the other hand, OpenGL ES 1.0 is obsolete, and OpenGL ES 3.0 is not supported by most Android devices yet.

Until now, we have covered almost every aspect of Android game development. However, finishing the implementation for the game does not define the completion of the development cycle. Developers need to polish the game after it comes to a release-ready state to improve its overall quality. We will discuss game polishing in the next chapter to indicate the completion of the game development process.

# 12
# Polishing Android Games

The quality of a developed game mostly depends on the final polishing. Polishing is basically a stage in development where the game is improved in every possible aspect to provide maximum user experience. There is no limit to such improvisation. Most game developers allocate a major time period to polishing.

In the polishing stage, the game should be ready for release. Most of the time, the developer faces a time crunch at the end of the development process. Polishing takes a significant amount of time. There are many examples where the developer chooses to polish the game after release. However, it is not recommended from the user experience and retention point of view.

The polishing job is carried out by the full development team, including designers, artists, and developers. It is the responsibility of the product manager and producer to ensure the target polishing level of the game.

Many developers choose to carry out play testing with a significant but limited number of users. Then, the issues and improvements are charted down for polishing. There are several approaches to polishing an Android game used by developers. We will discuss the general and widely used methods and practices of polishing in this chapter.

We will have a detailed look at the following topics:

- Requirements for polishing
- Play testing
- Taking care of UX
- Android-specific polishing
- Game portability

# Requirements for polishing

Polishing any game defines the quality of development. So, it is absolutely necessary to polish any game before releasing it in the market. A polished game performs far better than unpolished games in terms of visibility, smoothness, and user experience.

Polishing Android games covers all the three development components of a game:

- Development polishing
- Art polishing
- Design polishing

# Development polishing

Polishing the engineering or the technical aspect of the game development process to improve smooth playability of the game is the main target of development polishing. This section includes programming optimization, memory optimization, and stripping unnecessary code blocks to avoid any extra processing.

Development polishing can be further split into three phases:

- Memory optimization
- Performance optimization
- Portability

## Memory optimization

We have already discussed memory optimization in detail in the previous chapter. Memory optimization ensures that the game runs with minimum memory usage. In a way, it helps a lot to increase device support and game stability. A good game must have excellent memory management so that it can run smoothly even with limited memory capacity.

## Performance optimization

Performance optimization ensures that the game runs smoothly on each and every target Android device. However, it is not always possible to test such smoothness in all devices. Mostly, developers select a few devices that are almost equivalent to other targeting devices to test the game.

## Portability

Multi-resolution support and multi-platform support are also a part of development polishing. Thus the game can reach the maximum possible audience with minimal effort. Portability might be the key to success for many Android games.

## Art polishing

Game art is polished during this phase. The main target in polishing the game art is to provide better visual quality within the same art space.

Game art is the initial driving force of the game. So, the polishing of game art may create or destroy the future of the game in the market. Especially for Android, where a wide range of device variations are available in the market with different visual quality, game art polishing becomes extremely useful.

There are mainly three phases of art polishing:

- UI polishing
- Animation polishing
- Marketing graphics

### UI polishing

UI drives the game flow. So, the UI art should convey the desired path easily for users to roam around within the game. Thus, it becomes absolutely necessary to polish the UI art accordingly.

### Animation polishing

Almost every game uses animations for various purposes. Polishing animations means increasing the visual effectiveness and make a user see the game from a developer's point of view. Mainly for sports games, FPSs, and RPGs, animations are inevitable. Animations decide the character of gameplay.

### Marketing graphics

Marketing assets are the first thing to be visualized when it comes to a game. They create the hype and interest to start playing the game for the user. If marketing art is not polished enough to attract users to the game, then there may be significant loss, irrespective of the actual game quality.

# Design polishing

It may be a general concept that design is a phase of preproduction and can be improvised during production. However, it is very important to polish up the design after development so that the final application can have improved quality. It has five phases:

- Designing UX
- Polishing the game flow
- Polishing the metagame
- Game economy balance
- Game difficulty balance

## Designing UX

UX is the overall playing and browsing experience of a game from the user's point of view. There are several cases where a game failed to retain users because of poor UX designing. So, UX has to be polished with the help of actual user behavior.

## Polishing the game flow

Often in the game development process, the game flow might contain some unnecessary loops or actions. Users should have the maximum experience of the game with minimal action. Each action should be simplified enough for the users to understand without any tutorial. However, it is not always possible to simplify the game flow to that level. But it should be simplified enough to make it easy to understand.

## Polishing the metagame

A metagame is basically the container or packaging of the core gameplay. Polishing the metagame means polishing the packaging so that the game becomes more interesting and engaging for users. The metagame is also responsible for monetization. So, an extremely well polished metagame increases the chance of success in terms of revenue.

## Game economy balance

Many developers used to polish economy balancing along with metagame polishing. However, there are many aspects that need to be taken care of separately, depending on the core game model. Almost every game has an economical aspect associated to it. This aspect should be balanced throughout the game to keep users moving and give them a sense of progression.

## Game difficulty balance

As they say, all the fingers on a hand are never the same. Similarly, user efficiency is also not the same. It is the most likely thing to vary, and is reflected on the game leaderboard. So, the difficulty of the game should be balanced in a way such that almost each and every player has a chance to keep playing the game.

# Play testing

Play testing is a part of planning game polishing. Play testing is carried out after the game has been made according to the initial design. It basically reveals the entire user behavior throughout the game.

Here are the fields of exploration during play testing:

- User gameplay difficulty level
- User actions during gameplay
- User actions while browsing the game
- Whether the user is paying or not
- Whether the game is running smoothly
- Whether the user can adopt the gameplay
- User retention

Play testing is planned on a limited group of targeted users. Often, developers release beta versions of the game in a certain region to carry out play testing. The preceding points are basically the advantages of play testing. The only disadvantage of performing such an act is that the developer might lose some audience in the play test region because of a poor initial game plan, which can be improved after play testing. So, it is always recommended that you complete the game with the full game experience planned in the initial phase and make the game release-ready before performing play testing.

## User gameplay difficulty levels

Difficulty aspects of a game vary with game design and core gameplay. All users of the same game are not equally efficient in playing the game. Play testing reveals the difficulty faced by users while playing the game.

Game balancing is improvised after collecting this data from the play testing result. This has a direct impact on game polishing.

## User actions during gameplay

This section typically reveals the use of gameplay controls by users. For example, it reveals whether a gameplay mechanism supports few gameplay controls such as swiping, tapping on different buttons, choosing options, and so on. The developer collects data on all of these during play testing. Even the reaction time of each action may be considered.

Depending on this data, the developer can have an idea of the ease of game control. Whether the user can use the control properly or not determines the success of the game. Sometimes, developers change the game control if they encounter a serious issue with regard to user actions.

## User actions while browsing the game

All the user actions during UI browsing are recorded during the play testing phase. The UI flow and navigation style of the game are validated throughout this process. Sometimes, a UI section may be overlooked by the user. It is very difficult for developers to identify such UI sections from a user's point of view, although developers can easily browse those segments as they themselves have implemented those UI sections. Such cases indicate that the section of UI that is overlooked by a decent number of users is not highlighted enough by any means.

There may be several sections in the UI that are not a direct part of the main game flow, such as the leaderboard, offer wall, achievements, help, settings, IAP screens, secondary game mode, and so on. If a user does not visit such UI sections for a long period of time, which cannot be predicted by the developer, then the developer may choose to change the UI style or find out an alternate solution. The success of metagames mostly depends on this kind of polishing. Game monetization can also be improved a lot.

## Whether the user is paying or not

There are several game monetization models available. The basic three types are premium, free, and freemium. Developers adopt any model for the game to generate revenue.

As the name suggests, premium games are basically paid games. This means the full game is bought by the user in the first instance. So, in this case the user does not need to pay while playing. A free game is completely free to play and has no provision for paying to gain any advantage while playing. The developer can plan revenue through game advertising. User actions and behavior during gameplay can help place advertisements strategically. Users have an option to pay after starting to play the game in the case of the freemium model. The developer designs the metagame to make users pay for the game to gain advantage or increase game progression speed.

In the play testing stage, the developer monitors users when they are paying for the game. In the freemium model, the developer defines stages where the user should pay to progress faster or more smoothly. This plan is validated through play testing to project future revenue.

## Whether the game is running smoothly

As we have already discussed previously, from the optimization point of view, smooth gameplay is one of the major segments of game polishing. Initial testing is carried out on a few restricted devices. However, in the case of play testing, it is much more reliable to focus on real-time scenarios with a real device to validate smooth gameplay. However, a variety of hardware configurations are available on Android. The developer must decide the test configuration and set the benchmark before play testing.

The developer can take note of real-time FPS, crashes, and other performance data through play testing. The game is then further optimized to achieve target playability.

## Whether the user can adopt the gameplay

Not each and every game is easily understandable. It is a proven and common behavior of users that they do not pay attention to a separate game instruction section to understand the game. Instead, they directly jump into the gameplay. Hence, most of the time, it takes a considerable amount of time for a normal user to understand the gameplay.

Some developers use an interactive tutorial to help users understand game controls, gameplay, and game objective. Sometimes, it is mandatory to finish the interactive tutorial to continue playing the game. This is the best possible solution to the problem.

However, there are several ways to design the interactive tutorial. The game might not be understood through a poorly designed tutorial. It is not always possible to predict the time taken by the user to adopt to the gameplay. Thus, it becomes very important to know whether the user understands the game within the planned time or not through play testing. This has a great impact on user retention.

## User retention

User retention prediction is directly associated with predicting the game revenue, which signifies the commercial success of the game. If a user plays the game for the first time and never comes back, it means the user is not retained. User retention has a few segments: daily retention, weekly retention, monthly retention, and so on.

During the play test phase, developers count the number of users who are playing the game repeatedly and the number of users who left the game. Developers even collect data about the time and the specific point in the game where the user left it. This may reveal an issue with the game model. This issue can be rectified to retain more users.

## Taking care of the UX

When it comes to the quality of the game, UX or user experience is the most important factor to be considered. Thus, it becomes extremely necessary to polish the UX of the game.

We can categorize UX polishing into the following categories:

- Visual effects
- Sound effects
- Transaction effects
- Action feedback

## Visual effects

The user experience of a game is mostly visual. So, each visual effect adds an extra layer of polishing for the game to increase experience quality. There are several types of users. Visual effect ensures the engagement of the user. Basically, polishing visual effects means each action feedback should be visual.

For example, there are a few users who might be color blind. For them, only color visuals is not enough. This scenario may be improved by introducing visual effects with different shapes of objects or by some other action.

# Sound effects

Sound defines the mood of the game. Sound designers design sounds according to the game type. There are two separate types of sound effects:

- Theme music
- SFXs

## Theme music

The theme music is the music that plays in loop continuously. It creates an ambience for playing the game. Most of the time, it enhances the fun while playing the game or browsing through its UI. A good game must have a theme that complements the game.

## SFXs

SFXs are the event-based sounds that can be specified for a particular action or event in the game. A few common uses of SFXs are button clicks, user actions, game win, game lose, game start, and so on.

# Transaction effects

Most games have multiple stages of action. The main transaction is the one between the stages. Smoother transaction effects result in a better user experience as the user has a clear idea about the flow.

There can be other transactions as well. For example, if the game supports an in-game currency system, then there have to be currency transactions. Most of the time, the user does not pay attention to the numbers and text changes. However, a visible transaction makes the user notice the numbers.

# Action feedback

There are many games nowadays that strictly follow the action feedback system. There should be a feedback of each action made by the user. Feedback can be either visual, sound, or both. More prominent feedback results in a better user experience.

# Android-specific polishing

Android has a specific set of features and limitations. This opens up the possibility for Android-specific polishing. This can be done on the following features or limitations of the Android platform and devices:

- Optimum use of hardware buttons
- Sticking to basic Android features and functionalities
- Longer background running
- Following Google guidelines for Play Store efficiency

## Optimum use of hardware buttons

A typical Android mobile or tablet device has the following buttons:

- Home button
- Back button
- Menu button
- Volume up button
- Volume down button
- Lock/Unlock/Power button

Each button has its own functionality based on the Android standard. It is always a good practice to use these buttons for the exact same functionality in the game.

For example, pressing the Back button should take the user to the previous screen or previous state of the game. The most common use of the Back button for in-game play is to pause the game cycle. Similarly, the Volume up/down button should have a direct effect on the game sound in line with the native functionality.

## Sticking to basic Android features and functionalities

It is always a good practice to implement basic Android functionalities and use Android-specific features for an Android game. We just spoke about using the device buttons for Android devices.

From the features point of view, the Android standard features support killing the game application from the game itself. Unlike iOS, an Android game can be quit.

## Longer background running

It is a common practice for users to not always quit the gameplay in a conventional way. Rather, Home buttons are used to quickly get out of the game. In that case, the game goes to the background and keeps on running unless the user resumes it or the OS kills the process. The longer it can stay in the background, the quicker the game can be resumed.

Mainly, using low memory and low process overhead can increase the time the game persists in the background. A few times there might be several interrupts. In this case, it is a best practice to resume to the same state for a better user experience.

## Following Google guidelines for Play Store efficiency

Although Android is an open source platform, Google has some guidelines for Android applications; these are also applicable to games. It is obvious that the Google Play Store is the biggest platform to reach a global audience in the current market scenario. So, it is always a wise decision to follow their guidelines to get featured.

There are several millions of applications available on the Google Play Store. Without getting featured, it is very difficult to attract users to a particular game or application.

## Game portability

Polishing is the best phase where game portability should be increased to its maximum level without affecting the game itself. In this phase, portability can be increased in three ways:

- Support for various screen sizes
- Support for multiple resolutions
- Support for multiple hardware configurations

## Support for various screen sizes

Android has a lot of variety in terms of screen size. The game control system is the main segment affected by varying sizes. When a game is designed, the control system is also planned according to user convenience.

For Android mobile game development, Android tablet controls are usually a bit different from Android mobile controls. The screen size of tabs is usually bigger than mobiles. So, there is more space to be used by the user. The game should be optimized for both small and big screen scenarios for ease of control.

## Support for multiple resolutions

In contrast, there are Android devices that have the same screen size, but different resolutions. In this scenario, the main difference occurs in terms of visibility. So, supporting multiple resolution devices is more art-intensive.

Many developers use different art assets to support different resolution devices. We have already discussed the variety of resolutions in dpi for Android. So, it is possible to detect the device resolution and use art assets accordingly.

Specifically for Google Play Store games, Google supports four different application packages under the same application. So, the developer has the flexibility to create and use four different APKs for the same game. However, there are more resolutions. Hence, there are several other ways to achieve them.

Integrating a game-specific server is one of the most popular ways to do the job. Developers do not include the major chunk of art assets in the APK. Instead, they put different art packages for different resolutions on a game-specific server. Thus, the game can download specific resolution assets when required. In this way, the developer manages to keep the APK size to a minimum.

## Support for multiple hardware configurations

A single game cannot have equal visual and performance impact on every hardware platform. Game developers try to maintain a certain standard to run the game on several configurations smoothly.

Sometimes, the game is optimized specially for some hardware platforms. One of the common examples of such optimization is processor architecture. We have already discussed the variety of processor architectures used in Android games. So, games can be ported for a separate processor architecture.

It is very important to support as many possible hardware configurations as possible to target or acquire users. Developers might need to write separate code to perform such a game polishing function.

# Summary

Game polishing is an inevitable part of game development. However, game improvisation has no limit. Developers should plan polishing stages and changes to support and meet the development timeline. Game polishing helps a game acquire more users, more retention, and eventually more revenue. A highly polished game covers each and every section discussed in this chapter.

A game must look good, feel good, and be interesting enough to continue. Last but not least, it should be top-quality so that users pay for it or refer other users. Game polishing increases the life of a game. It helps developers plan updates and features, and keeps users in the game for a longer period.

So far, we have covered almost every aspect of game development for Android. However, a developer cannot be at rest even after developing the game. There are certain parameters to be fulfilled to make a successful game. For these reasons, the developer must include a few non-gaming features and functionalities in the game. We will explore these extra integrations through third parties in depth, and we will try to explore monetization techniques to make the game profitable in the last chapter of this book.

# 13
# Third-Party Integration, Monetization, and Services

Android game development or any other smartphone game development is not complete without implementing background services. Background services help the game spread and perform to reach the next level.

The style of game development has changed a lot with time. New styles and monetization techniques have been introduced. New game services have been created to support these techniques. Many tech companies start their own services to create a new industry. Any work we do professionally is mainly to earn our living, and the gaming industry is not an exception. However, this industry is targeting entertainment, fun, and interactivity between a device and the user. Developers make money based on this. All the third-party integration and services help developers monetize the game, which directly or indirectly helps increase revenue.

Services can be any background support that is not game specific and can improve the experience of a game. Mostly, services use the Internet and device hardware and software programs. Mostly, a server-based service works with the application to provide the service.

We will have a detailed look at these aspects in this chapter through the following topics:

- Google Play Services
- Multiplayer implementation
- Analytic tools
- Android in-app purchase integration
- Android in-game advertising
- Monetization techniques

- Planning the game revenue
- User-acquisition techniques
- Featuring Android games
- Publishing Android games

# Google Play Services

Google is currently the largest platform for Android applications. Moreover, Google is the owner of the Android OS. So, there can be no one better than Google to be the service provider for the Android platform.

Google Play Services is a background service for all Android devices to access all Google service product APIs. It was launched in 2012 to support Android development and take it to the next level.

The most used services in the Google Play Services package are:

- Google Analytics
- Google IAB
- Google Leaderboard
- Push notifications

# Google Analytics

Google Analytics is a service to track each and every event in the game. This can reveal user behavior, user actions, the number of users playing per day, each user's playing time, and so on. So, no data can go unnoticed by the developer. This analytic data helps developers identify the critical sections in the game. With this help, the developer can improve the game for better experience.

## Significance

It is not always possible to track down each and every issue in the game in the testing or play testing phase. When the game gets bigger, with a huge user base, then it is more likely that unknown issues will be exposed. Google Analytics helps in these fields, not only with the current behavior of the user, but with the game performance as well.

## Integration tips

Google Analytics is mostly used to track game events. So, the tracking events must be decided very carefully. The triggering points must also be placed in a strategic way. The developer might not require all the events and behavior data. More tracking may be even harmful to the application, as there would be more data use and more processing in the game.

The developer should always prioritize events. Events should be tracked based on the game flow design. They should then be validated by user action.

From the monetization point of view, it should always be a priority to track when the user is hitting the pay wall or which section is being visited more. A simple advertisement in the most visited section may increase the application's revenue.

## Best utilization

The best utilization of the Google Analytics tool is no different than any other Android application analytics tool. This tool is the best possible way to track user movement, and through the data the developer can easily predict the user's motive or intention with the game.

## Google IAB

In the modern world of gaming, there are many methods to monetize the application. In-app billing is one of the most popular methods. Google Play Services comes with the Google In-App Billing tool. This tool is directly associated with Google Play Store.

Through this tool, the developer can design some purchasable contents inside the game. For users, it is very easy to purchase from the built-in store of the Android application.

## The Google IAB model

Let's have a quick look at the three purchasable options in Google IAB. We will have a detailed look at them later in this chapter:

- Consumable items
- Non-consumable items
- Subscriptions

## Consumable items

Users can purchase this item multiple times from the store. Google does not keep track of these kinds of items. The most common example of this type of item is in-game virtual currency. Many games are designed around virtual currency, and most of the time, this factor is the backbone of game monetization.

## Non-consumable items

They are basically one-time purchases for the user. Google always keeps track of these purchases made by a user for any application through Google IAB. Even when a user uninstalls the application and reinstalls it, it is possible to restore the non-consumable purchases to the user's account.

The most common item under this category is game modes. In many games, there are some open modes and some can be purchased. This system also works with the try-and-buy monetization aspect.

## Subscriptions

Subscriptions are basically a time-based model of monetization. This is mainly used in typical service-based applications such as music channels, TV channels, library channels, and so on. Very few games, however, use subscriptions to monetize.

## Integrating Google IAB

Google Play Services comes with IAB APIs. The developer needs to register the application on Google Play Store to get live access. This system works with item IDs, which are called SKUs. Each SKU represents an item in the Play Store. The developer may not use all the SKUs created in the Google Play account for a particular game.

## Advantages and disadvantages of Google IAB

We have already noted that Google IAB provides a platform to implement a direct digital purchasing system within the application. This saves great effort and time for both developers and consumers. Let's have a quick look at the advantages of Google IAB:

- Google IAB provides a direct platform to purchase application components or services within the application
- Google IAB simplifies the monetization aspect of an application
- Google IAB provides multiple options for payment for consumer convenience
- Google IAB stores and manages purchases for non-consumable items

- There is hassle-free implementation and excellent customer support for Google IAB
- The easy refund process is completely managed by Google IAB

So far, Google IAB has proved to be an excellent system for both developers and consumers or users. However, there are several sectors where Google IAB is still lagging behind. Now, let's have look at the sectors where Google IAB needs to improve:

- Google IAB only provides billing services through Google Play Services
- Google IAB still does not support carrier billing
- Not every user is willing to provide credit card information to Google

Despite these issues, Google IAB is still the most popular platform for billing for Android developers. Google has started including carrier billing services within Google IAB, which may prove to be the most significant feature.

# Google Leaderboard

Leaderboard is a platform for games and similar competitive applications where each and every user can track their progress among other users. Leaderboard has proved to be the driving force of many games. Google Play Services comes with an in-built Leaderboard system for Android applications.

# Significance

Having a leaderboard integrated in games is always a plus, as it helps users compete with each other even when the game is not multiplayer. It is human psychology to try to become superior to others. Using this feature, there can be more user engagement than usual. However, the competing criteria on the leaderboard must be chosen carefully.

A good example of a leaderboard-driven game is Candy Crush. Users are very active, playing the simple game to stay ahead of their friends on the leaderboard.

# Integrating Google Leaderboard

There is no separate Google Leaderboard package. This can be included by integrating Google Play Services itself. However, Leaderboard has to be set up in the Google games account to use it.

The developer can choose any parameter or calculation to store leaderboard data. Google Leaderboard supports data from multiple leaderboards for a single game. Most of the developers use this feature efficiently to show different leader lists, depending on the time period, region, or some other customized parameter.

## Variety of leaderboards

Primary variations of Google Leaderboard are of two types:

- Social Leaderboard
- Public Leaderboard

## Social Leaderboard

Social Leaderboard lists only players who are connected with the player's circle. For this feature, the player must log in to their respective Google accounts. This has a limitation to players who have played and choose to share their activity in the same application.

## Public Leaderboard

Public Leaderboard stores data for players who choose to post scores publicly. Otherwise, this data won't be shown by Google Leaderboard, even if they have better score than the existing players on the public Leaderboard.

## Options for storing and displaying leaderboards

Leaderboard storage can be classified into two types, based on ascending and descending order. In terms of Google Leaderboard, they are called:

- Larger is better
- Smaller is better

A score is always a numeric value, which is again classified into three formats:

- Numeric value format
- Time format
- Currency format

In the case of a numeric value, the developer can specify the decimal placement. In the case of the time format, the developer needs to pass the score in milliseconds, and it will be automatically interpreted in the *hh:mm:ss* format. In the case of the currency format, the developer needs to specify the currency and its unit value beforehand. The Leaderboard will only take values in a unit and convert it to the specified unit format.

Leaderboard can have unique icons to display or indicate a unique leaderboard.

# Push notifications

The push notification service can be achieved through the **Google Cloud Messaging** (**GCM**) service. Let's have a quick look at the cloud messaging architecture.

There are primarily four components used to implement push notifications for Android using GCM:

- Database
- Server
- Target device
- GCM service

## Database

The database stores the registration details of a client or target device with the GCM service. So, each device is required to register only once. The same details are used to send push notifications to the registered target devices.

## Server

Developers need to put up a server to achieve and control push notifications.

## Target device

A target or client device is the platform where the message is pushed from the GCM. Each target device has a unique registration ID through the GCM. Without registration, a target device cannot receive any notifications.

## GCM service

The GCM service is responsible for registering devices and pushing messages to them. The server requests the GCM service with a list of registration IDs and customized messages. GCM is only responsible for pushing the given content to specified devices:

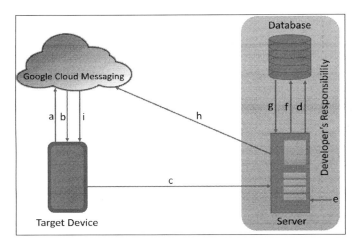

## Workflow of the push notification system using GCM

Now, let's discuss the push notification workflow. In the preceding diagram, the push notification system works according to the indicated indexes (for example, **a**, **b**, **c**, and so on):

1. **a**: The client or target device requests GCM to register with the application ID and sender ID.
2. **b**: GCM sends the registration ID back to the sender after a successful registration.
3. **c**: The device sends the registration ID to the developer's server.
4. **d**: The server stores the registration ID to the database.
5. **e**: The developer initiates the process to the push notification with customized content.
6. **f**: The server fetches the registration ID list from the database.
7. **g**: The database provides all the registration IDs.
8. **h**: The server requests GCM with developer-specified content and registration IDs.
9. **i**: GCM pushes the same content to the respective target devices according to their registration IDs.

# Integrating push notifications

Integrating push notifications is done in three steps:

1. Application integration
2. GCM setup
3. Server setup

## Application integration

The developer needs to set up a GCM client for the application, which is the medium of GCM communication. Here is a brief about client-side development for GCM communication services.

It requires a set of manifest permissions:

```xml
<uses-permission android:name="android.permission.INTERNET" />
<uses-permission android:name="android.permission.GET_ACCOUNTS" />
<uses-permission android:name="android.permission.WAKE_LOCK" />
<uses-permission android:name="com.google.android.c2dm.permission.RECEIVE" />
<permission android:name="com.example.gcm.permission.C2D_MESSAGE"
      android:protectionLevel="signature" />
<uses-permission android:name="com.example.gcm.permission.C2D_MESSAGE" />
```

The manifest will also require declaration of the GCM receiver and GCM service:

```xml
<receiver android:name="com.google.android.gms.gcm.GcmReceiver"
          android:exported="true" android:permission="com.google.android.c2dm.permission.SEND" >
<intent-filter>
<action android:name="com.google.android.c2dm.intent.REGISTRAION" />
<action android:name="com.google.android.c2dm.intent.RECEIVE" />
<category android:name="com.example.gcm" />
    </intent-filter>
</receiver>
<service android:name=".GcmService" android:exported="false">
    <intent-filter>
<action android:name="com.google.android.c2dm.intent.RECEIVE" />
    </intent-filter>
</service>
```

Let's have a look at the registration process for an application with GCM. Registration can be done in many ways, depending on the development style. We will follow the simplest processes within the main Android activity and store the registration ID for one-time registration of the application.

Here are the required declarations:

```
private final Context testContext = this;
private final String SENDER_ID = "<Application ID from Google developer console>";
private final String SHARED_PREF = "com.test.gcmclient_preferences";
private final String GCM_TOKEN = "testgcmtoken";
```

The registration code should be put inside `onCreate()`:

```
SharedPreferences appPrefs = testContext.getSharedPreferences(SHARED_PREF, Context.MODE_PRIVATE);
String token = appPrefs.getString(GCM_TOKEN, "");
if (token.isEmpty())
{
  try
  {
    InstanceID instanceID =  InstanceID.getInstance(testContext);
    token = instanceID.getToken(SENDER_ID,
      GoogleCloudMessaging.INSTANCE_ID_SCOPE, null);
    if (token != null && !token.isEmpty())
    {
      SharedPreferences.Editor prefsEditor = appPrefs.edit();
      prefsEditor.putString(GCM_TOKEN, token);
      prefsEditor.apply();
    }
  }
  catch (Exception e)
  {
    e.printStackTrace();
  }
}
```

Now, let's define `GCMService.java` to handle the GCM message:

```
public class GcmService extends GcmListenerService
{
  @Override
  public void onMessageReceived(String from, Bundle data)
  {
    JSONObject jsonObject = new JSONObject();
```

```java
      Set<String> keys = data.keySet();
      for (String key : keys)
      {
        try
        {
          jsonObject.put(key, data.get(key));
        }
        catch (JSONException e)
        {
          e.printStackTrace();
        }
      }
      try
      {
        sendNotification("Received: " + jsonObject.toString(5));
      }
      catch (JSONException e)
      {
        e.printStackTrace();
      }
  }

  @Override
  public void onDeletedMessages()
  {
    Log.d("Message is deleted …");
  }

  @Override
  public void onMessageSent(String msgId)
  {
    Log.d("Message is sent …" + msgId);
  }

  @Override
  public void onSendError(String msgId, String error)
  {
    Log.d("Sending Error … Msg" + msgId);
    Log.d("Error …" + error);
  }
  private void sendNotification(final String msg)
  {
    Log.d("Sending Msg …" + msg);
  }
}
```

## GCM setup

Google Play Services comes with a GCM system. GCM has to be enabled from the Google API console. Each registered application has its own unique application ID, which is required to configure the push notification system.

Here are the steps to enable GCM for the Android project:

1. Create a project on the Google Cloud platform.
2. Use the Google API to generate an API key.
3. Create a server key for Android.
4. Enable GCM for the application.

## Server setup

Notification server development can be implemented by any cloud connection server technology. The developer needs to set up the application server by satisfying the following criteria:

- The application server should be able to communicate with the application
- The application server should be able to send properly formatted requests to the GCM connection server
- The application server should be able to handle application requests and resend them using exponential backoff
- The application server should be able to store the API key and client registration tokens in a secured database

# Significance of push notifications

Push notifications are an inevitable part of modern day game development. Push notifications are used for the following reasons:

- User retention
- User control
- Knowing user behavior
- Alternative communication channel

## User retention

Push notifications provide users with current updates and information on the game. There are many cases where the user downloads a game and then forgets about it. Sometimes, users leave games in between. Push notifications help these users regain interest in the game. This procedure improves user retention.

## User control

Through device settings and the notifications center, the developer can control the content that the user will see, and the user can be navigated accordingly.

## Knowing user behavior

Using user controls, the developer can track user behavior upon notifications. Depending on the user actions, the developer gets to know what the user likes and dislikes.

## Alternative communication channel

There are several ways to communicate with end users. Mostly, users do not often communicate with the developer. So, a one-way communication channel proves to be fruitful. A push notification system fits the role perfectly. It is the best possible medium to deliver messages about the latest news, updates of the game, offers, and features. In some design models, it can be used to deliver game status information to users.

# Multiplayer implementation

There was a time when multiplayer was limited to conventional PC and console gaming. The modern day gaming industry consists of extensive use of social networking. This automatically opens up the opportunity for multiplayer gaming.

Improved hardware systems and continuous network support with modern connectivity have enhanced the world of multiplayer gaming. Multiplayer gaming can be classified mainly into two categories:

- Real-time multiplayer
- Turn-based multiplayer

## Real-time multiplayer

Real-time multiplayer is just like playing sports together, where every player reacts to any action by the game or other players at the same time. For example, a football game is played by 22 players, and each and every player acts as per the situation at the same time. If we imagine the same scenario from a digital gaming perspective, it will be called a real-time multiplayer.

In the general structure of multiplayer games, there should be a server where the gameplay runs with all the logics and calculations. The server interacts with the database when required, and the user does not have any control.

The client or terminal devices are the only medium that interacts with users. However, in many cases there are some extra layers used on the client side to perform a few actions without server validation to keep the spontaneity of the real-time multiplayer game.

Let's look at the general architecture of the real-time multiplayer system:

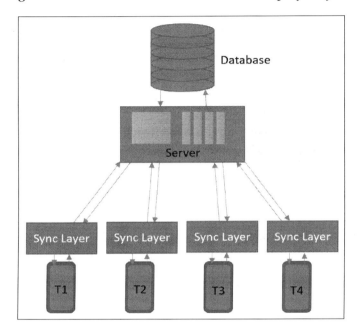

The best practice to implement real-time multiplayer is to introduce the sync layer on each terminal application layer. This layer acts as a medium between the terminal device application and server.

# Turn-based multiplayer

Turn-based multiplayer is a system where only one player gets the chance to play at a time. For example, in the game of chess, when a player plays their turn, the other player remains idle.

Generally, a turn-based multiplayer system is also controlled by a server. A server can be one of the clients itself. However, the execution layers work as shown in the following diagram. Many times, a database is also an optional part of the architecture. The server is responsible for activating UI control on particular terminal devices and should only listen to that device. Let's have a look at the architecture diagram:

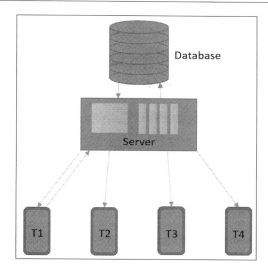

There are more types of multiplayer models possible in Android gaming. Until now, we have discussed only the models implemented over the Internet. Local multiplayer gaming is also possible in Android. We can classify these games into the following categories:

- Single-screen real-time multiplayer
- Pass and play turn-based multiplayer
- Local network multiplayer

## Single-screen real-time multiplayer

This kind of multiplayer game is dependent on the hardware features, other configurations, and feasibility. The device must support multiple inputs at a single point of time to support real-time multiplayer. For Android touch devices, it is recommended that the developers target large-screen devices to provide more space for control for multiple players at a time.

## Pass and play turn-based multiplayer

This is a type of single-screen turn-based multiplayer model. In this model, all the participants should manage the play order manually among themselves to synchronize with the game turn.

Here, one player passes the same device to the next player after playing their turn. Then, the next player reacts to the current state of the game. In this model, the game state does not change until the completion of each turn.

In both single-screen multiplayer models, no network connectivity is required, and the database is an optional component that can be stored within the device memory.

## Local network multiplayer

Both real-time and turn-based multiplayer models can be implemented using local network connectivity. In this case, one of the participating devices must act as a server and control the gameplay over local network connectivity using Bluetooth, Wi-Fi, or an infrared connection.

## Analytic tools

We have already discussed Google Analytics. There are several other analytics services other than Google. We will discuss analytics from a general point of view.

Analytics tools are inevitable for games. They help developers understand users better, which has a direct effect on game quality, user retention, and monetization.

## Requirement of analytics tools

Developers have been collecting and analyzing data from users in many forms for years. Often, we have encountered forms and analysis enquiries about many products. This data helps the developer or manufacturer modify or improve the product.

Let's have look at the variety of data from analytics and its importance through the following points:

- User behavior
- Game crash reports
- Game event triggers
- Gameplay session timing
- Gameplay frequency
- Game balancing
- User retention
- Piracy prevention

## User behavior

Analytic tools can track each and every movement of every user. This data can be further analyzed, and user behavior inside games can be guessed. This behavior validates the **meta** design of the application or game.

## Game crash reports

Almost all the analytic tools can report every crash event with the crash cause and location. However, an encoded package of game code cannot reveal the location completely, where the class and its members are encoded in meaningless symbols.

This helps developers identify the playing device and exact issue with the crash.

## Game event triggers

The developer can set triggers from the game itself to track any or every aspect of the game. These can be any event inside the game. It is a common practice for game developers to use this trigger system for the game start, game end, and a few strategic events such as IAP, advertisement display, mode selection (if any), and so on.

## Gameplay session timing

Analytic tools track gameplay timing by triggering two events between the application coming to the foreground or the application launch, and the application going to the background or the application exit. By calculating the time in between, analytic tools inform developers of the total amount of time when the user was inside the application in a single session.

## Gameplay frequency

This is basically the average count for launching the gameplay per user. So, developers can have the data increase or improve the sessions. Developers can classify the frequency at a given time, such as daily frequency, weekly frequency, or monthly frequency.

## Game balancing

Developers can collect data on user scores and playtime to detect the difficulty for each player. Then, developers can balance the game accordingly. However, every single player has a different ability and skill to play. Thus, developers must set some standards to balance the game properly globally.

## User retention

User retention is one of the most important aspects for developers to generate revenue from the game. This means the number of users playing the games repeatedly. User retention can be also time based, such as daily, weekly, and monthly.

## Piracy prevention

In the case of Android gaming, there might be a model of premium or freemium games. In this model, the user buys the game or some components inside the game with real currency. Piracy is an old practice for many hackers or trackers. They can hack into the payment system or decode the security layers to provide the paid game or paid components for free. Piracy is a major problem for developers in terms of generating revenue.

Analytics tools can check the game and provide the user details to validate the purchase, which adds an extra security layer to prevent game piracy.

# Monetization aspects of analytic tools

Analytic tools are useful in all the points mentioned earlier. All the features are connected to the game revenue directly or indirectly. Some features help developers improve the game quality, and the rest of the features can increase game revenue directly or can help developers plan for more revenue with the help of analytic data.

Depending on the analytic data, the developer can perform the following actions:

- Identify popular regions of the game
- Identify a user's likes and dislikes
- Validate and improve the metagame
- Track paying users
- Track and count advertisement display

## Identify popular regions of the game

Identifying the most popular regions of a game helps the developer plan more revenue in a region by advertising or through some paid content. Especially for free or freemium games, it is extremely necessary to find the part of the games that users are visiting frequently.

## Identify a user's likes and dislikes

There might be several segments of a game. Users might like some of them and dislike others. Unless the developer publishes the game or performs a play test on a decent amount of users, it is very hard to predict a user's likes and dislikes.

Through analytics data, the developer can easily point out the segments that users like or dislike. Developers can change the strategy or plan for a better update for the game.

## Validate and improve the metagame

A game generally has two segments of development: the gameplay and metagame. The metagame design is done by predicting user acceptance of the model. Only analytic tools can validate this prediction after launching the game.

## Track paying users

The developer can track which user is hitting a paywall and who is actually paying for the game through analytic tools. This data has a direct impact on game revenue.

## Track and count advertisement display

The developer can actually track the count of advertisement calls and advertisement display. Thus, it becomes easier to predict revenue from advertisements and the developer can even plan for better filling of advertisements.

# Some useful analytic tools

We have discussed Google Analytic tools under Google Play Services. There are many analytic tools available in the market that are as good as Google Analytics and can be a good option for replacement. There is no restriction for developers in terms of using analytics tools. Most of the tools are free and easy to use, and the developer can even integrate multiple tools for different purposes.

Let's have a quick look at such tools:

- **Flurry** (https://dev.flurry.com)
- **GameAnalytics** (http://www.gameanalytics.com/)
- **Crashlytics** (https://fabric.io/kits/android/crashlytics)
- **AppsFlyer** (https://www.appsflyer.com/)
- **Apsalar** (http://support.apsalar.com/)

- **Mixpanel** (https://mixpanel.com/android-analytics/)
- **Localytics** (https://docs.localytics.com/index.html)
- **Appcelerator** (http://www.appcelerator.com/mobile-app-development-products/)

# Flurry

One of the most popular game analytics tool is Flurry. Flurry has almost each and every feature for analytics purposes. This lightweight SDK is easy to install, and the developer can start getting data right away.

# GameAnalytics

GameAnalytics is a free and powerful analytics tool for game developers. It helps you understand player behavior and build better games through analytics data on a dynamic dashboard typically designed for games.

# Crashlytics

Crashlytics is the most powerful and efficient bug-reporting tool. It can intercept any error and exception with the maximum possible details. Crashlytics is lightweight and easy to use for developers.

# AppsFlyer

AppsFlyer is a single real-time dashboard for an all-in-one marketing tool with analytics features. It basically uses AppsFlyer's **NativeTrackTM** to provide analytic support for games.

# Apsalar

Apsalar is mostly used for advertising attribution. It gives a good look at the game marketing ROI. It also helps find out which marketing campaigns are working and which ones need to be avoided. They also offer great marketing tools such as **SmartTags**, which gives the developer a more detailed analysis of marketing efforts.

# Mixpanel

Mixpanel's benefit is mainly for non-technical people who can easily create custom queries, without knowing SQL. The powerful interface allows developers to segment users and see which segments are working best for the game.

## Localytics

Localytics provides most of the functions for data analysis. The platform provides real-time analytics, remarketing data, attribution, and more. Localytics's messaging features differ from other general analytic tools.

## Appcelerator

Appcelerator is an enterprise suite for mobile app testing, deployment, and analytics. The basic feature of this tool is an interactive tablet-based mobile app, which can be used on multiple platforms and provide immediate insight into the five key mobile metrics: retention, engagement, adoption, quality, and conversion.

# Android in-app purchase integration

In-app purchase is a feature through which the application's component can be bought from inside the application with the help of several payment gateways. This is one major aspect of monetization for Android games.

# What are in-app purchases?

In the modern day gaming industry, freemium games are booming. This means users can play the game for free, but they have to pay for certain components or for game progression advantages. This model has been proved to be a success, as it supports both free and premium concept in terms of digital gaming.

In-app purchases serve this purpose perfectly. We have already discussed Google In-App Billing services, which is just a means of in-app purchasing through Google. But there are other services that support the same thing.

In general, a game should offer in-app purchase items to give users a choice to buy the following types of content:

- Unlock certain features in the game
- Buy certain items to get an advantage over other players
- Unlock some modes inside the game
- Increase ease of play
- Remove annoying advertisements

There are many types of users who have different requirements from the same game with different skillsets. In-app purchase opens up the opportunity for all of them to play the game as per their convenience, and meanwhile, developers make some money.

## In-app purchase options

You learned that Google IAB is not the only option for Android in-app purchases. There are a few more that have almost the same features. There are different service types based on the payment methods. Users may not opt for one option to pay, but if several options are given, then it would certainly increase the chance of purchasing.

It is always a good practice to provide the maximum possible options to the user for payments. Several purchase options are required for the following reasons:

- All users might not have a credit card
- All users might not have a debit card
- All users might not have activated net banking
- All users might not have sufficient talk-time balance
- All users might not like to directly use real currency

The developer should provide the maximum possible options to overcome these issues and make users use real cash for the game. Currently, available billing services support multiple ways of payment, but we can categorize the services into two major divisions:

- Store billing services
- Career billing services

## Store billing services

Store billing services are based on the stores from which the user downloads the game. The game should be connected to a store with provided APIs in order to access this feature. We already discussed that Google IAB is a type of store billing service that includes several methods of paying, including credit card, debit card, selective career billing, and so on.

However, Google IAB is not the only store billing service available. The most mentionable store billing, other than Google, is Amazon billing service, which provides almost the same features as Google.

## Amazon billing services

Amazon billing service works exactly like Google IAB. However, API and integration is slightly different to Google IAB.

The developer needs to include the `com.amazon.device.iap` package to integrate Amazon IAP. This process has mainly three components:

- `ResponseReceiver`
- `PurchasingService`
- `PurchasingListener`

### ResponseReceiver

Amazon IAP is an asynchronous process. It works as a background service that requires a response receiver to be implemented. The developer needs to declare the receiver in the manifest file.

### PurchasingService

The `PurchasingService` class is used to retrieve various types of information about the user, execute purchases, and notify the Amazon purchasing service about the fulfillment of a purchase.

### PurchasingListener

The `PurchasingListener` interface is used to process asynchronous callbacks from the Amazon server. The application UI thread handles all the callbacks, which is why the developer should keep a check on the running process on the UI thread.

Amazon IAP is similar to Google from a feature and integration point of view. There are other stores that may support their own billing services. There is another option of implementing the developer's own payment portal. However, most developers of Android games prefer to stick to mainstream billing services.

## Career billing services

Some game developers use career billing services for monetization. Career billing means the user pays developers for in-app products from their mobile balance, which is managed by the connection provider.

Currently, Google IAB has started supporting career billing within store billing.

## Types of in-app purchases

Developers can design their IAP products in three types mainly. These types of products depend on game design and game genre. The types are:

- Consumable items
- Non-consumable items
- Subscription

### Consumable items

These items are meant to be consumed within the application. In the case of Google IAB, these products are termed non-managed products.

The billing service provider does not keep track of this consumption by the user. Mostly, in-game currency, power ups, extra life, and so on are the main genres of this type of products. Users can buy the same item multiple times.

Consumable items must be defined on the billing server to make them understandable to the billing service.

### Non-consumable items

Non-consumable items are those that do not expire on use. Billing servers keep track of these purchases.

When a user purchases this type of item and uninstalls the application, then upon reinstallation, these purchases can be retrieved. This means the user needs to buy this product only one time throughout the application's life.

### Subscriptions

This is a purchase of time or usability of some features inside the application. There are very limited uses for subscription in games. However, this is a good option to provide some feature or services for a limited time or limited use.

Within the span of the duration, the user may not buy the same item, however there is a renewable feature that allows the user to subscribe again for the same thing upon expiration of the service period.

# Android in-game advertisements

In-game advertisements are the most significant factor in monetization for both free and freemium games. Developers use their game platform to show advertisements in order to generate revenue.

Here is how it works:

1. Advertisers submit the advertisements to various advertisement agencies.
2. Each advertisement has a certain value and time duration limitation, which is called campaign cost and campaign time, respectively.
3. The developer subscribes with those agencies.
4. The developer integrates the agency advertisement platform to include and show advertisements.
5. The developer sets the parameters for advertisement types, genre, and level.
6. When the application triggers an advertisement call to the agency server, it looks for the available or running advertisement campaigns that match the criteria predefined by the developer.
7. Upon successful match, the server sends the advertisement elements to the client device application.
8. The application loads the advertisements.
9. The application shows the advertisements on request.
10. The server keeps a count of successful display of advertisements and calculates revenue as per the campaign cost.
11. The developer receives the revenue after meeting certain criteria from agencies.

# Requirement for advertisements

Completely free games have no source of revenue other than advertisements or sponsorships. We will only look at advertisements here. Let's understand the requirement for advertisements inside a game.

We all work to earn our living. Android is an open source platform, and most of its user base consists of free users. This means developers have only one option left. Compared to other monetization aspects, advertisements are a good platform to depend on.

Advertising as an industry is old and has proven its sustainability in the market. In-game promotion is just another way to display advertisements. This way, it is always a win-win situation for both developers and advertisers.

# Terminologies in advertisement monetization

Now, we will discuss typical game advertisement platforms. The developer needs to be familiar with a few terms to get used to in-game advertisement:

- eCPM
- CPC/CPA
- CPI
- RPM
- Fillrate

## eCPM

eCPM stands for **effective cost per mile**, which is the result of a calculation of advertisement revenue generated by a banner or campaign, divided by the number of ad impressions of that banner or campaign expressed in units of 1,000, which is represented by the letter $M$ at the end.

## CPC/CPA

CPC stands for **cost per click**, which means the developer will earn a certain amount if the user clicks on displayed advertisements. CPA stands for **cost per action** which is similar to CPC.

## CPI

CPI stands for **cost per impression**, which means the developer will earn a certain amount if any advertisement is successfully displayed inside an application. Generally, these earnings are lower than CPC.

## RPM

RPM stands for **Revenue Per Mile**. It indicates the total revenue generated from a thousand interstitial advertisements. RPM includes all types of revenue models. RPM is calculated by the following formula:

$RPM = (Total\ revenue) / (Ads\ served / 1000)$

## Fillrate

**Fillrate** is the percentage of successfully served advertisements by the server. We already know that the application requests the advertisement server for advertisements. This is termed a "request." If a server successfully serves advertisements upon request, then the advertisement is termed an "impression". So we have our fillrate, as follows:

*Fillrate = (Impressions/Requests)*100%*

## Types of advertisements

There are a few types of advertisement styles that can be used for Android games:

- Banner advertisements
- Interstitial advertisements
- Video advertisements
- In-game dynamic advertisements

## Banner advertisements

Banner ads are generally ads with a continual display feature, which users cannot close or hide. However, there is a very low campaign value for CPI, but CPC is acceptable. Many developers nowadays avoid using banner ads, as it occupies a significant space of the game screen. Banner ads are displayed at a given rectangular shape at the edge of visible display.

Possible banner display positions are as follows:

- Top left
- Top center
- Top right
- Bottom left
- Bottom center
- Bottom right

The size variations as per the current scenario are shown in the following table:

| Banner type | Target | Size in pixels |
|---|---|---|
| Standard banner | Phones and tablets | 320 x 50 |
| Large banner | Phones and tablets | 320 x 100 |
| IAB full-size banner | Tablets | 468 x 60 |
| IAB leaderboards | Tablets | 728 x 90 |
| Smart banner | Phones and tablets | Screen width x 32<br>Screen width x 50<br>Screen width x 90 |

# Interstitial advertisements

An interstitial advertisement is a full-screen clickable image advertisement based on various campaigns. Normally, an interstitial has a defined close button for users to close the advertisement and go back to the game.

When an interstitial ad is shown, the ad view comes to the foreground, pushing the main game view to the background. So, each time the game thread triggers an interrupt for the game thread.

This type of advertisement is widely being used in games because of decent revenue. Game monetization design has a significant role in interstitial advertisements. Each advertisement placement has to be strategically based on the analytic data.

## Integration best practice

Integrating interstitial advertisements should follow a few logical ad displaying cycles:

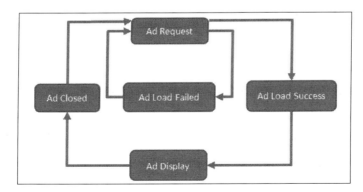

It is always a good practice to follow the cycle. An ad should be loaded and be in ready state before being displayed. Upon closing an advertisement, the next ad should be loaded immediately to avoid load delay.

## Video advertisements

Video advertisements are one of the latest procedures to generate revenue. This type of advertisement has the maximum rate. However, the availability of video advertisements is comparatively less than image interstitial ads. There are two types of ads:

- Full length ads
- Short length ads

### Full length ads

Full length ads are generally longer. These types of ads are generally skippable, which provides an option to skip after a certain amount of time.

### Short length ads

Short length ads are comparatively smaller and have no option to skip.

## In-game dynamic advertisements

This concept provides an option to show any available ad banner within the predefined position and size. No matter what the actual ad size is, this mechanism resizes the ad in the given size within the application.

# Monetization techniques

Monetization is basically a system or strategy to generate revenue from any application. The developer needs to decide their game monetization model based on the game requirements. We can classify these models into four categories:

- Premium model
- Free model
- Freemium model
- Try-and-buy model

## Premium model

This is a typical pay-before-play model. The user needs to pay for the game before downloading it. Normally, these games do not have in-app purchases or in-game advertisements. This is just a one-time buy for the user for the gameplay, and normally all users have the same opportunity for game progression.

## Free model

This kind of model offers the game for free but may include in-game advertisements to generate revenue. The user can play the complete game for free but does not have any extra privileges for any actions.

## Freemium model

This model offers the game for free, and the game can be played completely without any real currency spent on it. However, this model offers in-app purchases to provide extra content or facility for game progression.

## Try-and-buy model

This model is years old. However, very few developers prefer using this model. Developers create a separate build of the same game with different features.

The free version usually has limited content or limited use. This version may or may not contain advertisements. The full version of the game usually follows a typical premium game model. Sometimes, developers use in-app purchases within the free version of the game to unlock the full version, which is a smart way to do the job, as it eliminates the hassle of creating and managing two different applications.

## Planning game revenue

As far as we have discussed, we have a fair idea of game revenue generation. A game developer cannot keep on developing games without generating revenue or having strong financial support. Let's discuss game planning now, to keep a developer developing games.

# Revenue versus profit

Most new game developers do not know that revenue and profit are two different things.

Revenue is the gross amount of money that a game generates directly from users. Making a game may cost money to developers, and each third-party medium may charge a certain percentage of revenue or some amount for the services. After all the required payments and cuts, the remaining amount is called profit. So, high revenue does not mean high profit.

However, without generating revenue, there cannot be any profit. So, the developer must plan revenue in order to generate profit.

# Revenue sources

Now, we know that generating revenue is necessary. To generate revenue, the developer must know about the possible revenue sources. We will discuss the main sources here:

- Advertisement revenue
- In-app purchase revenue
- Other sources

## Advertisement revenue

Especially for free and freemium games, advertisements are one of the main sources of revenue. There are a lot of advertisement agencies that serve advertisements through ad servers. There may be separate values for separate advertisement campaigns.

There is another platform called ad mediation. This platform provides advertisements from different agencies. Sometimes, this platform helps find the highest rate among available advertisements. This special feature is called real-time bidding.

## In-app purchase revenue

This is a way of generating revenue for mainly freemium game models. The developer provides the game for free, but certain content and features are kept locked inside the game. Once the user is used to the game and feels like spending extra bucks to get a strong hold of the game, they use in-app purchases.

Planning revenue through in-app purchases entirely depends on the game design and market behavior. Some game models demand content, some demand features, and a few demand both.

In-app purchases can be made with several billing and purchasing services, which we have discussed. However, choosing a particular service may have an effect on revenue generation. So, the developer should always study market trends before tying the knot with a billing service provider.

## Other revenue sources

Other than advertisements and in-app purchases, there are other sources of revenue too. Offerwall and coupon systems are two other options. The developer might opt for branding and sponsorship for a game. This will certainly help make more money. However, these are not exactly means of revenue sources from a general point of view.

As the industry modernizes, new sources of revenue may come up to help developers grow and make better games.

## Regional variations of revenue plan

There are several types of users. Mostly, the game industry market varies with region, age group, and gender. If the developer plans to increase revenue, then they must consider these factors in a revenue plan.

However, it is not always possible to use all of these factors at one time or in a single plan. Mostly, developers in the current industry vary revenue plans on the basis of region. It has been established in the market that user behavior varies a lot based on region.

For example, Asian user action and behavior may vary from African or American users, so does the spending capacity. So, the developer should plan game revenue according to the spending capability and spending behavior of users. In some regions, users do not pay real cash. In those cases, the developer must have a different approach to generate revenue.

## User base variations

As we have already said, the user base varies with region. For example, racing is one of the most played genres on average throughout the world. However, generating revenue is not the same. In many regions, people value time more than money, and in other regions, it may be the opposite. So, if the purchasing element inside a racing game helps users save some time for game progression, it might not work in all regions. Some people like to spend more time to achieve that progression instead of paying. The developer has to have a plan to convert that play time into revenue by some means.

## User behavior variations

Typical user behavior data around the world indicates a lot of variation. One of the major variations is game genre. For example, cricket is an extremely famous and hot genre in a few countries or regions that are used to the game and connected to the game professionally, mentally, or sentimentally. In the American region, this game is not much appreciated. For the same behavior, baseball is not so popular among Asian people. The developer should always analyze the user behavior data of the maximum possible users to plan for the maximum revenue generated from a game.

# User acquisition techniques

If a game has no users, it is as good as scrap. This does not mean that the game quality or design is bad. In the Android gaming market, more than 5 million games are published. Hundreds of games are being published every day, which is increasing the competition.

In this immense crowd, a single game may disappear, irrespective of its quality, but due to having a poor or no marketing strategy. A game can only be successful if it has a significant number of users and good retention.

Let's have a look at few of the user acquisition techniques through the following topics:

- Game promotion channels
- Game blogs and forum discussions
- Paid user acquisitions
- Other techniques

# Game promotion channels

There are several ways to promote the game in the market. There are some game promotion channels that advertise in various mediums. A specific game genre channel promotes the same kind of games. Let's look at few of these mediums:

- YouTube channels
- Android forums
- Sports forums
- Facebook promotions
- Twitter and other social platforms

## YouTube channels

There are several YouTube channels that review and promote Android games. Many users follow certain channels for better games. Developers can approach these channels to review and promote their games in a way that users can get to know about the game.

A good game review from such channels can get developers a significant amount of users. However, such channels might charge developers for reviewing their games. Thousands of users may be found from such channels.

## Android forums

There are hundreds of Android forums available, and there are thousands of active participants that can be found talking about games, apps, development style and standards, and so on. Such forums are also good platforms to promote Android games. However, developers should be specific to the topic, and the game should have the potential to be talked about. A few hundreds of users can be achieved through such channels.

If a developer uses any Android-specific special feature and has implemented something new through technology, such forums are an excellent medium to reach out to users who are technology enthusiasts and hungry for new implementations.

## Sports forums

There are many forums for specific sports. This method works mostly for games in the sports genre. The developer should talk to other members of a forum about games of the same sport. For example, if a developer has made a cricket game, then the game should be posted and promoted through cricket forums.

This method has an added advantage. As the forum is specific to the same sport, then the developer might find a few people who are experts in the sport and can share their valuable opinion about the game, which may make the game better.

## Facebook promotion

Facebook is currently the largest social platform, with billions of users. It is a common practice for developers to use this platform for promotion of games. Social networking can find a significant number of users for a game.

Each game should have a page that should be maintained properly by the developer. This page is one of the communication mediums between the user and the developer. Such pages can be used to talk about the features and elements of the game so that new users have a good idea about the game even before they start playing it.

## Twitter and other social platforms

Twitter and other social platforms are also useful for game promotion and increasing the user base. Timely tweets about game updates and features can help increase the user count.

A social platform need not necessarily be a digital or web platform. It can be anything, like a social event in real life. Many developers organize events to showcase their games or participate in various events and competitions to get recognition. Good recognition for a good game can help gain more users.

# Game blogs and forum discussions

Game blogs and creating forums for developed games can help in user acquisition. However, this technique works after the game develops a decent user base so that there can be a significant number of people who will participate in the discussion.

The developer can create a game blog for the game, where users can share their opinions, criticism, or suggestions for the game. This can make a game famous, which always helps gain users.

# Paid user acquisition

There are many marketing agencies that find users for games. Usually, such agencies charge developers for user acquisition. If the developer has the strength to spend real cash to gain users, then this is probably the best possible solution.

User acquisition charges may vary with region. The developer needs to research more on this, depending on the game genre and type; the users gained can repay the developer with more revenue. Sometimes, the wrong choice of promotion and a wrongly acquired user base may lead the game to disaster.

## Other techniques

Besides the preceding techniques, there are several methods to gain users. Developers may come up with their own ideas for promoting the game. Some of them are as follows:

- Many times, the developer approaches users individually to promote games
- Many times, the game is promoted verbally through friends and family
- Many times, developers run campaigns for the game
- The developer may approach a good publisher to get help acquiring more users
- Sometimes, celebrities are used to promote the game

There is no fixed path for promoting a game and acquiring users. It is always a good habit to keep all the options open and aim for the maximum possible outcome.

## User retention techniques

Creating a good user base might not be enough to generate decent revenue to gain profit out of the game. Hence comes the term **user retention**. This means the number of users who are playing the game repeatedly.

Users may download a game, and after a few game sessions, they may never come back. In another scenario, the user may come back again and again to the game. User retention is calculated on time parameters such as weekly or monthly use. This means how many users are coming back to the game within the given time period.

Free and freemium game revenue mostly depends on user retention, because the developer converts the time spent inside the game into revenue through several revenue generations plans. That is why user retention becomes important for doing business with games.

There are many techniques to improve user retention other than the core metagame. Let's discuss the major techniques through these points:

- Daily bonus
- Leaderboards and achievements
- Offerwall integration
- Push notifications
- Frequent updates

## Daily bonus

Daily bonus is the most popular technique among game developers for user retention. In this system, the user gains something extra for coming back to the game each day. Consecutive days of playing rewards the user with more items and elements.

This system motivates users to keep coming back to the game. Thus, a developer gets more game session time to convert it to revenue.

## Leaderboards and achievements

Leaderboards and achievements are used extensively to retain users. Both give users competition and motivation to make progress in the game. To make progress in the game, users must come back to the game and spend time within the game.

## Offerwall Integration

The developer uses some real-world offers to keep users inside the game. Real offers such as coupons and discounts always interest users. It provokes them to come to the offerwall frequently. Offerwalls not only help retain users, but also help generate more revenue from various offer campaigns.

## Push notifications

Push notifications can inform users about the latest information and updates about the game. Even if the user is not playing the game, push notifications help them gain interest in the game, which may make the user start playing again.

Sometimes, a user downloads a game and forgets about it. In such a case, a push notification reminds the user to play the game. It also informs them about their progress inside the game.

## Frequent updates

The developer should keep updating the game frequently to keep up with the chart and to be in the sight of the user. This indirectly attracts more users and helps retain existing users.

Every game store informs existing users about the latest update information for a game or application so that users can update their game and keep playing.

## Featuring Android games

A successful game means both profits and fame. A game can be profitable with a good monetization design and marketing. However, getting famous is not that easy. A game becomes famous if it gets featured in various places.

A game can be featured with the help of the following qualities and criteria:

- Creativity and uniqueness
- User reviews and ratings
- Download count
- Revenue amount

### Creativity and uniqueness

There are many game critics and reviewers present in the game industry. There are many articles, blogs, magazines, and sites that follow, review, and talk about games. Game creativity and uniqueness are the biggest factors for such mediums. The quality of the game depends on these in terms of game art, game design, and playability. A good art style, good design, and playability can make a game get featured by game stores, magazines, or blogs. In such ways, the developer can make a game famous, which may lead to more users and revenue.

### User reviews and ratings

After publishing the game, the game's fate depends on users. New users cannot be attracted to the game if the game receives bad reviews and a poor rating. Hence, the game will not be featured and gain momentum. The developer should always keep an eye on the game ratings and user reviews. The developer should actively respond to the issues that users are having and be thankful for the good ratings and reviews. Often, it has been noticed that the game does not do well in the early stages of publishing. However, with a positive attitude towards user reviews, they perform well in the later stages.

# Download count

Download count is another game featuring criteria. As soon as the download count increases, there is more probability that the game will get featured by the store itself. However, the rating is also a factor in such featuring. The developer should concentrate on increasing the number of downloads as soon as possible to get featured or to be in the top list.

# Revenue amount

An Android game can be featured with the amount of revenue generation in the top grossing list. Being in the top grossing list means users are paying for the game or the game is generating a significant amount of revenue. Getting featured in the top grossing list always increases the visibility of the game, which indirectly generates more download count and revenue. However, to remain in the top list, the developer should always update the game as per user requirements and heavily focus on user retention.

# Publishing Android games

So far, you've learned how to reach users and how to make revenue out of the game. However, these are the steps after the game gets published in the market. There are two ways through which the developer can publish the game:

- Self publishing
- Publishing through publishers

Let's have a quick look at this segment of game development.

# Self publishing

When users publish under their own banner and name, it is called self publishing. In this case, developers keep 100% of the equity in the games and own the game IPs themselves. Self publishing games are totally controlled by developers. Developers take full responsibility for the game, game ratings and reviews, game revenue, and user satisfaction.

## Publishing through publishers

Often, a developer does not have bandwidth to take full game responsibility after publishing it. In this case, the developer may approach established publishers to publish the game. A few times, publishers have their own terms and conditions, and requirements for the game in order to publish it. The developer needs to keep up with the conditions to enjoy less responsibility and better marketing.

## Summary

You learned about the whole game development cycle in this chapter. Developers should be capable of taking the right decision for the game to taste success. It is a well-known fact that success does not come easily. This chapter shows all the factors of a game that need to be taken care of to achieve success.

Making a good game is not enough; making a unique game is not enough; making good graphics is not enough; and having a good design is not enough. A game's developers must take help from other third-party services if they are not capable of doing it on their own. Using social platforms is also a must.

Finally, choosing the right publishing place and targeting the correct audience for the game can bring success. In the case of Android-specific gaming, there are already established publishing houses, stores, and other third-party service providers available. The developer needs to assemble all of them carefully after the game has been made. Otherwise, there is a strong possibility that a good game might be lost in the crowd of millions of Android games.

# Index

## Symbols

**2D/3D performance comparison**
  3D processing, heavier than 2D processing 151
  about 151
  different look and feel 151
**2D assets optimization**
  about 147
  data optimization 147
  process optimization 148
  size optimization 147
**2D rendering pipeline 145**
**3D assets optimization**
  about 148
  model optimization 148
  polygon count, limiting 148
**3D rendering pipeline 146**

## A

**Acorn RISC Machine (ARM) 270**
**action feedback, UX polishing 281**
**ADT-1 27**
**advantages, C++ for games**
  CPU architecture support 262
  cross-platform portability 261
  faster execution 262
  universal game programming language 261
**advertisement monetization, terminologies**
  CPC/CPA 312
  CPI 312
  eCPM 312
  fillrate 313

**advertisements styles, for Android games**
  about 313
  banner advertisements 313, 314
  in-game dynamic advertisements 315
  interstitial advertisements 314
  video advertisements 315
**Ahead-of-time (AOT) compilation 2**
**allocation tracker 220**
**Amazon billing services**
  about 309
  PurchasingListener 309
  PurchasingService 309
  ResponseReceiver 309
**analytic tools**
  about 302, 305
  Appcelerator 307
  AppsFlyer 306
  Apsalar 306
  Crashlytics 306
  Flurry 306
  GameAnalytics 306
  Localytics 307
  Mixpanel 306
  monetization aspects 304
  requisites 302
**Android**
  about 2
  future, in VR 238
**Android application**
  life cycle 6, 7
  memory management 7
  performance 7
**Android build process**
  native shared library 256
  native static library 257

Android consoles
  development insights on 42
  exploring 28-33
  GamePop 32
  Game Stick 31
  Mad Catz MOJO 32
Android DDMS
  about 211
  connecting, to Android device filesystem 212
  device operations, emulating 214, 215
  heap information monitoring 213
  log information, tracking with Logcat 214
  memory allocation, tracking 213
  network traffic, managing 214
  network traffic, monitoring 214
  profiling methods 213
  thread information monitoring 213
Android Debug Bridge (adb)
  about 53, 250
  client, on development machine 53
  daemon 53
  server, on development machine 53
  using, on Android device 54
Android Development Tool (ADT) 50
Android device
  Android Debug Bridge (adb), using on 54
Android device debugging
  about 217
  usage, of breakpoints 217
Android device filesystem
  Android DDMS, connecting to 212
Android device testing
  about 215, 216
  full/complete testing 216
  prototype testing 216
  regression testing 216
  release testing/run testing 216
Android-enabled STB devices
  Arcadyan BouygtelTV 25
  Forge TV 25
  Freebox Mini 4K 25
  LG UPlus Android TV 25
  OgleBox Android TV 25
  Shield Android TV 25

Android game development
  about 1, 2
  challenges 4
  design constrains 5
  features and support 3
  user experience 4
Android games
  life cycle 6, 7, 101, 102
  memory management 7
  performance 7
  publishing 325
  publishing, through publishers 326
  self publishing 325
  success, reasons 2
Android games, featuring qualities
  about 324
  creativity and uniqueness 324
  download count 325
  revenue amount 325
  user reviews and ratings 324
Android in-app purchase integration 307
Android in-game advertisements
  about 311
  requisites 311
  working 311
Android library shaders
  about 160
  BitmapShader 160
  ComposeShader 160
  LinearGradient 160
  RadialGradient 160
  SweepGradient 160
Android.mk file, options
  BUILD_SHARED_LIBRARY 259
  BUILD_STATIC_LIBRARY 259
  CLEAR_VARS 258
  LOCAL_MODULE 259
  LOCAL_MODULE_FILENAME 259
  LOCAL_PATH 259
  LOCAL_SRC_FILES 259
  PREBUILT_SHARED_LIBRARY 259
  PREBUILT_STATIC_LIBRARY 259
  TARGET_ARCH 259
  TARGET_ARCH_ABI 259
  TARGET_PLATFORM 259

Android mobiles
  development insights on 36, 37
  exploring 18-20
Android NDK
  about 256
  working 256
Android PackageManager 14
Android programming structure
  about 76
  call hierarchy 77, 78
  class formation 76
Android RunTime (ART) 2
Android SDK
  about 50, 257
  used, for creating sample game loop 97-101
Android-specific polishing
  about 282
  Android functionalities and features, implementing 282
  Google guidelines, following for Play Store 283
  longer background running possibility 283
  optimum use, of hardware buttons 282
Android STBs
  development insights on 39, 40
  exploring 24-28
Android Studio
  about 65
  Android project view 65, 66
  memory and CPU monitor view 66
Android tablets
  development insights on 38, 39
  exploring 22-24
Android televisions
  exploring 24-28
Android TV game development
  development insights on 39, 40
Android Virtual Device (AVD)
  about 51, 207-209
  attribute factors 209
  configuring 51-53
  dedicated disk space 52
  hardware profile 51
  other features 52
  system image mapping 51

Android VR development best practices
  about 248
  better audio experience 250
  draw call limitations 248
  overheating problems, overcoming 249
  proper project settings, setting up 250
  proper test environment, using 250
  steady FPS, keeping 249
  triangle count limitations 249
Android VR game market, challenges
  about 250
  limited device support 251
  limited game genres 251
  long game sessions 251
  low target audience 251
  real-time constraints 252
Android VR games
  about 237
  current industry situation 238
  history 237
  technical specifications 237, 238
Android watches
  development insights on 42
  exploring 33-35
animation polishing 275
Appcelerator
  about 307
  reference 306
application memory distribution 188
Application.mk file, options
  APP_ABI 260
  APP_BUILD_SCRIPT 260
  APP_CFLAGS 260
  APP_CPPFLAGS 260
  APP_LDFLAGS 260
  APP_OPTIM 260
  APP_PLATFORM 260
  APP_PROJECT_PATH 260
  APP_STL 260
  NDK_TOOLCHAIN_VERSION 260
application priority
  about 188
  active process 189
  active services 190
  background process 190
  visible process 190

applications
  versus games 5
applications, as game
  qualifying criteria 6
application services
  about 191
  life cycle 191
  misconceptions 191
AppsFlyer
  about 306
  reference 305
Apsalar
  about 306
  reference 305
Arcadyan BouygtelTV 25
art assets 203
ART message log 218
art optimization 176
art polishing
  about 275
  animation polishing 275
  marketing graphics 275
  UI polishing 275
asset optimization tools
  about 60
  full asset optimization 60
  sprites, creating 61
ATC 267
attribute factors, Android Virtual Device (AVD)
  Android target version 210
  Android version API level 210
  AVD display size 210
  AVD resolution 209
  CPU architecture 210
  extended AVD settings 211
  hardware input options 211
  name of AVD 209
  other options 211
  RAM amount 210
audio assets 203
Avatar 236

# B

banner advertisements 313, 314
base port 56

best optimization practices
  about 201
  asset-using techniques 202
  cache data, handling 204
  data structure model 202
  design constraints 201
  development optimization 201
best practices, for making Android game
  about 10
  background behavior 13
  battery usage, maintaining 14
  extended support, for multiple visual quality 15
  game quality, maintaining 11
  interruption handling 13
  maximum devices, supporting 12
  maximum resolutions, supporting 12
  minimalistic user interface 11
  multiplayer, introducing 15
  social networking, introducing 15
best testing practices
  about 230
  APIs 230
  testing techniques 231
  tools 230
BitmapShader 160
build dependency
  about 257
  Android SDK 257
  C++ compiler 257
  Cygwin 258
  Gradle 258
  Java 258
  Python 258

# C

cameras
  first-person camera 145
  fixed camera 145
  moving camera 145
  rotating camera 145
  third-person camera 145
Cardboard
  headset components 241
Cardboard application
  upgrades 241

variations 241
working principle 241
**Cardboard development styles**
  display properties 243
  game controls 244
  in-game components 243
  VR device adaptation 243
  VR game, exiting 242
  VR game, launching 242
**Cardboard SDK**
  about 240
  basic guide, for developing games 242
**career billing services 309**
**C++ compiler 257**
**C++, for games**
  about 261
  advantages 261
  conclusion 263
  disadvantages 262
**Coby Kyros MID7047**
  configuration specifications 23
**Cocos2d-x**
  about 68
  cons 69
  pros 68
**color resources 192**
**common game development mistakes**
  about 149
  shortcut, during development 150
  substandard programming, using 150
  use of full utility third-party libraries 149
  use of non-optimized images 149
  use of unmanaged networking connections 149
**common optimization mistakes**
  about 199
  design mistakes 200
  incorrect usage of game services 200
  programming mistakes 199, 200
  wrong game data structure 200
**ComposeShader 160**
**Concurrent Mark Sweep (CMS) 219**
**Concurrent Partial Mark Sweep (CPMS) 219**
**Concurrent Sticky Mark Sweep (CSMS) 219**

**Corona**
  about 72
  cons 72
  pros 72
**cost per action (CPA) 312**
**cost per click (CPC) 312**
**cost per impression (CPI) 312**
**CPU architectures, supported by NDK**
  ARM 270
  MIPS 271
  Neon 271
  x86 271
**Crashlytics**
  about 306
  reference 305
**cross-platform tools**
  about 67
  Cocos2d-x 68
  Corona 72
  PhoneGap 71, 72
  Titanium 73
  Unity3D 69, 70
  Unreal Engine 70, 71
**custom shaders**
  writing 161
**Cygwin 258**

# D

**Dalvik Debug Monitor Server (DDMS) 55, 56**
**Dalvik message log 218**
**Dalvik Virtual Machine (DVM) 2**
**data file optimization 177**
**debugging for Android**
  while working with cross-platform engines 230
**design optimization**
  about 177
  game design optimization 177
  technical design optimization 178
**design polishing**
  about 276
  game difficulty balance 277
  game economy balance 276
  game flow, polishing 276

metagame, polishing 276
UX, designing 276
**development insights, on Android consoles** 42
**development insights, on Android mobiles** 35-37
**development insights, on Android tablets** 38, 39
**development insights, on Android TV and STBs**
  overscan 41
  UI and game design 41
**development insights, on Android watches**
  about 42
  correct libraries, including in project 44
  hardware compatibility issues, with Android versions 44
  wearable application, creating 43
  wearable application, setting up 43
**development polishing**
  about 274
  memory optimization 274
  performance optimization 274
  portability 275
**device configuration options, Android**
  about 152
  battery capacity 153
  display quality 153
  GPU 153
  processor 152
  RAM 152
**disadvantages, C++ for games**
  about 262
  high program complexity 262
  manual memory management 263
  platform dependent compiler 263
**Draw 9-Patch** 58
**drawable resources** 192
**DXTC** 267

# E

**Eclipse, for Android development**
  about 56
  benefits 57
  drawbacks 57

**effective cost per mile (eCPM)** 312
**example smart TV**
  specifications 26
**exception handling, in Android games**
  about 224
  scope 226
  syntax 224, 225
**exceptions, in game development process**
  arithmetic exceptions 228
  custom exceptions 229
  index out of bound exceptions 227, 228
  input/output exceptions 228
  network exceptions 229
  null pointer exceptions 226, 227

# F

**features and support, Android game development**
  Android device hardware configuration 3
  direct manipulation interface 3
  excellent support, of multimedia 3
  virtual reality 3
**fields, virtual reality (VR)**
  architectural design 236
  education and learning 236
  fine arts 236
  medical therapy 237
  motion pictures 236
  urban design 236
  video games 235
**fillrate** 313
**first-person camera** 145
**fixed camera** 145
**Flurry**
  about 306
  reference 305
**Forge TV** 25
**FPS system**
  about 110-112
  controlling 116
**frame rate** 7
**frames per second (FPS)** 101
**Freebox Mini 4K** 25
**full length ads** 315

# G

**GameAnalytics**
  about 306
  reference 305
**game controls**
  about 244
  control placement 246
  Fuse Button 244
  fuse button indication 245
  types 244
  visual countdown 245
**game design optimization 177**
**game design standards**
  about 85
  artificial intelligence 86
  art style 86
  change log 87
  game elements 86
  game overview 85
  gameplay details 85
  game progression 86
  level design 86
  storyboard 86
  technical reference 87
**game development, for VR devices**
  about 239
  VR game design 239
  VR game development constraints 240
  VR target audience 239
**game loop**
  about 7, 94
  frames, rendering 96
  game update 95
  state update 96
  user input 94, 95
**gameplay programming 78**
**GamePop 32**
**game portability**
  about 283
  multiple hardware configurations, supporting 284
  screen sizes, supporting 283
**game programming specifications**
  about 78
  gameplay programming 78
  graphics programming 79
  technical programming 79
**game promotion channels**
  about 320
  Android forums 320
  Facebook promotion 321
  sports forums 320
  Twitter, and other social platforms 321
  YouTube channels 320
**game revenue, planning**
  about 316
  regional variations, of revenue plan 318
  revenue sources 317
  revenue, versus profit 317
**game revenue, sources**
  about 317
  advertisement revenue 317
  in-app purchase revenue 317
  other sources 318
**games**
  versus applications 5
**game state machine**
  general idea 107, 110
**Game Stick 31**
**game tool programming 80**
**game update 102, 103**
**geometry shaders 159**
**Google Analytics**
  about 288
  best utilization 289
  integration tips 289
  significance 288
**Google Cloud Messaging (GCM) 293**
**Google Daydream 238**
**Google IAB**
  about 289
  advantages 290
  disadvantages 291
  integrating 290
**Google IAB model**
  about 289
  consumable items 290
  non-consumable items 290
  subscriptions 290
**Google Leaderboard**
  about 291
  integrating 291

significance 291
variations 292
**Google Nearby** 15
**Google Play Services** 288
**Gradle** 258
**graphics programming** 79

## H

**hardware dependency**
about 112
display 113
logical operations 114
memory load/unload operations 113
rendering 113
**HDPI** 153
**heap memory** 113, 194, 195
**Hierarchy Viewer** 57
**HTC Dream** 17

## I

**in-app purchase options**
about 308
career billing services 309
store billing services 308
**in-app purchases**
about 307
consumable items 310
non-consumable items 310
subscriptions 310
types 310
**industry best practices**
about 89
design standards 89
programming standards 90
**in-game dynamic advertisements** 315
**instrumented tests** 232
**interrupt handling** 106
**interstitial advertisements**
about 314
integration best practice 314, 315

## J

**Java** 258
**Java Native Interface (JNI)** 256

## L

**layout resources** 192
**LDPI** 153
**leaderboards**
displaying, options 292
storing, options 292
**LG G Watch**
specifications 34
**LG UPlus Android TV** 25
**libraries for game development,**
    **on wearable devices**
notifications 44
Wearable Data Layer 44
Wearable UI support library 44
**LinearGradient** 160
**local network multiplayer** 302
**local test** 231
**Localytics**
about 307
reference 306
**log messages**
about 218
ART message log 218
Dalvik message log 218
**Lower CamelCase** 90

## M

**Mad Catz MOJO** 32
**MDPI** 153
**memory footprint, monitoring**
about 217
heap update, checking 219, 220
log messages, checking 218
memory allocation, tracking 220, 221
memory leaks, tracking 222
overall memory usage, checking 221
**memory load/unload operations**
heap memory 113
Read-only memory (ROM) 114
register memory 114
stack memory 114
**memory management, in Android**
about 186
application memory distribution 188
memory allocation and deallocation 187
shared application memory 187

memory optimization
    about 178
    significance 195, 196
    tricks 179-182
memory segments
    about 193
    heap memory 194, 195
    register memory 195
    stack memory 193
menu resources 192
meta design 303
microconsoles 28
Micromax Bolt A24
    configuration specification 18, 19
Microprocessor without Interlocked
        Pipeline Stages (MIPS) 271
Mixpanel
    about 306
    reference 306
mobile game loop, with touch interface
    working 103
mobile phones
    market shares, since 2012 21
modern age Android console
    specifications 29
modern VR systems 235
monetization aspects, analytic tools
    about 304
    advertisement display, counting 305
    advertisement display, tracking 305
    likes and dislikes, identifying of users 305
    metagame, improving 305
    metagame, validating 305
    paying users, tracking 305
    popular regions, identifying of game 304
monetization techniques
    about 315
    freemium model 316
    free model 316
    premium model 316
    try-and-buy model 316
moving camera 145
multiplayer implementation
    about 299
    local network multiplayer 302
    pass and play turn-based multiplayer 301

    real-time multiplayer 299, 300
    single-screen real-time multiplayer 301
    turn-based multiplayer 300, 301
multiple architecture support
    integration, advantages 271
    integration, disadvantages 272

# N

native code performance 264
native project build configuration
    about 258
    Android.mk configuration 258, 259
    Application.mk configuration 260
native shared library 256
native static library 257
NativeTrackTM 306
Neon architecture 271
network programming 80

# O

OgleBox Android TV 25
OpenGL
    texture compression 267
    used, for rendering 265
OpenGL 1.x 265
OpenGL 2.0 265
OpenGL 3.0 266
OpenGL 3.1 266
OpenGL manifest configuration 268, 269
OpenGL rendering system 146
OpenGL version
    detecting 266
    setting 266
OpenGL versions
    about 265
    OpenGL 1.x 265
    OpenGL 2.0 265
    OpenGL 3.0 266
    OpenGL 3.1 266
optimization fields, in Android games
    design optimization 177
    memory optimization 178
    performance optimization 183
    resource optimization 176

**OUYA**
  about 28
  specifications 28
**overall performance optimization**
  about 196
  base resolution, selecting 196
  database management 197
  frame rate, increasing 198
  network connection management 198
  portability range, defining 197
  program structure 197

## P

**pass and play turn-based multiplayer 301**
**performance, and memory**
  balance between 115
  relation between 186
**performance optimization**
  about 183
  significance 198, 199
  tricks 183-185
**performance profiling tools 64, 65**
**PhoneGap**
  about 71
  cons 72
  pros 71
**pixel shaders 159**
**platform-specific specialties**
  about 44
  Android consoles 46
  Android mobiles 45
  Android STBs 45
  Android tablets 45
  Android televisions 45
  Android watches 46
**play testing**
  about 277
  gameplay, adopting 279
  monetization 278, 279
  smoothing running, of game 279
  user actions, during gameplay 278
  user actions, while browsing game 278
  user gameplay difficulty levels 277
  user retention 280
**polishing**
  art polishing 275

  design polishing 276
  development polishing 274
  requisites 274
**private RAM 221**
**processing segments, in Android**
  about 188
  application priority 188
  application services 191
  resource processing 191
**ProGuard 59, 182**
**Proportionate Set Size (PSS) 187**
**Public Leaderboard 292**
**push notifications**
  application integration 295, 296
  database 293
  GCM service 294
  GCM setup 298
  integrating 295
  server 293
  server setup 298
  target device 293
**push notifications, significance**
  about 298
  alternative communication channel 299
  user behavior, knowing 299
  user control 299
  user retention 298
**PVRTC 267**
**Python 258**

## R

**RadialGradient 160**
**Razor Forge TV**
  specifications 30
**read-only memory (ROM) 114**
**real-time multiplayer 299, 300**
**real-time operating systems (RTOS) 252**
**regional variations, of revenue plan**
  about 318
  user base variations 319
  user behavior variations 319
**register memory 114, 195**
**rendering pipeline, in Android**
  2D rendering pipeline 145
  3D rendering pipeline 146

requisites, analytic tools
  game balancing 303
  game crash reports 303
  game event triggers 303
  gameplay frequency 303
  gameplay session timing 303
  piracy prevention 304
  user behavior 303
  user retention 304
research and development programming 81
resource optimization
  about 176
  art optimization 176
  data file optimization 177
  sound optimization 177
resource processing
  about 191
  color resources 192
  drawable resources 192
  layout resources 192
  menu resources 192
  other resources 192
  tween animation resources 192
RISC (Reduced Instruction Set Computing) 270
rotating camera 145

# S

sample game loop
  creating, Android SDK used 97-101
Samsung Galaxy S6
  configuration specification 19
services, Google Play Services package
  Google Analytics 288
  Google IAB 289
  Google Leaderboard 291
  push notifications 293
SFXs 281
shaders
  about 156
  benefits 157
  consequences 157
  geometry shaders 159
  in 2D game space 169

  in 3D game space 170, 171
  necessity 156
  pixel shaders 159
  scope 158
  tessellation shaders 159
  through OpenGL 163-169
  types 159
  using, in games 169
  vertex shaders 159
  working 158
shaders, in games
  cons 173
  pros 173
shared application memory 187
Shield Android TV 25
short length ads 315
single-screen real-time multiplayer 301
SmartTags 306
Social Leaderboard 292
Sony Xperia Z4
  configuration specifications 24
sound effects, UX polishing
  about 281
  SFXs 281
  theme music 281
sound optimization 177
sound programming 80
stack memory 114
  about 193
  working 193
store billing services
  about 308
  Amazon billing services 309
strategic placement, of debug statements
  about 222
  memory allocation 222
  object state, tracking at runtime 223
  object values, tracking 223
  program flow, checking 223
styles, for different development engines
  about 88
  programming languages 88
  target platforms 89
  work principles 88
SweepGradient 160

# T

**target device configuration, Android**
　feature requirement 9
　game scale 8
　scope for portability 10
　selecting 8
　target audience 9
**target OpenGL ES version, selection factors**
　about 269
　device support 269
　performance 269
　programming comfort 270
　rendering feature 270
　texture support 269
**technical design optimization 178**
**technical design standards**
　about 81
　change log 84
　design pattern 82
　flow diagram 82
　game analysis 82
　other requirements 83
　resource analysis 83
　risk analysis 84
　scope analysis 84
　technical specification 82
　testing requirements 83
　tools 83
**technical programming**
　about 79
　game tool programming 80
　network programming 80
　research and development
　　　programming 81
　sound programming 80
**tessellation shaders 159**
**testing techniques**
　about 231
　instrumented test 232
　local test 231
**texture compression, OpenGL**
　about 267
　ATC 267
　DXTC 267
　PVRTC 267

**theme music 281**
**third-person camera 145**
**Titanium**
　about 73
　cons 73
　pros 73
**tools, for testing**
　about 61
　test case, creating 61
　test fixture, setting up 61, 62
　test methods, adding to verify
　　　activity 63, 64
　test preconditions, adding 63
**transaction effects, UX polishing 281**
**turn-based multiplayer 300, 301**
**tween animation resources 192**

# U

**UI polishing 275**
**Unity3D**
　about 69
　cons 70
　pros 69
**Unreal Engine**
　about 70
　cons 71
　pros 70
**Upper CamelCase 90**
**user acquisition techniques**
　about 319
　forum discussions 321
　game blogs 321
　game promotion channels 320
　other techniques 322
　paid user acquisition 321
**user retention techniques**
　about 322, 323
　daily bonus 323
　frequent updates 324
　leaderboards and achievements 323
　offerwall Integration 323
　push notifications 323
**UX polishing**
　about 280
　action feedback 281
　sound effect 281

transaction effects 281
visual effects 280

## V

**variations, Google Leaderboard**
  Public Leaderboard 292
  Social Leaderboard 292
**vertex shaders** 159
**video advertisements** 315
  full length ads 315
  short length ads 315
**virtual reality therapy (VRT)** 237
**virtual reality (VR)**
  about 234
  evolution 234
  fields 235-237
**visual effects, UX polishing** 280
**VR development** 252
**VR game design** 239
**VR game development constraints** 240

**VR game development, through Google VR**
  about 246
  Android NDK used 248
  Android SDK used 246
**VR game, exiting**
  Back button, hitting 242
  Home button, hitting 243
**VR gaming concepts** 252
**VR target audience** 239

## X

**x86 architecture** 271
**XHDPI** 153
**XXHDPI** 153
**XXXHDPI** 153

## Z

**zipalign** 182

Made in the USA
Middletown, DE
18 March 2018